Beaten but not Defeated

Siegfried Moos: A German anti-Nazi who settled in Britain

Beaten but not Defeated

Siegfried Moos: A German anti-Nazi who settled in Britain

Merilyn Moos

CHRONOS BOOKS

Winchester, UK
Washington, USA

First published by Chronos Books, 2014
Chronos Books is an imprint of John Hunt Publishing Ltd., Laurel House, Station Approach, Alresford, Hants, SO24 9JH, UK
office1@jhpbooks.net
www.johnhuntpublishing.com

For distributor details and how to order please visit the 'Ordering' section on our website.

ISBN: 978 1 78279 677 0

A CIP catalogue record for this book is available from the British Library.

Design: Stuart Davies

Printed in the USA by Edwards Brothers Malloy

We operate a distinctive and ethical publishing philosophy in all areas of our business, from our global network of authors to production and worldwide distribution.

CONTENTS

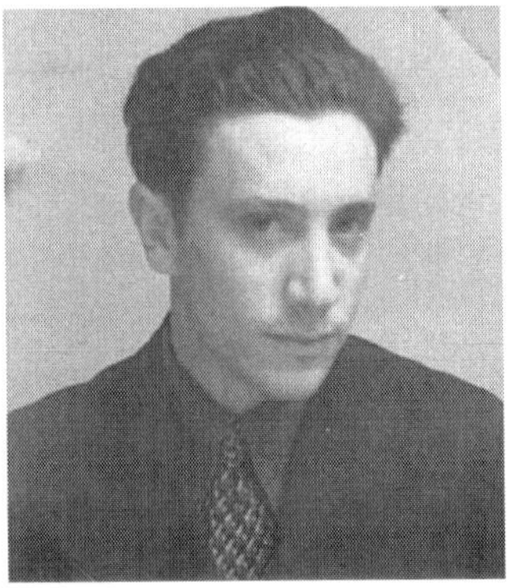

Berlin 1933

Oxford

Durham, late 1950s

To my parents, Siegi and Lotte Moos,
who gave me life.

Acknowledgements

This is a book which would never have been written, never mind finished, if it had not been for the help of a large number of people. I want to thank in particular Irene Fick for her commitment and good nature in translating so many documents from German to English and English to German without which this book would have been impossible; Richard Kirkwood for his detailed knowledge and analysis of the revolutionary left in Germany during the Weimar Republic, and for the moments of inspiration in his exploration of my father's role in Germany and then in Britain, and Ian Birchall for his generosity in translating my father's articles and for his astute comments on the text. My thanks also to Nick Jacobs for his translation of the biographies, in Hermann Weber's *Deutsche Kommunisten Biographisches Handbuch 1918 bis 1945*, of the men and women who pass through Siegi's biography. I particularly want to thank Kathryn Leander for stepping into the breach and sorting out the copy-editing. My thanks also to the following for their interest and encouragement: Charmian Brinson, Hugh Brody, Pete Cannell, Annie Duarte-Potter, Akan Leander and Sue Vice. Many other people provided me with useful material and ideas, either in document form or in discussion, all of whom I acknowledge in the endnotes.

My particular thanks go to Elfrieda Bruning, Hans Kohoutek and Rudi Schiffman, who has sadly died since I interviewed him. They all agreed to be interviewed aged 100 or over and gave me an invaluable insight into what it was like to be a Communist in the early 1930s in Germany. I thank also Dr Hans Coppi of the VVN-BdA (Vereinigung der Verfolgten des Naziregines - Bund der Antifaschistinnen und Antifaschisten: Association of Victims of the Nazi Regime) for arranging the interviews for me.

Although Chronos bore the greater part of the expense of publishing this book, it would not have been published if it were not for the generous financial support of Rudolph Moos, from the US, and Mairead Breslin Kelly, from Ireland. I suspect my father would have appreciated the historical irony that Rudolph's gift was in part a consequence of his finally re-acquiring and selling land that the Nazis had 'taken over' from Rudolph's family over seventy years ago. Mairead's heartfelt gift was also a product of a shared heritage – her father and my mother's good friend had both been murdered in the USSR under Stalin. I am deeply grateful to Rudolph and Mairead for making the publication of this biography possible. Their gifts also highlight that neither Nazism nor Stalinism, both systems that blighted my parents' lives, ultimately succeeded in their goals. We live to fight another day.

Finally, this book would never have been written if it had not been for my parents. My father may not always have been the easiest of dads, but I did not doubt his love for me. He encouraged in me a sense of my own uniqueness and potential, which has made writing his biography possible.

The world is a dangerous place to live in, not because of the people who are evil, but because of the people who don't do anything about it. Einstein, letter to Max Born, 1937/1938

Prologue

How do I present my father? How indeed do I present myself, his daughter, in this biography?

I started to write this biography a long time after my father was dead (not uncommon among familial biographers, I suspect). This had the great advantage that I was not constrained by what would almost certainly have been his refusal to cooperate. My father was a complicated man with a personal and political history he preferred to keep private.

How to find out about a man who had taken his many secrets to the grave? Researching any exile, uprooted from their country of birth, is complicated. What made this even more problematic was obtaining records about my father. A combination of the allied bombing of Germany, which obliterated many records, Nazi destruction, the dispatch of KPD papers into the locked archives of the USSR and my father's foresighted tendency to have hidden away – under trees and floorboards – his own papers left me thin on primary material. Happily, there turned out to be useful (!) SS and Gestapo papers about Siegi's time in Germany, and two volumes of MI5 documents resulting from their close surveillance of my parents. And, in the process of putting all this together, stories told me on those rare occasions by my father and mother came floating back into my memory.

I had left it too late to interview anybody who knew Siegi in Germany. But then who would I have interviewed anyway? As far as I could gather, my father's comrades had mostly been murdered. The one person who, from the letters in my father's archives, appeared to have survived – after nine concentration camps – I failed to trace before his death, hard though I tried.

Moreover, almost everybody from my father's immediate family had perished and the mother and daughter who did survive the camps were dead before I started this biography (one from old age; the daughter, I suspect, from suicide). Siegi's parents had both died very young. His brother, Adolpho, had committed suicide in his early 20s. Hermann, who unofficially adopted Siegi, had no children of his own and 'died' in Theriesenstadt. There is a dispersed extended family, as is the way with those fleeing Nazism: Brazil, Italy, Switzerland and the US, with whom generally I have had little contact; indeed my father had not been one to keep close ties with distant relatives. Even had I started far sooner, gaining information about my father from his German days would have proved difficult. Such complexities are one reason, I suggest, why writing the stories of anti-Nazi refugees is so rare.

I was fortunate that some of my father's articles about agitprop had been preserved by Weber: and I thank him for allowing me to reproduce them. Siegi's lyrics to accompany Wolpe's music from the early 1930s also miraculously surfaced during my research. So between one form of record and another, I built up a picture. I was helped in understanding the texture of the early 1930s by interviewing three centenarians who had been in the KPD at the same time as my father, even though they did not (sadly) know him.

Gathering information on my father's time once he arrived in the UK was helped along by MI5 records. They seem to have opened all my parents' mail until some time in the 1940s (opening mail being their chief means of keeping tabs on German Communist refugees) so I have a fairly full – though still partial – picture of Siegi and Lotte's time in the 1930s.

My personal knowledge of Siegi, except as a dad, was limited. While I knew my parents came from Germany and were anti-Nazis, very little else was allowed to penetrate our home. My parents wished to keep me protected. Another way of putting that is that they kept me in a cage. So my own knowledge of my father as a public figure is exceedingly limited.

I look back now on both my parents with sadness. They had been too damaged to be able to provide much of the gentle skill of parenting. My father, less paranoid than my mother but far sterner, had dedicated himself – with extraordinary success – to the creation of a new world for himself of books, lecturing and writing, in which a daughter did not have a part. He had lost so much, not just his family, his comrades and his 'country' but also of himself, that accessing his past was impossible for him. I was brought up ironically without a history, and to feel that the world was a threatening and insecure place. But with that came a sense of uniqueness. The little my father told me, for example, the story of his escape from Germany, defined me and gave me lifelong courage.

But I am left with how far to put myself into the biography. My relationship with him was far from easy. His past gave him strength but also sapped him. He was a tender man who was regularly consumed by rage. He expected respect and never to be contradicted. He could not bear closeness, physical or emotional. I both loved and feared him. I avoided his company. It is in these pages, that I have tried to find my father. But I have chosen to leave on one side his and my relationship, though it inevitably pushes its way into the narrative. It is his remarkable political life which should be better known.

My father died when his grandson, Josh, in whom he delighted, was only one and Josh does not remember him. But I have written this biography in my father's memory and I am proud of him.

P.S. There is an issue about the use of the word 'murdered' in this biography. As is the norm here, I have used it to apply both to people who were gassed, shot or otherwise deliberately killed and to those who died as a result of gruelling work, a starvation diet and grotesquely unhealthy living conditions. Germans use the word *unkommen* to refer to the second group who died as a result of gross mistreatment but were not directly killed. Though I was tempted to make use of this distinction in this study, I decided *unkommen* was too unfamiliar a word to use in an English-language context. So I use 'murdered' throughout to refer to both groups of Nazism's victims.

Part 1

An anti-Nazi in Germany

Chapter 1

Introduction

It took me a long time to come to terms with how little I knew about my father. As a child, I knew his date of birth, but where he was born and to whom were not matters that were talked about. Indeed, my timid questions about his parents or siblings elicited a sharp response. 'It's bourgeois to be concerned about matters of family,' though when I was little, he said something more like: 'Families don't matter. You do understand that.' I learnt when little not to try to open up the door to my father's past and to horrors I only sensed.

When young, I was told little stories to furnish me with some explanation of how I came to be born in Oxford. My father had had to flee the Gestapo in 1933 because he had been active in left-wing theatre. This, I understood, was something to be proud of. He had walked out of Germany and had fled to the UK. It had taken him a long time and it was luck he survived. His life had been saved by a rural cobbler who had asked no questions and not given him away, when my father had appeared in his shop, the soles of his shoes worn right through.

Much later on, my father had also told me that he was the secretary of the Freethinkers (but left me believing this was simply a Humanist organization). It never struck me to unearth the stories that lay beneath my father's tales. I learnt early to understand my parents' unspoken wishes. I became terrified of asking questions and, even more, of receiving answers.

Later in my life, I began to develop a curiosity about both my parents' pasts. My father died twenty years before my mother, and it was only in her declining years, that I got my hands on their archives. Well versed in the ways of paranoia, I knew to unravel every blanket for what might lie hidden in its folds, go through the pockets of every suitcase, look deep into the heaped carrier bags, and check all files for the papers which mattered. There slowly opened up a hidden history.

There had been a few earlier intimations. A couple of years earlier, a friend had turned up a reference in the India files to my father acting on behalf of the Russian party. 'Rot,' I had declared. My father had always denounced Stalin. One of my first memories was my abstemious parents opening a bottle of wine when they heard of Stalin's death. My father had worn a red tie as the three of us had sat and toasted Stalin's demise.

The other clue had come via a researcher into my mother's past. His news was unwelcome –and again, clearly untrue. My mother, he had informed me via an initial letter, had had an affair with a Communist spy. 'But she was already married,' I remember protesting to him, after checking the date. I should have been more suspicious. I had been the spectator, as a young woman, to my mother's many arguments with Richard Kirkwood as to why the USSR had got it wrong, crucially over collectivization, although I had been puzzled at the detail of her knowledge. She opposed Stalinism if anything more than my father, I told the researcher. He had given me that researcher's glance. 'Well. I didn't expect you to take it well.'

I had already contacted Kew about my parents' files and they had fobbed me off. I had been met with surprising resistance, which I failed to understand. Now I again approached them, indeed started to badger them to release both my parents' MI5 files. When I was finally informed they would be released, I had expected to find a thick file on my left-wing activist father, and nothing much on my mother.

But the reverse was the case. To my astonishment, my housewife boring mother had two thick files; my father nothing. This continues to intrigue me. My guess is that in the trawl in the 1960s, my father's files, along with thousands of others, were discarded. But it is possible that they are still 'under wraps' because of his association with either the Free French or Harold Wilson (he was one of the – then unusual – special advisers in the Wilson government of 1966–1970). Fortunately, it has been possible to glean some information on Siegi from Lotte's copious files.

Siegi had left behind little to help with the reconstruction of his history. He had failed to talk systematically about his past, as far as I know, to anybody at all. His writing was of a theoretical not personal nature. Even the poetry he wrote in old age has a wonderfully polemical character; it says a lot about his politics but little about the man.

Sadly my father's consideration of writing his own autobiography, which is referred to in a letter (6 June 1966, in personal possession) to him from Philip Andrews (Nuffield College), never came to fruition. We have Andrews' responses to the reasons that Siegi must have given for not writing an autobiography. It is the same reply he gave me when I asked him, when he was already quite old, why he did not write an autobiography. There were no such things as facts in a history such as his, he told me. This is more understandable to me now than it was at the time. The older Siegi did not completely identify with his younger self. His other reason, I suspect, was that he did not see himself as more worthy of attention than his many comrades, too many of whom did not live to tell such tales. Now I know rather more as to why he could not write that autobiography. But it can only be regretted that Siegi could not have 'owned up' to his past. As I have only recently discovered, his life was far fuller than I had realized.

I had always been told by both my father, and, after his death, my mother that Siegi had not belonged to the Communist Party. Very late in Lotte's life, she told me, her lip curling in disdain that, yes, Siegi had belonged to the German Communist Party. In the months before Lotte's death, she also told me that Siegi had belonged to the Rotfrontkämpferbund (the offensive/defensive anti-Nazi group, loosely affiliated to the KPD, discussed later). 'But they never fired a shot at the Nazis,' she told me, adding something like: 'What an idiot.' It came as a great – and not welcome – surprise, therefore, to discover that Siegi was not just an active member of the KPD in the early 1930s, but probably one of their leading cadres in Berlin.

So here I am writing my father's biography, with the help of Richard Kirkwood and Irene Fick. It is a biography which focuses on the man in the public sphere, not my father as I knew him, but inevitably some of Siegi as a father and also as a husband is included. It should not be forgotten that it is his daughter who is writing this and while this gives me a unique view of the man, my view of Siegi will inevitably be affected by my sympathies for and conflicts with him, and may at points have the too close-up view of a daughter.

It has not been possible to fill all the holes in knowledge about him. My parents never talked to me of themselves, in the past or the present. So some of this biography will be written as a search for my father's past. But then, no biography, or indeed autobiography, can ever be complete. My father was right on that one. It's impossible to tell the truth about oneself, he had also insisted.

There has to be an attention here to records which are partial, both because at least some of the records are hidden away, if they exist at all, in the Moscow and ex-East German archives, and partly because of the inherent nature of records, particularly from such a politically tumultuous 80 years. The people who knew my father are almost all dead, too many of them murdered. Some of the material has been gleaned from MI5 records, some from the very limited family records. The partial nature of the information here has been forced upon us by the unavailability of sources.

It is time to rescue my father's life, because it is the life of a man forged into a revolutionary by the struggles in 1920s Germany, who becomes deeply involved in the activities and debates about how to stop the Nazis and who saw agitprop theatre as one means of winning over the working class. He had to start a second life and learn a second language in the UK, became deeply disillusioned with some of his previous beliefs, but never gave up his socialist opinions.

But it is not just my father's life I am rescuing. The history of the revolutionary left in Germany between 1918 and 1939 is remarkably unknown, even in Germany but more so in the UK. The zigzags of the Communist International (Comintern) have been thoroughly studied as have the KPD's official twists and turns, but not the rank and file. Certain acts of heroism have made it into the history books or been given media attention, for example the Bavarian White Rose student group, the attempt on Hitler's life in 1944, or some people who 'saved Jews' but, in fact, these acts of bravery have almost nothing to do with the revolutionary left, working-class activities or the resistance from 1933 onwards.

Why did the East German government, who had a culture of celebrating their heroes, and who if anybody did, should have inherited the mantle and memory of the German working-class revolts and resistance, not celebrate more fully both the early attempts at revolution in 1918 and 1923 (beyond Luxemburg and sometimes Liebknecht) and later those who had stood and fought, and too often died, opposing Nazism? I suggest that the East German government, who were theoretically in a coalition with the Social Democrats from 1948, were not always in sympathy with the politics of the earlier 1918–1923 revolutionaries and the often less than 'respectable' members of the resistance. This government preferred to honour those who had visibly contributed to the fall of Nazism rather than the thousands who were working underground and largely out of sight and who, after all, 'failed' to stop Nazism. No doubt the erratic opening of the Moscow and East German archives will now facilitate further research.

The other reason is to do with the other side in the Cold War, where a belief in 'our side' held an ideological influence over academia as well as politics, which started to significantly reduce only in the mid-1960s (though there were some brave early swallows). The Allies did not honour revolutionaries or often even the resistance. Amongst the 'leaders' in the second world war, Churchill was an exception in holding to the tactic of building up a group (the Special Operations Executive) who worked with resistance fighters across Europe. Roosevelt and many of the top-brass in the British military preferred a more conventional war.[1] Add to that that we are here discussing the 'enemy', the Germans, even if these were the 'good' Germans, and the lack of recognition and attention becomes easier to understand. Moreover, these men and women were often Communists and often working class, and, during the academic freeze which so often went along with the Cold War, 'on the other side'.

Two of the few authors who write in English (Rosenhaft[2] and LaPorte[3]) who look at the grass-roots politics in the German working class during this period will be referred to frequently in this text. So this study of my father I hope will help illuminate the grass-roots activities and fates of those brave men and women who worked for a revolutionary Germany after the end of the first world war and in particular stood up against the rise in Nazism.

This book's structure in part reflects this dual purpose. In Part 1 which takes us up to 1933, there are chapters which are specifically about my father, two early separate chapters which address the political background in Germany, and a final chapter which combines the two. People who want to keep to Siegi's story may want to miss out the political chapters, although readers will find they do provide a background to Siegi's activities.

I was also exceedingly fortunate in being given the opportunity to interview in autumn 2011 three very old members of the KPD, activists in the 1930s, whom I refer to as the Berlin 3, and who gave me the insight one gets only from talking to people who actually were there and allowed me to get some sense of what my father's Berlin had been like. I refer to their observations intermittently throughout this study. Not much work has been done on the experience of the 'Third Period' on the ground. Almost all studies have been of official KPD policies, and of its many vacillations and zigzags. It is in this context that the interviews with the three Berliners were so valuable in that they give a long distance but intimate view of what was happening on the ground between 1929 and 1933 and the degree to which the political activities of the Berlin 3 were as much driven by their experiences as by the Party line.

I am not writing this biography as an academic historian and do not delve into the (interesting) debates about how to interpret this period of history – whether it is better top down or bottom up. My perspective is moreover decidedly anti-Stalinist and I do not give time or credit to a Stalinized historiography. I also do not read German – a serious limitation when studying German history and I have to thank Irene Fick for her generous translations from German into English on my behalf. Nevertheless, I have largely depended on English translations and texts and what they have to say about German sources. So, for example, I depend on secondary sources to know that Weber, a key German left-wing writer about the German revolutionary left and the KPD up to 1945, demonstrates the Stalinization of the KPD[4], a position LaPorte suggests has limits. I have taken what fits the story of my father and do not get into the rights and wrongs of the different positions.

In the last season of Siegi's life, he returned to his earlier writing, pouring out lyrical left-wing poetry and musing on how to bring about change. He remained a socialist till the end. As he lay dying, I sang him the Internationale (to the horror of the nurses used to a more reverential atmosphere by the bedsides of the dying) and, by now unable to speak or virtually to move, he wiggled his toes to the beat.

Endnotes

1. I owe this point to Steve Cushion.
2. Rosenhaft, *Beating the Fascists? The German Communists and Political Violence 1929– 1933*.
3. LaPorte, *The German Communist Party in Saxony, 1924–33: Factionalism, Fratricide and Political Failure;* and *Bolshevism, Stalinism and the Comintern. Perspectives on Stalinization, 1917–53* (with Kevin Morgan and Matthew Worley).
4. Weber argues in *Die Wandlung des Deutschen Kommunismus* (1969), that by the 1930s the KPD had been transformed into a disciplined and centralized instrument of Stalinism. (See Appendix 6 for further details.)

Chapter 2

1904–1928 Early life. The makings of a revolutionary

Siegi was born into a knot of contradictions, which framed him from an early age. Born in Munich, on 19 September 1904, he was the second son to Johanna and Albert Moos. We know that Albert lived at a variety of addresses during Siegi's early childhood (at the time, as now, any move in Germany had to be registered, so it is possible to check Albert's many addresses). Not all was well in the Moos household.

Albert was a joint owner of a factory in Ulm, but kept moving, ending up near to Monte Carlo, where he gambled compulsively, before leaving for Paris where he died, aged 45 (from family correspondence). Albert left his wife to look after herself and their two young boys.[5] Siegi was only six or seven. My father's passing suggestion to me once that his father was some sort of bohemian artist was somewhat economical with the truth! Siegi's mother was left to struggle alone to bring up the two little boys and, most probably, without any regular source of income. Thus Siegi was marked at an early stage by emotional disruption and material poverty.

Siegi's aunt Rosa, his father's sister, had married into a well-off Bavarian family. Hermann Binnswanger, Rosa's husband, and his two brothers ran three highly successful liqueur and vinegar factories (Likoerfabrik zum Magister) across Bavaria. Rosa and Hermann had no children. Though it is impossible to now know exactly how close the relationship was, it appears that Rosa and Hermann unofficially took over some of Siegi's care, a pattern more common at this time when, if needed, childless couples would 'adopt' a brother or sister's child.[6] Certainly, there are a variety of photos of a beaming Hermann posing with the young

Siegi in his lush garden at their summer house outside Munich. In later life, Siegi used to talk to me as if Hermann's house was his home. Siegi had told me of how easy it was to 'steal' some of the booze as a child and how he would then go to sleep in the barn. Indeed, I was startled to discover this was not the full story. I had been allowed to believe that Siegi grew up in an opulent household, which made wine and liqueur for its living.

But Siegi did spend some time with his mother. Siegi told me that towards the end of the first world war, when he was around twelve years old, he had lived on turnip stew, turnip jam and stewed nettles, which he had foraged from local farmers' fields.[7] Whatever the exact nature of the different relationships, Siegi went between his mother's 'social need' housing, and his uncle's opulent houses. It cannot have been easy for him. This contrast between poverty and affluence may well have radicalized the young boy.

Siegi told me that when still quite young, he went to pay homage every year at the memorial to those who fell in the German revolution of March 1848 (which forced King Ludwig of Bavaria to abdicate). I now suspect that this was probably in Augsburg. One piece in the complicated jigsaw of Siegi's early life is that at least one part of his adopted family, the Binnswangers, seems to have belonged to the radical – and 'modernist' – wing of the bourgeoisie. Gabriel Binnswanger, it appears, played a minor role in the 1848 German uprising, and is noted to have taken down a notice placed by the state on 1 May 1849, which he trampled into the ground. Siegi probably saw himself as paying homage to a member of his own family, his great-uncle, but was also supporting the general cause of those early fallen revolutionaries. Hermann's later letters to Siegi once he was in the UK (considered in Appendix 3), also show a deep humanism and sympathy for his revolutionary, wayward and brilliant nephew.

Aged only 14, Siegi was in attendance when sailors declared

a Soviet republic[8] from the steps of Munich Town Hall, an event he described to me in some detail. Later in life (and this will be considered in a subsequent chapter on the 1970s), he wrote an excoriating article against Ebert's betrayal of the 1918–1919 revolution, written with the passion and knowledge of one who was there. Siegi's presence on the steps of Munich Town Hall tells us that he was already at least interested in radical politics. Having grown up under the wing of Hermann and Rosa, radical minded representatives of the Bavarian haute-bourgeoisie, and also presumably influenced by Germany's defeat and the victory of the Russian revolution, Siegi seems to have developed an early attachment to revolutionary politics.

Even Siegi's schooling raises issues over identity. His mother had moved the children from Munich to Amberg, where Siegi attended the *Humanistische Gymnasium* (equivalent to a grammar school). This was a Catholic school, run by Catholic priests. Yet the original inscription next to Siegi's name in the school's entry book, where religion had to be stated, has 'Judische' scratched out and 'Protestant' overlaying it.

Why he was finally registered as a Protestant cannot now be known nor why he was sent to a Catholic school, though one can guess that it was because it was the best available. Certainly, although the Hermann household were secular Jews, Jewishness was not a concern; indeed is not mentioned at all in Hermann's many letter to Siegi. (We do not know about Siegi's mother.) Siegi certainly told me he was brought up as a Catholic, and would quote parts of the Catholic catechism at me. ('You can always recognize a Catholic,' he informed me on several occasions, 'by the look of guilt in their eyes.') But later, while still in Bavaria, he is documented as choosing to relinquish his Judaism, indicating that he saw Judaism as his original 'faith' and that he took this sufficiently seriously to need to reject it. Maybe he took this decision because he was no longer a believer; maybe he never was. Maybe he already saw religion as 'the opium of the masses'.

But this flurry of religious identities probably discouraged a belief in any particular religion (and led to his active role in the Freethinkers). The rest of this biography will consider Siegi's later politics. But, with such a background, it is not surprising that Siegi showed an early political awareness.

He did not do especially well at secondary school and went to study for an Economics degree at Munich's Technische Hochschule (equivalent to a cross between the old Further Education colleges and polytechnics), maybe staying with Hermann.[9] But he did not finish his degree. Though continuing to study Economics in the evenings at Munich University proper, he went to work at the biggest Bavarian bank, Bayerische Vereinsbank, where he stayed for over five years, working his way up to Head Office. Then he joined the management of his uncle's factory, Likoerfabrik zum Magister, where he stayed for another two and a half years. Finally, he moved to Berlin in 1928, still only 24, to work at the liqueur factory: Hermann Meyer. It appears from a great-uncle's letter, he also worked for a paper: *Neue Zeit*.

The late 1920s is also the time his brother commits suicide. My father never mentioned that he had a brother. I was only to find out when I emptied out my parents' possessions from their house, to discover his brother, Adolpho's, christening mug and ring, lying in the drawer in which my father kept his cheque books, a drawer my father went into probably once a day. Then I also found, buried deep under my father's papers in his study, Adolpho's christening book. The letter from Adolpho, which I now possess, suggests he killed himself over a failed love affair. Another part of Siegi's world must have fallen apart.

Endnotes

5. Although the history of my father's family is fragmentary, as happens when families are either dispersed or/and murdered, some distant relatives, in particular Rudolph

Moos, have put much effort into reconstructing a family tree. But nothing is known of Siegi's mother. I tried to trace her but had no luck. My father never mentioned her and I do not know for sure how she died, though my mother told me (never a reliable source on causes of death as I was to discover) that she died young of breast cancer. In the photo albums I acquired when I cleared their home, there appears a beautiful young woman, white ruff round her neck, eyes softly out of focus. I assume it is Siegi's mother.

6. Siegi was the chosen one; his brother, Adolpho seems to have been left in the care of their mother. Adolpho committed suicide in his early 20s.
7. Turnips were the only food my father banned my mother from cooking! But Siegi did show me on his and my occasional walks together how to pick nettles for cooking so that they didn't sting.
8. The Bavarian or Munich Soviet Republic, based in Munich, was a part of the German Revolution of 1918–1919, led by Eisner. The sailors, who were deeply engaged in resisting the continuation of war by their leaders, were probably in Munich, which is far from the sea, on their way home to now revolutionary Austria (Harman,2008). This event is discussed further in Chapter 3.
9. Apparently, Munich University, even during Weimar, did not welcome Jewish or socialist students of economics (Crohn, 1996: 178). It is still notorious for its association at this time with its fencing clubs. Whether all this influenced which university Siegi went to, can only be guessed at.

Chapter 3

Bavaria: the early stamping ground of the Nazis. KPD resistance

This is the period when Siegi's politics are developing, and it is therefore not the main focus of this study. Nevertheless, the activist from the early 1930s had his political birth in Munich; indeed I would argue that his later acute awareness of the threat of Nazism was born out of his experiences in Bavaria, where, and we shall see, he will have witnessed and probably experienced the early growth of the Nazis, their influence over the Bavarian government and their lethal activities against the left.

So this section will look in some detail at the tumultuous politics in and around Munich from 1918, through the Kapp Putsch and the events of 1923 by when we know Siegi was again in Munich, to when he leaves for Berlin in 1928. Siegi's personal/political trajectory parallels and illustrates two of the major events in German history between 1918 and 1933 – the revolutionary uprising in Bavaria in 1923 and the failed attempts by the revolutionary left to stop the rise of Nazism in Berlin from 1929 to1930. The first section will be on the revolutionary left, the second on the rise of the Nazis. We begin with a brief diversion into the birth of the Weimar Republic which provides a backdrop to subsequent events.

On 29 October 1918, the sailors of the German fleet mutinied when ordered to continue the fight against the British. They took over the naval base and city of Kiel and elected a workers' and soldiers' council (Hobsbawm, 1973).[10] On 9 November, the Kaiser abdicated, handing over government to the Social Democrat, Ebert. The German republic was declared on 9 November 1918. The army chiefs transferred their loyalty to Ebert but on the condition that he fight Bolshevism. In that they were united. But the army itself had become militant and was not to be trusted, so Ebert turned to the reactionary Freikorps (Hobsbawm, 1973). On 15 January 1919, Luxemburg and Liebknecht, the two great leaders of the German revolutionary left, were murdered, following the failed first attempt at revolution in Germany.

Munich: the unlikely seat for revolution, 1918–1919

Munich became the fulcrum for the revolutionary left after the defeats in Berlin. As we know, Siegi witnessed the historic struggles of 1918 and 1919.

Bavaria, one of the more conservative and Catholic areas of Germany with a population at the time of around 8 million, long dominated by the right, was an unlikely place for the revolutionary days of 1918 and 1919. But Krupp had built a new munitions factory, employing 6,000 out of its 60,000 population in Munich (Harman, 1982),[11] its employees at the forefront of the insurgency. Moreover, it was a staging post for demobbed and often radicalized soldiers: in December 1918, there were about 50,000 of them (Harman, 1982).

Towards the end of the war, Eisner,[12] the leader of the Independent Socialist Party of Germany (USPD),[13] called for a general strike in Munich, which was conceived of as political and peaceful (Frohlich, 1972). Proletarian workers' militias, usually only modestly armed, were formed. On 7 November 1918, the city was paralysed by the strike; Eisner led his units of armed soldiers and sailors to the barracks; many soldiers, with their arms, deserted their barracks and flocked to support the demonstration (Harman, 1982).[14] Strikes occurred in Munich, Nuremberg, Fuerth, Schweinfurt, and Ludwigshafen. About 75,000 defence workers participated in the strike, demanding the end of the war. The biggest rally was in Nuremberg, with 45,000 strikers, since MSPD (the majority Social Democratic Party) and the USPD had called for joint action. In Munich, there were over

10,000, with the USPD enthusiastic to continue beyond the agreed time in order to enforce specific policy concessions.

Workers' councils and committees were established but were never properly coordinated. Armed groups of workers and militia took over the streets of Munich. In a situation where neither the soviets nor the government held power, Eisner briefly formed a left coalition government with the Social Democrats in early January 1919, which survived the collapse of the revolution in Berlin. The soldiers declared they would not oppose a general strike (Harman, 1982). However, Eisner was outmanoeuvred, and in February 1919 decided to resign but was murdered on his way to Parliament (Harman, 1982). Workers were in uproar.

The revolutionary ball kept rolling. Despite the defeats of the revolutionary left elsewhere, in Bavaria, hardly a stronghold of the labour movement, there was continuing revolutionary pressure. In April 1919, the Sparticist leader, Max Levien, declared the establishment of the Bavarian Soviet Republic in Munich. Again, workers' militias were created, especially in the large metalworking companies and working-class areas, but this time they were largely defensive. Huffman's government was declared deposed. (For an analysis post-hoc by Siegi of these events and the attempt to establish soviets, refer to Chapter 8.) Lacking a sufficient working-class base and any sort of armed insurrection, the soviet stood little chance (Frohlich, 1972).[15]

Leviné was dispatched by the KPD Central Committee (CC) to avoid another blood bath as in Berlin. Harman argues that, with Leviné now in leadership and emphasizing the role of workers' councils (though Harman's use of Leviné-Meyer's biography, 1973, could be more critical), the Bavarian revolution entered into a second more hopeful stage. But as Hobsbawm puts it: 'Leviné... knew all was lost but also that it had to fight.' Leviné was deeply aware that this was a revolution without working-class roots and was rightly suspicious of the leading role of the Social Democrats.[16] Leviné wrote of how the factories were still working, the press still lying, the military still intact. 'Noske is already whetting his butcher's knife.' (Rosa Leviné-Meyer, 1973) Johannes Hoffman, who has already appeared above, fled and began gathering about 8,000 troops outside of Munich to attack the Bavarian Soviet Republic. On 7 April, a council republic was proclaimed (Broué, 2005: 280)[17] made up of everybody from the Social Democrats to the anarchists and denounced by Leviné as a masquerade and pseudo-council republic. There was a massive general strike in Munich, but nowhere else. Hoffman essentially blockaded Munich which ran out of food. (Was my father's talk of living off turnips and foraging in the fields as much to do with these days as hardships during the war?)

On 13 April 1919, after the Soviet Republic was declared in Munich the Social Democratic Cabinet under the Bavarian Prime Minister. But there was an attempt at a counter-revolutionary coup. Hoffman finally called on the Freikorps to attack the defenders of the Republic.[18] (Similar had already happened in Berlin under Ebert when he let loose the Freikorps on the revolutionaries.) Ebert, the SD President of Germany, then gathered 30,000 Freikorps to take back Munich, welcomed by the reactionary Bavarian middle class. The Freikorps clashed with, and first lost to, Ernst Toller's troops, including army conscripts, at Dachau (Leviné-Meyer, 1973; Broué, 2005). But Toller and the Communists were bickering. Munich then fell over a couple of days and the Soviet Republic ended on 1 May 1919.

The repression was brutal: an estimated 700 men and women were captured and executed, including Leviné (Mitchell, 1965; Broué, 2005), and including 186 military executions (Harman, 1982). (It was during his 'trial' that Leviné said: 'We Communists are all dead men on suspended sentence' (Broué: 281).) Harman (1982) quotes Frohlich that the Bavarian Republic started as farce and ended as tragedy. Serge estimated that, between 1918 and just 1921, 15,000 workers were killed. The final defeat of the

Bavarian uprising was also a defeat in the belief that the working class would take over in Germany. Although it is not possible to know whether Siegi played any part, though he was only fifteen, the hope of these heady and turbulent revolutionary months appears to have inspired him and influenced his world view for the rest of his life.[19]

In the midst of this political turmoil, the KPD was established in Munich in 1919 (Mühldorfer: op.cit.) as a loose grouping. But the violent suppression of the 'Soviet Republic' in early May 1919 by government troops and the Freikorps squashed the youthful Bavarian KPD (Mühldorfer). The Sparticist leader Max Levien (1885–1937) and the more anarchistically inclined P. Erich (1879–1934) brought their organizations in with the KPD at this point. In 1920, the Independent Socialists, the USPD, until then the significantly larger organisation, whose stronghold was North Bavaria and who also had a mass base in the local unions, also joined (though one faction refused and later rejoined the Social Democratic Party of Germany. This led temporarily to the KPD having around 200,000 members – but this rapidly declined to around 10,000.

By 1920, the main grouping in Munich had approximately 500 members.[20] Nuremberg, a more developed industrial centre, had 3,000 members. These two centres sustained the KPD. Despite the apparent militancy of these years, the character of Bavaria – low industrialization, the lack of a tradition of a working-class movement and its strong nationalist and rural perspectives – was not fertile ground. Moreover, many of the leaders of the 1919 uprising had not survived or were in prison, leaving the new movement relatively rudderless (Mühldorfer).

The level of repression against the Communists and others was acute. From 11November 1923 to 14 February 1925, the KPD was banned; there was a state of emergency till 19 October 1921, and then again from September 1923 to February 1925, resulting in the right (often implemented) banning the press and public meetings which led to further restrictions on KPD activities at the local level (Mühldorfer). Members of the KPD were under constant surveillance by the state security and the police.[21] The list of political prisoners at Dachau concentration camp some years later, also reveals a roll call of Communist members from Munich, including some leading cadres, during the period between the failed revolution of 1918–1919 and 1928.[22]

Nevertheless, there was a small increase in membership in Munich during the mid-1920s, though in northern Bavaria, the number of members halved. Munich and Augsburg (the two cities Siegi was most connected to) remained the cities where the KPD membership was strongest. The membership of the KPD in Bavaria shows a gradual but irregular rise: from 3,500 in 1919 to 10,000 in 1921; then a fall to 5,000 in 1923; a rise to 7,000 in 1926, but a fall to 6,000 in 1930, rising to 10,000 in 1931 (and an estimated 15,000 in 1932). Despite the ban on the KPD, it was allowed to participate in elections in 1920 and 1924 but the Munich election committees were already working illegally. At least the election of deputies to the Reichstag and in the Bavarian state parliament gave them a limited immunity to liaise and organize (Mühldorfer). The Bavarian state elections between 1920 and 1932–1933 show a similar pattern: 1.7 per cent in 1920 (2 seats), 8.3 per cent in 1924 (10 seats), 3.8 per cent in 1928 (6 seats) and 6.6 per cent in 1932 (9 seats) (Mühldorfer). By 1924, the KPD got a remarkable 8.3 per cent of the regional vote overall, 16 per cent in Munich, 17.5 per cent in Nuremberg, 11.5 per cent in Augsburg[23], partly a result of increasing social impoverishment and unemployment.[24]

There were also a number of significant KPD associated organizations in Munich. The Young Communists League, led later on by Alfred Andersch (1914–1980), though it was weak, supported Red Aid (see Chapters 3 and 4). (Siegi is only around 20, so quite young enough to have belonged.) The League of Struggle against Fascism was banned as a military organization, as was the Proletarian Freethinkers (another key organization for Siegi – see Chapter 5) and the community sports Red Unit. By the mid-1920s, there was also the official possibility of being a fellow traveller to the KPD.

There was also the Red Front Fighters (RFB), initially established in Nuremberg and instantly banned (again, a possible link with Siegi – see Chapter 5). The attempt to set up a Young Red Storm group in Munich also was unsuccessful. An RFB group also existed in Munich, but it was not large. The RFB was constantly being threatened with being banned. In the summer of 1928 there were 14 branches of the RFB with 800 members, 350 of them registered in Nuremberg – apparently the RFB's job was even then to protect workers' sports gatherings, Communist meetings and other such events against the Sturmabteilung (SA) and the Nazis. They also leafleted and joined the bike caravans around the rural areas of Bavaria advertising the KPD. During the short time of its legal existence, the RFB played an important role, although its membership would have been under 1,000 in Bavaria. Especially after the events of 1919, there were regular clashes with right-wing groups, especially in factories and working-class neighbourhoods, which they defended against the Nazis.

There were also a series of Communist or aligned papers: *Neue Zeitung*, the Munich-based *Red Flag*, the *North Bavarian People's Daily* from 1930 and finally, there were the intermittent productions of the *People's Will* from September 1919 to April 1922, and *Red-Flag Bavaria* from October 1921 to May 1923 in Augsburg. This plethora of papers and journals gives us some small sense of how broad and lively the Communist 'scene' in Bavaria was at the time.

As there is no evidence about Siegi's activities in this period, one can only surmise. But as will be seen in subsequent chapters, Siegi became involved in many of the organizations he will have known about, or encountered, during his time in Munich – the

RFB in particular. Another question is whether he felt sympathy with the USPD before it amalgamated into the KPD. In 1918–1919, Siegi was only 14–15 but old enough to have got to the declaration of the Soviet in Munich. The USPD was after all the dominant left organization in Bavaria up till 1920, so Siegi's introduction to politics was almost certainly via its politics. Did the romance of Toller and the bravery of the USPD during the Munich Soviet and its aftermath capture his youthful imagination? He certainly talked glowingly of Toller, but as a playwright. According to Ken Worpole, Siegi had told him he knew Toller, Ken assumed in Bavaria. Ken's impression was that this was more than a 'formal' acquaintanceship. It is possible therefore that Siegi maintained an attachment to the less 'Leninist' politics of the USPD, when he joined the KPD. The USPD contained factions with inconsistent tendencies – some looking towards replacing the SPD in the Reichstag, others far more concerned with building it up as a mass party. As will be discussed in Part 2 of this book, Siegi in his 40s, was combining (published) left-Keynesian articles with attempts at (unpublished) socialist analysis; in his 60s, he was combining working for a Labour government with (unpublished) articles damning the SPD in 1918. Are the tensions in these different positions understandable against the background of an early allegiance to the USPD? Maybe, to again run ahead of ourselves, Siegi's distancing from the KPD was partly rooted in his early experience of the USPD as a mass party and a consequently more acute awareness of how bureaucratized and unresponsive to its membership the KPD had become by the mid-1930s, a theme that will be returned to in Part 2.

One personal story: my father used to suggest I read B.Traven's novels. I did, and loved Traven's vivid depictions of the daily lives and travails of the exploited Mexican and South American workers. Having grown up with Traven, I was always nonplussed that so few, even on the left, had heard of him.

(Indeed, many still haven't.) So I was fascinated to discover that Traven was a member of the Soviet Republic in Munich, was arrested on 1 May 1919, and then imprisoned. He had been publishing a much censored radical/anarchist paper called *Ziegelbenner*, or Brickmaker/burner, and fled Germany around 1924.[25] Siegi would have come across him and/or his writings when he was himself a youth.

In fact, Munich, despite being at the heart of reactionary Bavaria, had a flourishing and 'progressive' cultural scene, which may also have influenced Siegi's emphasis on culture as being politically of significance. Rilke, whose poetry my father loved so well, lived and worked intermittently in Munich at the turn of the nineteenth century. Thomas Mann, whom my father seemed to detest, also lived in Munich from 1891 to 1933.

Another person Siegi might have come across in Munich was Brecht, whom Siegi was to know (and dislike) in Berlin. Brecht was born in Munich in 1898 and lived there till 1924, dates which largely overlap with Siegi's. Brecht went to school in Augsburg and then enrolled at Munich University in 1917. He became involved in the Workers' and Soldiers' Council in Augsburg in 1918–1919. (Augsburg was also the home of one of Siegi's rich uncles.) He made frequent rail journeys to Munich to watch and join in the demonstrations there (Rosenhaft, 2006).[26] Valentin, an early agitprop artist and clown in Munich, who made fun of employers, influenced Brecht. (Indeed, my parents retained an interest in the clown as a 'political' medium.) Brecht later attended lectures in 1928–1929 at the Marxist workers' college in Berlin, but he never seems to have actually joined the KPD. Even if their paths never crossed, Brecht and Siegi emerged from a similar political/cultural milieu.

The fate of the left in 1923 in Bavaria will be considered in the next section on the rise of the ultra-right. It is impossible to now know in what ways Siegi's experience of repression, the crucial strategic debates on the revolutionary left, or the combinations of different working-class and military actions in 1918–1919 and subsequent years, influenced him, but it is known that, within a short time of arriving in Berlin, he had become a leading cadre, which certainly suggests he was already active and probably known to the KPD.

Bavaria: the birthplace of the Nazis

Bavaria was the birth place and centre of the far-right after 1919. Indeed, its location (next to Austria), its strong tradition of independence from Germany from before 1914, its deeply reactionary politics outside of the main cities and its failure to industrialize suggest that Bavaria was not at all a typical German state.[27] But its historical significance to this story (and to future events in Germany) is great, as it was here that the Nazi party was founded, and later the SA as an amalgamation of the Nazis with sections of the violently anti-Communist Freikorps (Thomas Grant, 2004).[28] The precursor of the Nazi party, The Committee for Independent Workmen, was first set up by Drexler in 1918 in Munich. Hitler joined in 1919. Certain policies were already visible – opposition to the Versailles treaty and the new Weimar Republic, a belief in the Germans as an Aryan race, and the claim that the Jews were responsible for international capitalism and war profiteering.

In 1919, Drexler was involved in creating the 'German Workers' Party', an essentially secret organization, out of the original group and another similar organization. Hitler, who was stationed in Munich, joined the Party (after a debate about Bavaria joining Austria!). By 1920, partly under Hitler's guidance, the Party had grown from a few dozen to thousands. It also added 'National Socialist' to its title (National Socialist German Workers' Party or NSDAP or Nazi Party). By the end of July 1921 (P. Hoser),[29] there were nine local groups in Bavaria; by the end of 1922: 44; and in the rest of Germany, by spring 1922: 56; by 1923, there were 178 groups – a remarkably fast expansion. In

1921, the local group in Munich, the Nazis' main centre, alone was large enough to be divided into seven sections. By 1923, the Nazis already had an estimated membership of 35,000 in Munich; in Bavaria: 150,000. They already relied on their paramilitary organization SA, when they went into the 'public'. Serge (1997), [30] in his remarkable reports from Munich in 1923 written at the time, quotes a German journalist who succeeded unusually in penetrating Hitler's premises at this time. Even then, Hitler intended to be the Mussolini of Germany and to march on Saxony to root out Marxism. He anticipated that Prussia would then rise in his support. Hitler was already attacking parliamentarianism for ruining Germany. Marxists were Jews and the Jews were responsible for the impoverishment of the masses and for supporting parliamentarianism (Serge: 1997).

The first time that the Nazis as a party entered the public stage in Munich was in the Kapp Putsch of March 1920.[31] Its aim was the overthrow of Weimar and its government. Kapp, a right-wing journalist and politician, received support from one of Germany's foremost military men, General Ludendorf, as well as from the paramilitary Freikorps and many army officers. The military and the Home Guards' leadership of the putsch demanded the Bavarian government resign.[32] Although it is not known how many rallied (Gunther Gerstenberg from Walter Roos, 1998, Bavarian archives),[33] there was a call to workers in Munich and Nuremburg to form workers' militias to counter the Kapp Putsch. Ironically, the Kapp/Luttwitz putsch, led by the Bavarian Civil Guards and the Freikorps, forced the Social Democratic Prime Minister, John Hoffman (1867–1930),[34] out of office. So the Kapp Putsch did succeed in Bavaria. But after the Kapp Putsch, both Social Democratic and KPD groups encouraged the formation of workers' militias and this led to many clashes with the Nazis, including, in Nuremberg on 17 March 1920, the murder of more than 20 workers.

While the middle class had generally been against the Kapp Putsch, the right were growing in strength, particularly in Bavaria, the one region where the Kapp Putsch had had a lasting impact, throwing out a 'left' government and putting into power an extreme right government, briefly under von Kahr succeeding Hoffman. It collaborated with the Nazis and welcomed in every far-right group who were banned elsewhere.[35] Worried at the NSDAP's growing influence, especially in Bavaria, the German Social Democratic government tried to ban the NSDAP, but the Bavarian state authorities ignored this (Harman, 1982). In March 1921, the KPD called the ill-fated 'March Action'. Bavaria then called a state of emergency and banned left-wing meetings and papers, but not the ultra-right papers which the Federal government had previously banned. A variety of ultra-right militaristic organizations, with hundreds of thousands of supporters, took to the streets (Price, 16 September 1921).[36] Berlin tried to ban the Bavarian emergency, on the grounds that they were exceeding their powers, but essentially failed. In the following couple of years, the Bavarian army high command secretly collaborated with the NSDAP and other paramilitary organizations (Rose,1999 from Price, 23 November 1922).

By 1923, the ultra-right in Bavaria was holding power. Van Knilling, the Bavarian prime minister, had opposed the overthrow of both the German monarchy and of the home-grown Bavarian monarch.[37] He and his government loathed the federal Social Democratic government and in effect declared semi-autonomy. Rumours of repeated Nazi putsches rocked Munich. Storm troopers marched through Munich and beat up people they disliked. They did not discriminate between the Social Democrats and the KPD; indeed members of the SPD even manned the barricades in response (Landauer, 1959).[38]

Information on the political turbulence of 1923 can be found elsewhere (see Price in particular). But, briefly, in Munich, the shock waves of the French occupation of the Ruhr had led to a variety of trade-union organizations campaigning to refuse to handle Ruhr coal. To quote from Price's dispatch of 5 April 1923 'Armed Reichswehr troops wearing steel helmets and with a hint of a goose-step in their marching passed. A cluster of... Swastika wearers roaring, "To Hell with the French beasts!" "Down with the Jews!" Hitler's shock troops were daily parading through Munich.' Price adds, however, that what united the right was their common purpose to fight organized labour.

Following on from the strikes and revolts in parts of Germany in early–mid 1923,[39] the federal military leadership had declared an emergency ban on demonstrations. But in Bavaria, explicitly anti-Semitic fascist organizations were openly organizing and mobilizing, unchecked locally or by the national government, to the degree where Serge, an astute observer, saw them as organizing for civil war (Serge: 1997). To quote Serge, 23 September 1923, from his *International Correspondence*: 'Fascist Bavaria has thus in no uncertain terms put itself at the head of the movement of protest by the bourgeoisie ...'

Price, in his dispatch of 23 January 1922, talked of how in Bavaria, from 1921, there was a systematic anti-Semitic campaign (which Price sees as a capitalist conspiracy) by a group called the Constitution Council: 'With them, Jews are vermin.' Price sees this anti-Semitism as inspiring the murders of Rathenau (see endnote 31) and Erzberger (see endnote 201). This organization, which Price saw as even to the right of the fascists, also organized against workers' centres and Jewish shopkeepers, and plundered banks and mail trains.

Another early example of the strength of the ultra-right in September 1923 was the so called German Day in Nuremberg. 'German Day' was established as a deliberate provocation to the 'red' city workers, in part a response to the attempt to organize a soviet. Hundreds of thousands of supporters turned up, including Hitler, Goering, Streicher and Ludendorf. Serge (1997) quotes Captain Heis, addressing a fascist meeting on 23

September in Augsburg (where Siegi's uncle had his distillery): 'The time has come for rifles, machine-guns and...cannons [for civil war]. The Bavarian fist will resolve in Berlin the problem of German liberty.' The Nazi rally was met with resistance and, according to the sources, there was much blood.[40]

Von Kahr, on whom the Bavarian government had conferred dictatorial powers, declared martial law and was expected to reach a deal with Hitler and Ludendorf: to strike at Bolshevism and 'to wring the neck of Ebert's republic' (Serge).[41] The federal government's response, under (the 'Marxist') Stresemann, was to declare martial law throughout the country (Serge, 1997).

The coalition government's espoused aim may have been to curb the Bavarian government but it was the ultra-right who benefited from martial law – in Bavaria strikes were banned and the death penalty threatened for acts of sabotage. In October 1923, the next conflict erupted when the Nazis prepared for their 'March on Berlin', inspired by Mussolini's success in Italy, with Munich as its base. The demand was for Chancellor Stresemann's resignation.[42]

Then, at the beginning of November 1923, the Nazis used a patriotic rally in a Munich beer hall to launch an abortive putsch, demanding the regional and national governments, including President Ebert, stand down and the establishment of a right-wing dictatorship; otherwise, Bavarian troops would march on the capital in order to install Hitler, von Kahn and Ludendorf. Most of the members of the Bavarian government were there (Price, 1999). It was backed by around 600 armed storm troopers. With Hitler, were already Rohm of the Bavarian army, Goering, Hess and others, including General Ludendorf. Fascist forces mobilized for one million to march on Berlin, supported by the Stadhelms' five thousand local groups (Serge, 1997). The next morning, they gathered something between two and three thousand supporters to march through Munich. The troops opened fire and 16 Nazis were killed. In the few hours when the fascists held Munich, they ransacked the SPD editorial office and the home of the SPD local leader, and arrested, with the intent to execute, the KPD and SPD councillors (Serge, 1997). Hitler and others were sentenced for treason but received light sentences. The leniency with which the plotters were treated contrasts with the extreme severity of the sentences, including execution, of those on the left who had been arrested.[43]

It seems exceedingly unlikely that Siegi would not have been aware of the rapid growth of the extreme right and of the composition of their leadership. Certainly, he talked to me and Richard Kirkwood of the Bierkellers of Munich, of the gatherings of the early Nazi boot-boys, and of how important it was to understand that the Nazi thugs presented a popular 'socialist' programme to appeal to the 'masses' but, as was his wont, did not refer to his own involvement. My guess is that he spotted early on the contradictory nature of the Nazi party – appealing not only to the workers but also to German nationalism and the bourgeois right. He used to tell me: 'Always remember what the name 'Nazi' stands for: National Socialist.' Siegi's understanding of Nazism was rooted in his time in Bavaria.

Despite much effort and the help of the Bavarian library archives, it has not been possible to find any political trace of Siegi till his arrival in Berlin. But Siegi will have been deeply affected by the cauldron of revolutionary and Nazi activity in Munich and the unusual level of early political repression, and will have developed roots in Munich's rich cultural seed bed. The person who arrived in Berlin in 1928 was about to become an active anti-Nazi and revolutionary and at a minimum his experiences in Bavaria had helped form his future politics.

By 1928, it might have looked as if the worst of the political earthquakes, which had almost consumed the Weimar Republic, were over. After the ferment of 1918–1923 and the following years of economic depression and stagflation, the economic and political situation had stabilized. In 1928, the NSDAP picked up a mere 2.6 per cent in the Reichstag elections. But the 1929 Wall Street crash finally upset the Weimar apple-cart (Hobsbawm, 2003) – just in time for Siegi's arrival in Berlin.

Endnotes

10. Hobsbawm, *Introduction to Leviné.*
11. Harman, *The Lost Revolution.*
12. Eisner, 1867–1919, first a member of the SPD, joined the USPD because of his opposition to the First World War and war credits. Sentenced to prison, he was released in 1918. He was shot by Count Arso on 21February 1919.
13. The USPD was a break away from the Social Democrats in 1917, opposing its support for Germany in the war. Within months, it had a membership of 120,000 to the SPD's 150,000 and was a magnet for the striking sailors, as well as thousands of working-class activists. But its orientation was as much towards the Reichstag and its main unifying demand was an end to the war (Harman).
14. Siegi, after retirement, took to painting. One of his pictures is of the revolution in Portugal in 1974 when the paramilitaries led by de Carvalho came out against the right-wing Salazar government. Siegi's picture shows them on the roof of their barracks, pointing their weapons at the counter-revolutionaries. (I have it up in my bedroom.) Maybe Siegi's awareness of how crucial it was which side the armed forces were on stems from his experiencing this inspiring support of the revolution by these Bavarian soldiers.
15. If one accepts Rosa Leviné-Meyer's version based on the account of her husband, Leviné, there was also acute factionalism between the USPD with Toller, and the Sparticists/KPD.
16. Although this can only be supposition, Siegi, as we will see in later chapters, never joined, or, as far as I know, was even tempted to join the British Labour Party. Many British ex-

comrades since the 1930s have done so and, indeed, at least before his time in Durham, his closest friends were in the Labour Party. My hunch is that, as a young man, he had observed how the Social Democrats betrayed the revolution in Bavaria, as well as having the more usual association of the Social Democrats as the killers of Luxemburg and Liebknecht.

17. Broué, *The German Revolution 1917–1923*.
18. In addition, there were the 'Bavarian white guards', a force of about 9,000, referred to in Price's submissions to the *Manchester Guardian* (7 December 1920). Price argues that France no longer saw the conditions of the Versailles treaty as applying to Bavaria and was giving the White Guards financial assistance. The suggestion is that the ultra-right forces in Bavaria were keen enough on separating from Germany to be willing to collude with Germany's enemy. In another instance of Bavaria protecting the ultra-right, Price (in dispatch to the *Daily Herald* on 16 September 1921) described the Erhardt Brigade (made up largely of Munich students) – responsible for the murder of Ezberger, an influential member of the Centre party who in 1917 unusually called for the ending of the war, and also responsible for the murder of thousands of workers in 1919, which then took part in the Kapp Putsch and had theoretically been banned – as existing illegally under the protection of the Bavarian government and police.
19. Lukacs too was inspired by similar days in Hungary. I owe this point to David Renton.
20. Albert Buckman (1894–1973), who had moved to Munich in 1920 and joined the KPD, became its leader from around 1923 to 1932. Briefly imprisoned, he then became the political director of the Southern Bavarian district from 1929, as well as being a Reichstag deputy (1924 to 1932/33). He was sent to a variety of concentration camps over twelve

years but survived to die a natural death.

21. A fascinating detail, which I have not been able to get more information about, but the KPD apparently partially relied on bases in England for their southern Bavarian network (Mühldorfer).
22. The sole representative of Bavaria in the highest governing body of the Communist Party in 1929, F. Stenzer (1900–1933) was the secretary of the district leadership in southern Bavaria; he was also on the city council in Chessington since 1932. In 1932, he was elected a full member of the Reichstag. In 1933, he was sent to Dachau where he died within the year.
23. The KPD representatives from northern Bavaria were: G. Karl (1882–1964), Member of Parliament from 1923 to 1928, member of Communist Party from 1930; J. Schlaffer (1891–1964), Member of Parliament from 1924 to 1926 and from the mid-1920s, head of the illegal Communist Party; J. Meyer (1889–1950), political leader of the district from 1924 to 1930, member of the Reichstag from 1924 to 1933, and J. Boulanger (1897–1968), political leader from 1930 to 1933, Member of Parliament in 1932, twelve years in concentration camps and jails. In 1932, the Munich locksmith, Hans Beimler (1895–1936), who had been a member of the Landtag and the Reichstag since 1932, and of the political leadership of the district of southern Bavaria, fell fighting for the International Brigades during the Spanish Civil War.
24. The Bavarian KPD was as faction ridden as every other bit of the KPD and was dominated by the squabbles and changes of line of the Comintern. What apparently particularly taxed their members was whether it was right to have delegates in the Reichstag and the local parliament (Mühldorfer).
25. Nobody is sure who Traven was, as this was a pseudonym and after his German experiences, he seems to have become a bit of a recluse, but he was almost certainly Ret Maput.

After he had escaped Germany, his book, *White Rose*, a condemnation of capitalism, was published in 1929; it is thought that its name may have inspired the heroic anti-Nazi 'White Rose' group (June 1942–February 1943), who were based at Munich university. A final twist for me is that one of the leading experts on Traven, Michael Baumann, turns out to have been my second cousin on my mother's side.

26. Rosenhaft, Eve, 'Brecht's Germany 1898–1933', in *Brecht*, eds. Thompson, P. and Sacks, G.
27. After a serious flirtation with its neighbour, Catholic Austria, in the nineteenth century, Bavaria joined Germany, but managed to retain, nominally anyway, its own army, post and railways. The demand of independence from the German republic was even used to support their demands by the leaders of the Munich Soviet in 1918–1919, such as Eisner.
28. Grant, *Stormtroopers and the crisis in the Nazi movement: activism, ideology and dissolution.*
29. Hoser, *National Socialist German Worker's Party, 1920–1922.* Accessed 11.10.10. http://www.historisches-lexikon-bayerns.de/suche/abfrage?type=volltext&schnellsuche=Hoser&x=-163&y=-209
30. Serge, 1997, *Witness to the German Revolution.*
31. Hermann Ehrhardt was one of the leaders of the Putsch and was to be involved in the murder of the Jewish cabinet minister Rathenau in 1922 (a distant relative of Siegi's wife, Lotte). The Social-Democrat, Noske, defending Ehrhardt concerning the Putsch argued for him that he had formed an elite corps which had been highly useful in suppressing Bolshevism. Ehrhardt was sent to prison but escaped, with official collusion (I. Birchall's notes in Serge, 1997).
32. Bavaria was not their main target – the ultra-right organized an attempted military coup in Berlin, when sections of the

military moved on Berlin (and Ebert et al fled) and were ultimately defeated by the trade unions and workers declaring a general strike. Kapp was ousted and the Social Democratic government then took back the reins of power, only to attack the forces which had protected them.

33. Roos, *Die Rote Armee der Bayerischen Räterepublik in München 1919 (The Red Army of the Bavarian Soviet Republic in Munich 1919)*, Heidelberg, 1998. Accessed 10.10.10. http://www.historisches-lexikon-bayerns.de/artikel/artikel_44654 (12/11/2009).
34. Hoffman, who had been a SPD deputy to the Reichstag before the first world war, was Bavarian minister of education/culture under PM Kurt Eisner after the November 1918 revolution, when he removed the Bavarian schooling system from the supervision of the church (another possible ideological link to Siegi's later interest in the Freethinkers). Hoffman became elected Bavarian President. The soviet ousted him, but he returned to Munich in 1919 after the crushing of the soviets and briefly resumed being President.
35. Price writes of Bavaria in January 1923 to *Labour Monthly* that Bavaria was the area most removed from normal 'traffic', where the workers were sparse and scattered and not generally politically effective, the peasants had become landowning junkers, and were 'boorish, superstitious... and politically backward'. It was a situation easily exploitable by the ultra-right and the army high command.
36. Price, *Dispatches from the Weimar Republic*, ed. Tania Rose.
37. Crown Prince Rupprecht would have been heir to the Bavarian monarchy, abolished in 1918.
38. Landauer, *European Socialism*.
39. The tumultuous months of 1923, when the revolutionary left finally decided to go for revolution, are not considered here as they did not have a direct impact on Bavaria. For those interested, a good starting point is Harman's *The Lost*

Revolution. For more detail, go to Broué.

40. Bavaria was not unique. In other parts of Germany, the fascists were taking on the left, such as at Jena, where the fascists and municipal police together killed demonstrators. In Halle, the fascists of the Stadhelm attacked a left newspaper office (Serge).
41. One month later, von Kahr declared himself to be a temporary replacement for the Bavarian king!
42. The Stresemann government's response was typically – but tragically – to attack the left at this point, not the fascists. Stresemann only lasted from August to November 1923.
43. The causes of the failure of the Putsch fall outside this narrative but Serge essentially suggests that the bourgeoisie and rich industrialists (some of whom were already financing it) took fright, at least for the time being.

Chapter 4

1918–1933 Political background to the KPD

Siegi's time in the KPD in Germany was relatively brief – as far as we know, from 1929/30 to 1933 – but it was at the centre of his life for those four years and framed his thinking for the rest of his life. It is worth first reminding ourselves of the position of the KPD as a backdrop to Siegi's activities up till 1933. A brief glimpse into the twists and turns of the KPD is a necessary prelude to understanding Siegi's political choices and activities; moreover, given that we will find Siegi actively resisting the Nazis, it is worth providing a background to enable us to analyse in subsequent chapters how his activities followed, or failed to follow, a KPD line. In a period of political and economic turmoil, the faction fighting around the KPD took on a far more than normal significance – its bare bones are summarized (and simplified) below. (Readers interested in the alphabet soup of different grouplets, whose internecine feuding was to determine all our fates, should keep an eye on this chapter's endnotes and the appendices.)

The threat from the NSDAP in Berlin in the years up to 1928–1929 was growing, but was vastly outnumbered by the left and was largely unobserved. We do not know the membership of the newly established NSDAP Berlin branch, but by 1926, the NSDAP were beginning to draw people from right-wing paramilitary organizations and right-wing athletics clubs, as well as campaigning amongst the ever increasing numbers of unemployed (Rosenhaft, 1983:18). Already in 1927, hundreds of the SA had the confidence to confront a carload of the Rotfrontkämpferbund (RFB or Red Front) following a Nazi meeting at Trebbin, close to Berlin (Rosenhaft, 1983:18).

By early 1929, the SA in Berlin had a membership of about 800.

By comparison, the membership of the KPD in 1927 in Berlin was greater: 15,000, one tenth of German membership (Rosenhaft, 1983:11); the RFB in 1929: 11,000 (Rosenhaft, 1983:18). The left far outnumbered the right – which contributed to the KPD's failure to pay sufficient attention to the right. In the 1928 elections, the Nazis received only a very small proportion of the Berlin vote (nationally 2.6 per cent, against the KPD with 10.6 per cent and the SDP with almost 30 per cent). Two years later, in 1930, the Nazis gained 18.3 per cent and in 1932 their share nationally had risen to 37.3 per cent, though 'only' 30 per cent in Berlin (Rosenhaft, 1983:19). (In the November 1932 election, the Nazis lost votes, creating further illusions.) This was the context in which KPD policy needs to be assessed.

1918–1928

Any observer would have predicted that, if any country were to move towards socialism, then Germany would be the first. By the early 1900s, the SPD was already both the biggest socialist party in the world and the main opposition in Germany. It had been founded by associates of Marx and Engels and held a formally Marxist position of class struggle and the need for the overthrow of capitalism. However, many of its leading figures were already committed to a 'reformist' perspective. Dating back to its founders' opposition to the 1870 Franco-Prussian War, one of its key principles was never to vote for the military budget. The SPD vote for war credits in August 1914 led eventually to the split in 1917 with a pro-peace, if not anti-war, minority. This formed the Independent SPD (USPD) and alongside them a number of hard-line and actively anti-war revolutionary groupings, principally the Spartacus League around the leading theoretician, Rosa Luxemburg, and the former leader of the SPD youth, Karl Liebknecht. These groupings came together in December 1918 under the leadership of the Spartacists to form the new German Communist Party (KPD), which became the biggest and most influential Communist Party outside the Soviet Union. Germany was seen by most revolutionaries as the key to the success or otherwise of the Russian, indeed the world, revolution. In this sense, Siegi was an important participant in one of the most important struggles in world history.

From its foundation, the KPD suffered from divisions, factions and splits between those who saw themselves as continuing Luxemburg's struggle to build a mass party and a mass workers' movement, and those who stigmatized them as passive and opportunist and who were, in turn, accused of irresponsible and sectarian leftism. But, unlike in the period from 1929, the overwhelming majority of the KPD had, from 1921, with Comintern approval, upheld the tactic of the united front. In late 1920, at its Halle Congress, the majority of the USPD had voted to merge with the KPD (the minority were to rejoin the SPD in 1922). The new party's policy was for a united front with the trade unions and the SPD, which had been crucial in the defeat of the Kapp Putsch (see previous chapter). The tactic of the united front involved attempts at uniting all organizations linked to the working class, from the 'ultra-left' Communist Workers' Party of Germany (KAPD) to the SPD, around a militant, and if necessary armed, defence of workers' living standards and struggle against authoritarianism. The KPD's argument was twofold: if the SPD accepted the alliance, they would be able to pull over a significant section of the SPD into joint activity leading towards revolution; however, if the SPD rejected the approach, then the KPD could win over their membership.

In 1923, the KPD, now led by the 'centre-rights' Brandler and Thalheimer, decided to plan for a full-scale revolution, with the hope of bringing on board as much of the SPD as possible. In Saxony and Thuringia, where a strong SPD leaned to the left,[44] KPD leaders had become ministers in SPD dominated governments and it was hoped this would give the revolution financial support, control of local police and distribution of arms to militias (LaPorte). But the left Social Democrats started to pull out; no arms were distributed in Saxony and Thuringia and, following the failure of the 'United Front' Chemnitz conference of 21October to agree plans for a general strike, the rising was called off at the last minute by the KPD CC (after a strong intervention in favour of doing so from Radek on behalf of the Comintern). The failure of the 1923 events is a turning point: it marked a fundamental defeat for the revolutionary left and laid open the space for the growth of an ultra-right alternative to the Weimar fiasco.

At this point the factional struggles in the KPD became entangled in the factional struggles within the leadership of the Soviet Union and the Comintern (Radek, the main link between the KPD and both the Comintern and the Soviet Communist Party, held responsible for the defeat, was a supporter of Trotsky against the 'troika' who took over after the death of Lenin). The Brandler-Thalheimer leadership were excluded from all influence following the April 1924 KPD conference and were moved to Moscow to work for the Comintern (during 1924 similar 'purges' were carried out in several European Communist Parties). The Comintern became increasingly dominant in providing a leadership and settling bitter internal disputes, to the point where it is often thought that KPD policy was effectively decided in Moscow.

The 1923 defeat also opened the door to the dropping in practice of the united front policy. The Berlin-based leftists, Ruth Fischer and Arkady Maslow, who had opposed the united front tactic, in particular the entry of KPD members into government in Saxony and Thuringia, now took over. Then, from 1926 to 1928, following the 'leftists' removal by the Comintern, the KPD was led by the 'Centre'.[45]

1928–1933

Siegi's main period of political activity occurs once he arrives in

Berlin – he is still only 24 – and it is therefore an analysis of the KPD's policies between 1928 and 1933 which is of most importance as it provides the background to all Siegi's activities. It coincides, moreover, almost exactly with the 'Third Period'. It is also worth noting that the Berlin KPD had, from its earliest days, been strongly influenced by the hard-line 'left' of the party.

The Social Democrats and the KPD saw the working class as a battle ground (certainly in Berlin, Siegi's stamping ground), who, having undergone mass unemployment and poverty, were generally deeply disaffected from the main parties and parliamentary system. For every 'front' organization of the KPD, we will find an alternative with the SPD. It is important to recognize how significant the division between the KPD and the SPD was in the years leading up to 1933 and how far it framed the KPD's lack of attention to the rising NSDAP. While what is written here will focus almost entirely on the KPD, it is fully recognized that the SPD was as sectarian as the KPD but, unlike the KPD, was in some areas in power and in control of the police – therefore in a very different 'locus' of power to the KPD. Nevertheless, the SPD's responsibility for the rise of Nazism has to lie outside this book.

In 1928, the 6th Congress of the Comintern introduced the Third Period, a profound shift from the 'second period': a period of consolidation and of the tactic of the United Front, already described. Now, however, the Comintern saw a period of rising economic and political crisis and increasing class conflict – capitalism would consequently look for solutions outside capitalist 'normality' (even if an extension of it). The bourgeoisie would rationalize capitalism, using increasingly authoritarian methods. The Social Democratic leadership would place increasingly severe restraint on the working class and thus compromise with, and become an open vehicle of, the ruling class. Like the actual fascists, the 'social fascists' would gain a popular base with fake policies appealing to the less well off.[46] Thus the KPD came up with the infamous position that Social Democrats were 'social fascists'.[47] The major alternative was that capitalism would turn towards Fascism itself (Rosenhaft, 1983: 30–32). Both the 'social fascists' and the real fascists were defined as 'national fascists', both equally seen as enemies, (Rosenhaft,1983: 59; Carr,1982: 15 passim).[48] So, the choice was one form or another of fascism or the Communist movement taking over the leadership of the 'inevitable' mass protests and seizing power.

Early on in the Third Period, once the Social Democrats were defined as 'social fascists', the KPD rejected making even formal appeals to the Social Democrats – or 'social fascists' – for proletarian unity, as they had done earlier. As Carr (1982: 15) states about the position of the Politburo in April 1930: 'Nothing...suggested any weakening in the determination to brand *the SPD* and *its leaders* as social-fascists and as a prop to the bourgeoisie'. [My italics; note Carr's distinction here.] Crucially, it was implied and sometimes openly argued, that such appeals would be counter-productive as workers and other 'popular' classes would rapidly move to 'pre-revolutionary' consciousness and action such as strikes and street protests, and away from confidence in both parliamentary politics in general and social democracy in particular.

Though the interpretation of the 'Third Period' varies between leading members of the CC between 1930 and 1933 (Carr, 1982: 29–83, passim), the CC position was generally not a refusal to work with Social Democratic workers as the Third Period is frequently represented. Rather the emphasis is on pulling SPD workers away from their leadership and into the Communist fold, so that the KPD would become the leadership for the whole working class (Carr, 1982: 35). It is the leadership who (generally) are referred to as 'social fascists'. This is very different from the normal concept of 'united front'. Indeed, the criticism that both Trotsky and Brandler, removed from leadership of the KPD in the aftermath of the failure of 1923, made of this position was that attacking the Social Democratic leaders, even though not apparently the workers, would actually drive away the working-class members of such organizations, and therefore split the German working class and the left (as so tragically proved to be the case). I did not hear any evidence from the Berlin 3 that the policy of pulling Social Democratic workers into the Communist fold was put into practice. The one area where there was sometimes joint activity: the Red Front (discussed below, and in which Siegi played a role), I would argue was as much a product of circumstance – the increasing local power of the SA and Nazi thugs – than policy.

In subsequent chapters, there is a discussion as to whether Siegi himself adopted the concept of 'social fascist', a term that was not universally employed. Indeed LaPorte (2002: 305) (partly based on research by Gert Reuter) documents that in 1929 the KPD leadership purged those who resisted the use of this term and its implementation, but that these currents continued to exist latently as a basic tendency within the party.

LaPorte's (2002: 183) analysis of the relationship between KPD leadership's line and the activities of the membership is instructive and unique. Though his focus is Saxony, many of his conclusions have a far broader pertinence – and, as will be seen in later chapters, are borne out by my interviews with the three old KPD Berliners. Even before the implementation of the Third Period line in 1928, the leadership of the KPD, a 'Stalinized' party, was already 'unable to impose the Comintern's ever changing line on a membership which remained rooted in their local environments.' Party policy was already decided 'from above', and opponents from not only the KPD but also RFB were purged. Nevertheless, the strength of the factions, on right or left, was rooted in the local environment in which activists campaigned and this gave them an independence of thought. LaPorte (2002) indeed argues that in general the KPD leadership (unlike the SPD) failed to bring the rank and file with it in its many changes of line, and (particularly relevant here) in its confrontational attitude to the SPD.

LaPorte (2002) argues that already by 1929, the attempt of the party leadership to impose ideological uniformity generally destabilized the relationship between the party and its membership. The KPD leadership in late 1928 tried to bed down the new turn to the left. At the Second Party Workers' Conference in Berlin (its delegates were not elected but appointed), Neumann, one of the leaders of the German KPD whom we shall soon re-encounter, insisted that the term of 'social fascist' was merely the application of past principles to present conditions and pointed to a radicalization of the workforce, such as displayed in the strike in the Ruhr iron and steel industry (in fact, a lock-out in which the KPD had little influence). The link between party organization and the implementation of party policy was also tightened by the introduction of 'organizational discipline' (*Körperschaftsdisziplin*) (Rosenhaft, 1983: 266–268). Party debate must end after a decision was reached by a higher authority and trade-union and other delegates were restricted to their own organization and level.[49] LaPorte (2002) quotes Weber that the Opposition already stood no chance against the party machine.[50]

Talking to the Berlin 3 gave me an insight into how meaningful the 'social fascist' line was. Rudi and Hans had observed and undergone arrests, harassment and beatings before 1933, of course by the SA, but more significantly here, by the police under SDP control and the SDPers themselves.[51] Moreover, Rudi at least remembered the 1929 events in Berlin (discussed in the next chapter) when demonstrators were shot down by the police under Social Democratic control. It is also likely that he knew older comrades who would have experienced and remembered similar events of 1918 and 1923. The lived experience of these rank and file KPD members prejudiced them to see the SDPers as no better than the Nazis. LaPorte (2002), looking at the relationship between line and membership in his analysis of the KPD between 1924 and 1933, similarly argues that KPD directives were interpreted and responded to in specific political contexts.

Though Siegi was not active in a trade union, it is worth briefly examining the KPD's Third Period policy towards establishing and joining separate unions as an example of how far KPD leadership were successful in enforcing the 'line'. The Party's so called independent revolutionary trade union was the Red Union. To take Hans as an example of a rank and file trade union member: Hans lived in Leipzig, Saxony, and belonged to the Social Democratic Union, not the Red Union. This was almost certainly because it was the stronger union, maybe also because there was no Red Union there or it was not viable. He could not easily be forced to carry out policies that 'failed to account for the realities of their own specific political environment.' Moreover, Hans said that he actually did not carry out much political work in the union. Indeed, LaPorte (2002), referring to the very beginning of the period that interests us (1928, in Saxony), records the reticence of Communists to do political work in the factories because of their fear that this would lead to their expulsion from their union. Whatever the reasons for his non-involvement, Hans' case is an example of the limitation of the KPD policy of separate Red Unions. Membership of a SDP dominated union was presumably seen at a rank and file level as politically appropriate.

LaPorte (2002), examining the causes for the multi-fracturing of the working class and the relationship to the KPD, argues that there is no evidence that the Party members – whether unemployed or employed, skilled or unskilled workers – supported the policy of Red Unions and that this policy was instead a 'radicalisation from above', which found very little support in the factories.

In fact, a close reading of the KPD's debates on the formation of separate Red Unions shows much ambiguity, as to the desirability of separate formations, though in general the line supports this position. LaPorte (2002: 288) argues that the purpose behind the separate union position was to 'push the gulf between the SPD and KPD at national level into the parties' social bases.' The KPD wanted to end the internal party political consequences of contact with the wider workers' movement, even calling on the replacement of long serving Communists, who were frequently former Social Democrats. In reality, the KPD rather demanded that KPD candidates were put forward for shop steward positions. But, '[o]ften Communist union functionaries, as well as rank-and-file members, simply ignored party directives for drawing up independent candidate lists in the factory council elections' (LaPorte, 2002: 286).

LaPorte (2002) argues strongly that the Third Period line, rather than distancing their members from the SPD, actually loosened the influence of the KPD line on its trade union rank and file, certainly in Saxony. We will consider the implications of this analysis when examining Siegi's trajectory in the next chapter.

There was limited opposition to the Third Period line within the circles of the KPD but Siegi does not appear to have been directly influenced by any of the KPD factions. Very few comrades adopted any sort of true 'united front' position from 1929 onwards. A few SPDers who wished to oppose Nazism within a united front joined the Socialist Workers' Party (SAP), founded in 1931, and also joined by a few dissident Communists, a few KPD dissidents joined the Leninbund, (which the former chairman of the KPD, Ruth Fischer, joined)[52] and the KPD Opposition (KPDO or KPD Opposition), a kind of right-wing KPD opposition.[53] (Those interested in the minutiae of the (nevertheless) crucial divisions amongst the revolutionary left at this point should refer to Appendix 6 and endnotes below.)

Outside the brief of this study, but worth a mention, is that, on

31 December 1932, the SAP, Brandler's KPDO[54] and what was left of the Leninbund joined together, calling for the creation of a united defence organization. This initiative took place weeks before the January 1933 elections and was too late, even though it provided a challenge to the two 'parent' parties. These oppositionists to the KPD and the SPD had had to leave their parent organizations in order to organize against the Nazis. The SPD was so opposed to working with the KPD on an anti-Nazi front, that they would expel anybody who did (Private conversation with Harald Marpe, November 2011).[55]

LaPorte's crucial and distinctive argument about how far the KPD line was followed at a rank and file level highlights the importance of the balance of forces and local circumstances. Rudi's role in the Youth Red Front did not follow closely the vagaries of the KPD line on combating Nazism. Semi-unemployed Rudi, a youth activist in the Red Front, was running a daily campaign against the SA and the police well before 1933, which appeared to be based largely on necessity and experience, rather than the Party line. He was the leader of a group of the Youth Red Front in Wedding, and would have accepted non-Communists if he thought he could trust them against the almost daily onslaught of the SA before 1933. Yet, as LaPorte (2002) reminds us, the Party leadership remained focused on 'destroying' the SPD in order to 'clear the path' for revolution, at the time when local rank and file activists were increasingly confronted with Nazi violence on the streets. (This relative autonomy of the KPD from the leadership has been used by a few historians, for example K. Mallman (see Appendices), to argue against the thesis of the Stalinization of the KPD.)

Indeed, it is the 'exception' to the absence of joint anti-Nazi activity, which suggests how far local conditions could affect and limit KPD attempted dominance over anti-Nazi activity (though this is not meant to suggest that the Comintern's line was not a major determinant). In Saxony the SPD's response to the rise of the NSDAP at local level, particularly after the September Reichstag elections of 1931, was to hold meetings, which attracted considerably more workers than the KPD (LaPorte, 2002: 338,339).[56] (This position was at odds with the SPD's parliamentary policy of 'tolerating' the Brüning government.) In the localities in which the SPD was almost completely dominant in Saxony, Communist activists took part in political campaigning and genuine joint actions and became involved in umbrella organizations under SPD leadership to coordinate activity against the Nazis. 'The KPD leadership's prohibition on contact with the SPD at any level had an unexpected consequence: as street violence surged and the SPD organized counter demonstrations in middle and working class districts, working-class self-defence often took place under the banner of the SPD's local organizations' (LaPorte, 2002: 338) and, despite the KPD line, a significant number of Communist activists in the neighbourhoods joined those of the SPD in countering Nazi terror against workers' organizations (338).[57] As LaPorte (2002: 362) puts it: 'Nazi violence against organized workers was creating *ad hoc* co-operation between Social Democrats and Communists outside of the KPD leadership's immediate control.' Although parts of LaPorte's analysis of Saxony have a specificity, his emphasis on the failure of the KPD to hold many of its members to the Third Period line is relevant when we come to analyse Siegi's activities and attitudes in the next chapter.

Deadly mis-estimation of NSDAP

Siegi's involvement in the Red Front, a leading KPD dominated anti-Nazi organization, has to be understood within the context that, during 1930–1931, neither the Comintern nor even the KPD prioritized the Nazis' rise or significance. Carr (1982: 15) suggests that in mid-1930, 'national fascism', the SA and other paramilitary organizations scarcely were mentioned. The Nazis were not taken seriously. Carr (1982) writes that the first articles drawing attention to national fascism in Germany appear in mid-1930. (One of them is signed just with an 'S' –one possibility is that this was by Siegi.) Social Democracy remained the enemy, with its large membership and roots in the working class, and the NSDAP remained safely unseen in its shadow. Indeed, in one of those classic quotes from after the elections of September 1930, when the NSDAP increased its number of deputies from 12 to 107, the Rote Fahne announced that these elections marked the high point for the Nazis and that they would henceforth decline and fall (Carr, 1982: 25). Indeed, Heckert, one of the KPD leaders, attributed the NSDAP's enormous gains simply to a 're-grouping of the bourgeois camp' (Carr, 1982: 25).

As late as 1931, at the 11th plenum of the Comintern, held after the Nazis gained almost 20 per cent of the 1930 vote, Neumann, at the time a leading member of the KPD CC and representing the KPD, stated that the main struggle should be directed against the fascist bourgeoisie and its chief supporters, the Social Democratic leaders of the working class, adding that the danger of the actual fascists had to a large extent been removed (Carr, 1982: 36). At the same plenum, Manuilsky, the leading Comintern spokesperson at that point (and according to Trotsky the originator of the term: Third Period), also equated fascism to a form of bourgeois dictatorship and Thaelmann[58] equated it to the Brüning government (though Martynov, Stalin's ally, was a touch more subtle, describing the Brüning government merely as 'the carrier of the fascist danger' (Carr, 1982: 36, 37).) As Manuilsky put it: 'the *central task* of the KPD is to win over a majority of the working class from its allegiance to the Social Democrats' [original italics] (Carr, 1982: 35).

The profundity of the KPD's misunderstanding of the balance of power and the role of the fascists is argued by Trotsky (1971):

> 'On October 14, 1931, Remmele,[59] one of the three official leaders of the Communist Party, said in the Reichstag, "...once

> they [the fascists] are in power, then the united front of the proletariat will be established and it will make a clean sweep of everything." (Violent applause from the Communists) Remmele ... thus prepares the way for Hitler's domination ...The united front of the proletariat is achievable – for Remmele, as he has told us – only after Hitler assumes power.'

But the increasing threat of mass mobilization by the SA and the rise in street violence in 1931–1932, which their members were actively involved in countering, led the KPD to (briefly) identify the struggle against the Nazis as their central goal and to approach the SDP leadership in an attempt to agree joint demands in 1932. Finally, on 25 April 1932, the KPD policy appeared to have taken a sharp U-turn, offering the SPD leaderships the prospect of 'fighting together' against the Nazis (LaPorte, 2002: 356). This would have given the KPD access to the SPD membership or shown the SPD leaders up as rejecting vital collaboration. However, already by 5 June, the CC insisted that the KPD's united front offers had been directed at the Social Democratic workers as individuals, not their 'reformist' leaders (LaPorte, 2002: 356). Their presentation of the Social Democratic leadership as actively counter-revolutionary, indeed as 'social fascists', seriously undermined the possibility of cooperation.[60]

Too late, the Comintern paid heed. A variety of resolutions, declarations and articles appeared from the Comintern and the KPD, each one more ambiguous than the last, but which finally emphasized the importance of appealing to Social Democratic workers for a united front against Nazism, a marginal move towards recognizing a difference between the SPD and the Nazis. But as Carr argues, the overall tone of their condemnations of the SPD leadership was only slightly milder than before (Carr, 1982: 57). There was not even a clear – even if shifting – KPD line. In May 1932, Thaelmann in a fit of realism rejected the equation between fascists and social fascists. Yet in June 1932, a KPD circular stated that the struggle against the social fascists must not weaken (Carr, 1982: 57). But by June 1932, Thaelmannn was writing that there had not been a shift from the line of the 11th Plenum as one had to attack both the fascists and the social democrats (Carr 1982: 60). Trotsky, on the other hand, argued strongly from 1931 for the importance of a united front, and that damning the SPD leadership as social fascist, while calling for a united front, discouraged the SPD membership from any real united front activity.

KPD functionaries and rank and file were by now confused about the line on the SPD: how far were they supposed to become involved in joint action? Moreover, what was to be made of the KPD conducting negotiations with representatives of the SPD parliamentary fraction in the Prussia *Landtag*, on the one hand and the Berlin KPD calling on the Iron Front to take part in a joint demonstration on the other (LaPorte, 2002: 359)?

Though the KPD/Comintern by 1932 had become more aware of the Nazi threat, there is no clear break from the basic position held at the beginning of the 1930s. For example, the KPD CC was still stating in February 1932 that the SPD and the NSDAP were political twins and equally evil (Carr, 1982: 50). At the 12th Comintern in September 1932, Kuusinen, amongst others, condemned Trotsky for opportunism, for wanting a bloc with the Social Democrats. Two months later, in elections in April 1932, Hitler drew 13.4 million votes, Thaelmann 4 million. (Carr,1982: 55) suggests that a few millions of previously Communist voters had switched to the Nazis.) Amazingly, four months before the Nazis gained power, Kuusinen still argued that the principal blow should be at social democracy (Carr, 1982: 66).

Manuilsky[61] was still claiming that the rise of fascism meant the disintegration of capitalism, and that the German bourgeoisie would not let Hitler gain power (Carr, 1982: 69). Only Ulbricht, Carr argues, addressed the real situation and called for a broad united front movement, a position the plenum did adopt but not without adding the caveat that this must not detract from the struggle against the SPD, a position Ulbricht agreed with (Carr, 1982: 69).This confusion of policies made effective leadership against the growing Nazi threat near impossible.

Why the KPD membership went along with the 'social fascist' line, in so far as they did, raises questions which largely fall outside this study. But LaPorte's explanations are distinctive enough to deserve a brief reference. Drawing from Wickham's research in Frankfurt-am-Main, LaPorte (2002) suggests that the level of unemployed in the KPD separated them out from the SPD dominated trade unions and the consequent absence of debate undercut their confidence to challenge the KPD line. He also refers to Stolle's thesis that the KPD leadership had become isolated and bureaucratized, and introduced the 'social fascist' policy as a substitute for both the absence of a mass revolutionary movement and the absence of roots amongst skilled workers. As the KPD's leadership became increasingly centralized, the KPD became far less aware of what was happening on the ground, which repelled its activists. There was also a rapid turnover of members (313) – thousands momentarily passed through the KPD. (In Saxony, there was an 80 per cent turnover of membership in the mid-1930s (313).) The transient nature of the membership and the falling away of many of its activists will have lessened the KPD leadership's ability to persuade the rank and file of the Third Period line and have its instructions acted upon. Thus the rank and file's attachment to the KPD became ever weaker. (Siegi's relative prominence can also be understood in this context, explored in the next chapter.)

Whatever one's perspective, the Berlin working class became profoundly divided in the fight against the Nazis. Moreover, the suppression of the different uprisings under the aegis of the Social Democrat controlled government of 1918–1919 and the many murders of comrades created a seemingly uncrossable 'river of blood' between the KPD and the SPD leaders.

This is the contradictory state of affairs in which Siegi became a Party member. As shown in the next chapter, his involvement in the anti-Nazi struggle from a very early stage was not always 'on-line'. The KPD leadership as a generalization continued to see the SPD as their main target. It was unusual, at an official level, both within the KPD and the Comintern, to prioritize, as strongly as most commentators think they should have done, the fight against Nazism over the fight against the SPD, almost up till 1933. This position undermined the KPD leadership's ability to understand the distinctive threat posed by the Nazis or to develop a coherent strategy against them.

Indeed, the failure to distinguish the Nazis from other right-wing forces helps to explain the KPD's initial inability to understand the significance of the January 1933 elections. Their analysis, including the infamous statement of Remmele, one of the KPD leaders, that after the fascists would come the Communist revolution, further debilitated any fight back.

I emphasize this point here because, unlike what is now often assumed (and Hobsbawm, representing a modern Communist view, professed), many people in, or associated with, the KPD neither were strongly committed to active anti-Nazi struggle as opposed to holding an anti-Nazi position, nor understood the meaning of the January elections or of Hitler becoming Chancellor. My father did so, and this study examines why.

Endnotes

44. The history of Saxony in this period is far from typical but important because it reveals both what might have been and also the limits of the KPD. Much of this material will be drawn from LaPorte.
45. The 'Centre' was made up of former 'lefts', such as Thaelmannn, Neumann and Remmele, former 'rights', such as Heckert, Pieck and Ulbricht (the last two were to launch

the 'Popular Front' in 1935 and, remaining loyal Stalinists, were to end up as the key leaders of the GDR) and the one genuine leading figure from the centre: Ernst Meyer. During this period of relative calm for the KPD, there was a return to a version of the 1921–1923 United Front tactics. Ironically, Meyer was the only one of this group to oppose the Third Period line before his death in 1930. (Meyer had been head of the Party with Levi, was the chief editor of *Rote Fahne* and held a number of top positions. Consistently critical of the 'ultra-lefts', including on the Comintern, he had stood down for Brandler in 1923.)

46. Serge presents this in terms of the fascist movement being born of the wretched condition of the middle class, impoverished by the struggle of the imperialist epoch and disappointed by democracy...and with socialism.
47. As already noted, the KPD had always seen the Social Democrats as a counter-revolutionary obstacle, given their smashing of the 1918–1919 uprising and their behaviour in 1920, 1921 and 1923. Indeed Brandler's report on 1923 referred to the resultant SPD-led government as having 'established fascism in the form of the dictatorship of general Von Seekt.' (Von Seekt claimed to be the 'republican general'.) But, even under the Fischer-Maslow leadership, the KPD had continued with the United Front tactic of making formal demands of the SPD leadership for 'proletarian unity' against the authoritarian right and against attacks on workers' living standards. The murders of 1May 1929 only reinforced the social fascist position (see next chapter).
48. Carr, *The Twilight of the Comintern.*
49. The effect was that only a handful of right-wing Communists were able to present their factional critique of the KPD's return to an ultra-left policy – that the effect of the previous left turn under Fischer was to limit their

influence on the working class.

50. LaPorte gives three of the standard reasons, which he is critical of, for the ability of the KPD leadership to shift the line leftwards: 'the regional weakness of the Right [faction], such as in the Ruhr; the ZK [CC] majority's rapid control of the Bls [district leadership]; and the view that the new General Line gave expression to strong anti-reformist tendencies long held at all levels.'
51. The frequent battles between Social Democrats and Red Front/Communists are confirmed in Dewar's biography.
52. Ruth Fischer, 1895–1961, joined the Austrian Communist Party in 1918, left for Germany and became leader of the Left Opposition with Maslow. Not always consistently, she tended to support the 'theory of the offensive'. Supported by Zinoviev and the anti-Brandler current (see endnote below), she reached the leadership in 1924, but was replaced by Thaelmann in 1926, following her ultra-left position of withdrawing candidates from the second round of the Presidential elections. She was expelled in 1926 and founded the Leninbund. She fled to France in 1933 (Broué, 2005) and subsequently became rabidly anti-Communist.
53. In 1929, the CC purged any members of the right opposition who did not sign a solidarity declaration. (What the purge of these right-wing Communist activists did mark, argues LaPorte (2002), was the KPD's break with its roots in the German workers' movement, maintained in certain important localities such as Saxony, which had led them to regard SPD colleagues as potential Communists rather than the social basis of 'social fascism'.)
54. Brandler almost certainly influenced my parents' politics, particularly Lotte's. Lotte, Siegi's wife, suggested she supported him, if only over his opposition to the forced collectivization from 1929 in the USSR. The details of Brandler's position cannot be fully explored here but it is

worth giving him some attention as he was an influential figure during this decisive period.

Born in 1881, a building worker from the Sudetenland, with its profound mix of languages, national identities and cultures, he was an active SPD trade unionist. He joined the Spartacus group, then the USPD in 1917, and subsequently the KPD. He crucially supported Paul Levi, a long-time associate of the recently murdered Rosa Luxemburg, who had pushed a decision through the KPD's October 1919 congress that all members had to take part in parliamentary elections and fight the union bureaucracy from inside the trade unions. The left wing could never be expected to accept this; indeed, the KPD quickly lost about half of its hundred thousand members. In 1920, the Communist Workers' Party of Germany (KAPD) was founded in opposition to the KPD, initially drawing significant support among workers, but it did not flourish.

Brandler organized and subsequently chaired the election of workers' councils in Chemnitz after the Kapp Putsch, a crucial activity in the Putsch's defeat, and then started to develop his theme of the workers' united front, a position with which he continues to be closely associated. He was elected to the CC in 1920 and took over from Levi as Chair in 1921 and assumed Party leadership during the March action. (Levi, who saw himself as the heir to Luxemburg and had been the main spokesperson of the 'right', had already been expelled for breach of party discipline following his public criticism of the 1921 March Action, and is seen by some as the leader who never was.) He called off the planned insurrection of 1923 at the Chemnitz Conference, after the Social Democrats retreated, and was subsequently held responsible for the defeat of the 1923 uprising.

From 1920 onwards, the Party was decimated by a series

of splits and splinter groups but the failure of the 1923 uprising created divisions which were never resolved (Broué, 2005: 964; van der Linden, 2004). Brandler (and Thaelheimer), critical of the bureaucratic nature and some of the policies of the KPD, founded the KPDO (or KPO) in late 1928 and, along with hundreds of others, were expelled in 1929. It aimed to change the politics of the KPD, not to rival it. Brandler strongly favoured the immediate establishment of a united front against Nazism (something which would alone have appealed to Siegi and Lotte) to include trade-union and Social Democratic leaders as well as the rank and file. Brandler fled early in 1933 and wandered the earth, finally returning to Germany in 1949, where he founded his own group, 'Arbeiterpolitik', in Hamburg. He died in 1967.

55. There were exceptions to this, as LaPorte (2002) shows, in parts of Saxony. Local Communist support for the United Front policy was actually reinforced by the local ideological traditions of a radicalized SPD. The local KPD organization had grown out of the Spartacus Bund and remained loyal to the early party leadership's policy of working for revolution within the wider workers' movement, above all at local level; a factor easing the political defection of radicalized Social Democrats. It even contributed to support for the 'class war group' around Max Seydewitz, Kurt Rosenfeld and, later, the former KPD chairman, Paul Levi. Those in the KPD who were still campaigning locally for united action, were already running up against the KPD CC's 'social fascist' line. Although both party leaderships aimed to hold their distance at an official party level, their mutual belief in grass-roots 'proletarian solidarity' contributed to the local climate of viewing the other wing of the workers' movement as misled class brothers to be won over. But in many districts in Saxony, the SPD closed the door on United Front collaboration.

56. The statistics on meetings gives a bitter insight into what was happening on the ground: Nazi meetings in Greater Leipzig increased from 1,157 in 1931 to 2,386 in 1932; meetings held by the SPD, and its affiliated organizations, increased from 240 to 1,056; meetings held by the KPD, and its auxiliary organizations rose from 695 to 1,575 (LaPorte, 2002).
57. In the Erzgebirge-Vogtland district of Saxony, left-wing activists were frequently members of the SAP who were strong in the textile industry. The SAP had absorbed the SPD's membership and many KPD members attended SAP meetings – indeed there were no KPD local groups. This situation encouraged the local KPD to approach both the SAP and SPD for joint anti-Nazi collaboration. The KPD on the other hand failed to pull SPDers to it. At a regional KPD Conference in June 1932, from 264 delegates only three were members of the SPD, two were Reichsbanner members, five were in the SAP and three belonged to the Socialist Youth League (SJV); one unemployed Nazi worker represented the other prong of Communist tactics. The fear of genuine cooperation became so acute that the local KPD leadership instructed local groups to end their discussions with the KPD (O) and the SAP and to concentrate on 'unmasking' the SPD leadership (LaPorte, 2002).
58. Ernst Thaelmannn, 1886–1944, came into KPD via the Hamburg USPD, where he played an important role in the 1923 uprising. He was a member of the CC from 1923 and president of the KPD after Fischer and Maslow were pushed out. Arrested in March 1933, he was sent to Buchenwald where he was executed in August 1944 (Broué, 2005).
59. Hermann Remmele, 1880–1939, came into the KPD via the USPD; as a youth, he was in the SPD. In 1920, he was elected onto the CC, and played an important role in preparing for

the insurrection in 1923, with some responsibility for the Hamburg rising. He supported the Centre tendency, then the Thaelmann faction, then opposed him. He fled to Moscow in 1933 where he 'disappeared' (Broué, 2005).

60. The bitter disputes about tactics in the CC culminated in the removal of two members of the three-man Secretariat, Neumann and Remmele, in the course of 1932 (LaPorte, 2002, from Weber).

61. Manuilsky's report to the Executive of the Communist Youth International, February 1933, is a 'good example' of the social fascist line and I quote it at some length as an example:

> 'That in a series of countries fascism is based on the petit-bourgeoisie cannot change the fundamental fact that it is an agency of monopoly capitalism. Every political party, whatever it may say about itself, is, inasmuch as it stands on the ground of capitalism, a party of bourgeois dictatorship, independently of whether it stands for the fascist or parliamentary form of this dictatorship. In fact social democracy is now a party whose whole post-war history shows that it is for the preservation of capitalism.... To many social-democratic workers it still seems unjustified for us Communists to call social democracy a party of social fascism. But this characterisation does not contain the slightest shade of polemical exaggeration. It is a simple observation of a historical fact in the general evolution of social democracy. If the general tendencies of development of monopoly capitalism in the epoch of general crisis lead to fascistisation, i.e. to the suppression of the gains of the working class and the sharpening of terror methods, so it is quite impossible for a party, which has in practice renounced proletarian revolution and hence stands on the ground of capitalism, to do other than go along with the whole

evolution of capitalism.' (My thanks to Harald Marpe for drawing this quote to my attention, and to Ian Birchall for translating it.)

Even at the end of 1933, Pieck was saying: 'Germany is marching towards the proletarian revolution' and that the undefeated working class would gain strength again. The Nazis had gained power only because the Communists lost the majority of the working class through the policy of the social democrats. (*Beide Zitate nach Peter Lübbe: Kommunismus und Sozialdemokratie,* J.H.W. Dietz Nachf., Berlin/Bonn 1978, S. 141. I wish to thank H. Marpe for the source.)

Chapter 5

1928–1933 Resistance

It is difficult to follow all of Siegi's activities during this period, not least because much of it was 'underground'. But there will be an attempt to consider the three main areas of his activities in the movement: the Red Front, the Proletarian Freethinkers, and his considerable role in the agitprop movement up till 1933. Each will be considered separately but will also be set against the politics of the KPD at the time. The section on agitprop will include a discussion of Siegi's significant theoretical writing on the nature of revolutionary agitprop and his work with the composer Stefan Wolpe. The three areas of his political work were interconnected, both in that Siegi in all cases was representing KPD policy at some level, and because Siegi himself embodied the connection between these different areas of work. The final section of this chapter: 'Going underground', will consider why Siegi fled in February 1933, within the context of KPD's strategy, and why he finally came to the UK. The first section, however, will focus on 1 May 1929, the day which sealed the Third Period position as well as the relationship between my parents.

First, a quick overview of what was happening in the Reichstag between 1929 and 1933 provides a useful guide to the parliamentary decline of democratic practices and the rise of the NSDAP. By 1928, the Nazis had gained only 12 seats, but, with unemployment again rising, in 1931, they had 107 seats, making them the second largest party. In the 1930 elections, the Nazis received 18.3 per cent, the KPD 13.1 per cent, against the 24.5 for the SDP, the largest vote; in the presidential election of March 1932, Hindenburg gained 49.6 per cent, Hitler 30.1 per cent, Thaelmann 13.2; by July 1932, in the Reichstag elections,

National Socialists received 37.4 per cent, Social Democrats 21.6 percent, KPD 14.6 percent (marxists.org/archive).

Between the summer of 1930 and February 1932, the Reichstag was no longer functioning: it was in session for merely about 10 weeks; otherwise Weimar was ruled by emergency decree (Hobsbawm, 2002). Brüning, the Chancellor from 1930 to 1932, introduced what he called 'authoritative democracy', that is, rule by presidential decree; his policy of savage wage and welfare cuts, combined with rising prices and unemployment, contributed to his fall. The ultra-right von Papen, who had conspired to get rid of Brüning, briefly became Chancellor, but in those few months, pushed wide open the door to Hitler: he tried to form a pact with Hitler, repealed Brüning's (far from implemented) ban on the SA and overthrew the Social Democratic Prussian government. Against a background of the Nazis picking up an ever increasing percentage of the vote in the three elections in 1932, Presidential and for the Reichstag, Hindenburg, the President, fired von Papen and brought in von Schleiser on the basis of forming a coalition with Hitler. This was the tumultuous background which Siegi was operating against.

1 May 1929

The demonstration of 1 May marks the beginning of Siegi's relationship with Lotte as well as being a defining moment in the KPD's policy towards Social Democrats and a political turning point for Germany (as well as forming my own politics).

In December 1928, the police chief, Karl Zörgiebel, a Social Democrat, banned all public demonstrations and then renewed the ban specifically for the 1929 May Day demonstrations, asking the trade unions to abstain from public demonstrations and to organize only indoor meetings. Unlike the Social Democrats, the Communists, however, decided to challenge the ban and to demonstrate on the streets. Significantly, the KPD leadership was reticent to challenge the SPD police chief and hesitated before endorsing this move, but in a sign of what was to come, gave way to their members and local demand to go ahead with the march (Rosenhaft, 1983: 33). The police mounted a deliberate and violent attack, using their guns indiscriminately.

Both Siegi and Lotte were on the demonstration. Lotte often told me that the gutters ran with blood. It was a story which ran through my blood from a very early age.

The next day, barricades went up in working-class parts of Berlin. For days, fighting broke out over much of the 'Communist' working-class areas of Berlin (Rosenhaft, 1983: 33). The RFB were at the forefront of the action locally (to be discussed later in this chapter), giving rise to a fear amongst the Party centre that they were losing control (Rosenhaft, 1983: 33). It took the police three days to restore order.

There is not a fine agreement on figures: Rosenhaft (1983: 33) states there were 30 people dead, all of them demonstrators; 200 were wounded, and 1,200 arrested. But LaPorte (2002) argues that, of the 33 dead and some 160 wounded, only one was a Communist, two were Social Democrats, while the vast majority were residents, even passers-by, who were not involved in the events organized by the KPD. But the precise figures hardly matter.

The KPD's ambivalence towards violence at this point is exemplified by their refusal to distribute arms, which the insurgents blamed them for, and indeed for their attempt to stop the action completely (Rosenhaft, 1983: 33). LaPorte (2002) tells a complementary story: The 'Class War' group in the Saxon SPD, which advocated 'proletarian unity', wrote about the role of the KPD leadership:

> 'There can be no doubt that the KPD leadership has heavy responsibility for this loss of blood. The workers were almost led into police fire. To the KPD's Zentrale it was irrelevant whether people died or not. For them it was only about

> creating facts from which their poisoned agitation against the SPD could be supplied with new poison. [...] The events of May Day in Berlin have filled the gulf between Social Democrats and Parteikommunisten with workers' blood. The fissure in the working class is even greater than before.'
> (LaPorte, 2002, quoting from K. Rosenfeld, 'Berliner Blutmai', in *Klassenkampf*, 3 (10) (15 May 1929), 292–293.)

1 May was turned into a powerful symbol by the KPD but this lengthy quote from the time reveals how far these bloody events could be interpreted as damning the KPD, a position I strongly suspect Lotte held.

The Social Democrats were blamed for the slaughter on 1 May; indeed the onslaught on the 1 May demonstrators was turned by the KPD into an unassailable reason for its Third Period line, and these factors all combined: the Communist leadership and sections of the rank and file wanting nothing more to do with the Social Democrats.[62] The CC also used the defeat as a reason to eliminate opposition to the Third Period line.

1929 was an extension of the earlier events in Germany: the left who had been crushed during the different attempts at revolution not that many years earlier (1918 and 1923), became remobilized. But it was also a prelude to what was to come. For all the KPD leadership's talk of social fascists, if one observes what is happening on the ground from then on, the rank and file of the Communist party generally saw the SA and the Nazis as their prime enemy, not the Social Democrats. Frequent street battles occurred in the period from 1929 to 1932, in which the Communist street fighters succeeded in killing some hundreds of Nazis and injuring many more (for all the good this did).

The slaughter on 1 May had one personal and beneficial outcome. Both Lotte and Siegi were on the demonstration. Siegi had been in Berlin for about eight months, and he and Lotte had met at an agitprop performance (she was acting, Siegi directing). Lotte told me that she had become separated from Siegi. Indeed, as Siegi was a member of the RFB (see below), which played the leading role in confronting the police and the SA, Lotte had good cause for concern. Terrified that he had been hurt or even killed, she realized that she loved him. They seemed to have lived together from then on, getting married in October 1932, because, according to Lotte, they might need to flee. (Siegi was late for his wedding, one of the few stories Lotte regularly recounted.)

Their concern about the need to plan for the possibility of flight from Germany was well founded. The RFB was already illegal, followed soon after by the Proletarian Freethinkers (see later section). One month after their marriage, in November 1932, Siegi appears in a KPD list of 'illegals'.

Rotfrontkämpferbund (RFB)

Earlier, maybe as soon as Siegi, aged roughly 24, arrived in Berlin, he had joined the Rotfrontkämpferbund (which will now be referred to either as the RFB or the Red Front). My mother, when already very old, had mentioned Siegi's involvement in the Red Front. She told me sardonically how the Red Front went off to the woods to practise shooting and that my father had a gun but was a useless shot, shrugging in the way only she knew how, which said more loudly than any words, that they had not been successful. Gestapo papers corroborated Siegi's membership (kindly sent me by Dr Weber, from the archives on the SS), which showed that Siegi lost his German citizenship, at least partly, according to the SS, because of 'improper conduct', associated with his membership of the RFB.

I have no definite clues as to why he became involved in an organization, as will be discussed, which, after 1929, was primarily based on the 'local community' actively resisting (or defending against) the SA's intrusions into their area. I have no knowledge of what local group Siegi was attached to; he was living around Mitte – at the time, as now, an area of students and 'bohemians', though in the 1930s, probably with a higher Jewish constituency as it is near the main Berlin Synagogue.

How far the RFB changed from its offensive character prior to May 1929, and became an essentially defensive organization is reflected rather than focused on here, but certainly it was not just my mother who saw 1929 as the point when the RFB turned away from its initial purpose of providing the 'shock troops' in a revolutionary situation. As the concern here is with 1929 onwards, the RFB was already entering its more defensive period.

The significance of the RFB is not usually appreciated – it was the primary local defence against Nazi thugs and, unlike the CC, it was operating on the ground, where changes in Party line made little or no difference to daily experience. Moreover, though my father was almost certainly representing the KPD in his Red Front 'unit', the KPD regularly, if not consistently, distanced itself from the RFB and, more profoundly, did not see the fight against the Nazis as the primary – and sometimes even secondary – issue (as discussed earlier). My suspicion as to why Siegi, actually an unlikely Red Front activist given his background and age, became involved in this group was that he had witnessed (or more) the early strutting of the Nazis in Bavaria. I have no further detail about Siegi's role in the Red Front so the following section will consider this organization in general and then draw out some probable implications for Siegi.

I am aware that the KPD established a variety of other defence organizations, particularly after their disaffection with the RFB in 1929–1930, but none relevant to Siegi, and none, besides the RFB, which survived till 1933 so they will not be considered. It was both the RFB and its youth organization, which did most of the fighting against the SA. In so far as the RFB is analysed in histories of Germany up till 1933, there is a tendency either to reduce it to being no more than the military front of the KPD, or to present it as being essentially autonomous. Both positions, I suggest, are flawed, as the interviews with the Berlin 3 testified, and as LaPorte reveals.

The Red Front Fighters' League (which was to become the Red Front Fighters' Association) had been created in 1924, following a brawl at a Stahlhelm rally in Halle in May 1924. (The Stahlhelm was the oldest, and very right-wing, paramilitary organization in Germany.) The RFB's first leader was Ernst Thaelmann, the District secretary of the KPD (later to become the KPD's main leader).[63] Not much is written about the Red Front but LaPorte (2002), with his emphasis on the importance of activity at the grass-roots, gives a few significant details of its pre-1929 history. The RFB, set up to rival the Right's paramilitary organization and the SPD dominated Reichsbanner, was first involved in campaigning: marches, speeches and leafleting, usually, though not always, on behalf of the KPD. It drew its recruits from the same layer as the Reichsbanner, mainly unemployed, mainly youth, and often not KPD members (Grant, 2004: 43). Its original purpose included an important propaganda function –spreading an anti-militarist message, including in the army and other paramilitary formations, as did the Reichsbanner. By 1928, it had about 100,000 members. Following the first world war, and given the background of other quasi-military organizations, the Red Front too adopted a uniform of green Russian blouse, hat, belt, breeches and boots. The RFB had an official paper: *Die Rote Front*, and, from 1928, an official song: 'Der Rote Wedding' by Eric Weinert, with music by Eisler. According to a rare reference in the Bavarian archives, from 1928, the Red Front, in particular the subdivision, the Red Youth Front, increasingly carried out military exercises across Germany. The RFB went in for serious paramilitary physical training and training (illegally) in the use of fire arms (as I know from my parents), for use against the police, Stadhelm and the SA, and to protect the KPD members and supporters in public and factory settings (Rosenhaft, 1983:

89). Crucially, their training was supposed to equip them to take over in the event of a revolutionary situation.

LaPorte (2002) suggests that the RFB in the mid 1920s was often better at galvanizing its audience than the KPD. The RFB's emphasis on activity rather than discussion was a crucial counterbalance to the paralysis within the KPD, induced by factional feuding.[64] The RFB moreover attracted the young, and this was recognized with a specific youth organization: Rote Jungfront (Young Red Front) for ages 16–21. (This is the organization which Rude led locally.) Although not documented, my suspicion is that the RFB drew in youth far more than the KPD. According to LaPorte (2002: 308),[65] during the middle years of Weimar, only 12.3 per cent of Party members were between 18 and 25, of whom only two per cent had come through the Communist youth. New members of the KPD around 1932, aged between 18 and 25, amounted to 8.1 per cent of total recruitment, a probable increase on earlier, but nevertheless revealing the difficulty the KPD was having in recruiting the young. Although Siegi was older than that, it is worth reminding ourselves that when he joined the RFB, he was probably a mere 24, an appropriate age for a youth leader, and younger than the average age of 30 in 1933 for KPD members (Merson, 1986: 19).[66]

The RFB was the main organization involved in the – very serious – fighting against the police on 1 May 1929 and in the insurrectionary days that followed. The KPD was slow to endorse this violence, anxious that it could cause them to lose touch with their grass roots (Rosenhaft, 1983: 35). 1 May 1929 was a prelude to an intensification in the many street battles between the left and the Nazis when the SA attacked local KPD strongholds. (My mother told me they knew all was lost after the May events – though that may partly be hindsight speaking.)

Crucially, the RFB was banned a few weeks later. From then till the Nazis took power, the RFB operated as an illegal and underground organization. Berlin's police superintendent gave as his excuse the likelihood of renewed fighting between the SA and the RFB. Nominally, the RFB then was replaced by the League of Struggle against Fascism, but in reality this was the same organization (Merson, 1986: 16).

The RFB's members started to desert after 1929 (Rosenhaft, 1983: 90). The KPD dithered over whether to let it die. It seems, though, that by August, so many local groups already existed underground, with cover names (as indeed Siegi had), safe addresses and other ways of continuing illegally, that the CC agreed to their continuing and even endorsed their use of weapons (Rosenhaft, 1983: 105).

But this period marks a reorientation in the RFB's purpose, though there were KPD twists and turns on what it thought was the main purpose of the RFB, its unruly offspring. If we go with my mother, Lotte (whose opinion, even if disparaging, has tended to be accurate), its purpose changed from being offensive up till 1929, to defensive afterwards. Rosenhaft (1983: 88) also argues that after the May events, the RFB's main purpose was generally seen as 'Proletarian self-defence'.

The increasing attacks by the SA in 'red' working class districts, like Kreuzberg in August 1929, led Neumann, at this point still on the KPD CC and the editor of the *Rote Fahne*, to advocate a less centralized system where local – KPD and RFB – cells could take the initiative against the Nazis. 'Hit the fascists wherever you meet them,' became Neumann's motto (Grant, 2004: 43). This was enthusiastically supported by many rank and file RFB supporters. (Some of us will be aware of very similar debates going on in the 1970s and now amongst the revolutionary left as to how to confront the National Front/British National Party/English Defence League.) Rosenhaft (1983) confirms that, after the tensions arising from the events of 1 May 1929 between the RFB and the CC of the KPD, members of the RFB did not all toe the Party line. By the end of 1931, many of its members, including, and/or supported by, some of the younger members of the KPD, were in open revolt against the KPD leadership, and their opposition to individual and local terror.

The issue of the use of violence, which exercised the KPD leadership – whose line vacillated considerably, sometimes almost monthly, in the period between 1929 and 1933 – partly pivoted upon the importance they gave the NSDAP. It is not till 1930 and the September elections, which gave the NSDAP eight times the number of deputies as in the 1928 election (though remarkably the CC declared afterwards that the NSDAP had passed its peak), that the Nazis came to be seen as a sufficient danger that the possibility was considered of a physical fight against them as part of the wider struggle against fascism (Rosenhaft, 1983: 26, 71). The KPD in abstract distinguished their support for street demonstrations from a concept of insurrection, and they supported collective, but not individualistic, action (Rosenhaft, 1983: 39). They made a crucial – though, in real life, fuzzy – distinction between the RFB fermenting proletarian mass terror and mass action, and eschewing individualist, terrorist, action (Rosenhaft, 1983: 71–79). This tight rope act became even shakier after 1931, when on the one hand, the threat of Nazism was being taken more seriously, and on the other, the KPD started to place greater emphasis on cooperation with some Social Democrats (Rosenhaft, 1983: 75).

LaPorte (2002: 338) argues that, by 1931, the Party leadership no longer sanctioned the policy of physically beating back the Nazis, instead favouring a general strike. Increasingly, the KPD were worried about the use of violence in case it increased the likelihood of their being made illegal (Rosenhaft, 1983: 60–85, passim). But the ambivalence is illustrated by Ulbricht in 1931, a district leader, supporting 'blitz demos', and the use of guerilla tactics by small groups of people, with even the possibility of carrying arms now up for consideration (Rosenhaft, 1983: 39–41).

The seriousness of the CC's anti-RFB line in 1931 is illustrated by their move against Heinz Neumann, up till then a leading CC member (a position he had briefly shared with Thaelmann). Neumann's support of aggressive tactics was increasingly opposed among the leadership, who compared it to the use of fascist violence, and because of his 'advocacy of individual terror and his adventurism'. Thaelmann also had a go at Neumann in November 1931, condemning illegal terror squads, though he accused the Nazis of initiating the use of guns and knives. Neumann was then removed from the CC but in part because he opposed the Comintern's/KPD's downplaying of the struggle against the Nazis. The RFB came to be seen, disparagingly, as 'Neumanites' (Rosenhaft, 1983: 82, 83).[67] A resolution directed against Neumann by the CC in November 1931 prohibited the use of individual terrorism, a position adopted at least in part because of their fear of the KPD being banned.

The RFB objected (Carr, 1982: 48).[68] The KPD were afraid, the RFB protested, of illegality; the RFB were the protectors of working-class areas against the Nazis. They refused to adhere to the CC's ruling. They were not part of the Party, but semi-autonomous, they insisted (Rosenhaft, 1983: 84). Some left (Rosenhaft, 1983: 84). In October and November, the KPD went so far as to attack the RFB in Berlin, though Rosenhaft (1983: 85) does not give further detail. Both positions reveal how far the Red Front operated at a distance from the KPD.

Partly in order to reassure the SPD leadership and membership, in November 1931, the CC, at its meeting with the Comintern in Moscow, took a strong position against individual violence. Taking out individual fascists would not destroy the fascist movement, they argued. Moreover, as already discussed, the CC, with some support from RFB members, had wanted to bring SA sympathizers, even members, and nationalist unemployed workers over to the left, which would have been unlikely if the SA was being attacked (Grant, 2004: 43).

There was also the connected contradiction, which the KPD CC never finally resolved, as to whether the purpose of the RFB was to be a mass or a cadre organization and whether illegality made a limited membership preferable, especially given its quasi-military function (Rosenhaft, 1983: 100). Another tension was between its political and military purposes. Its original political functions – propaganda, campaigning and agitation amongst the 'masses' – were supposedly maintained after illegality. Yet it purportedly continued to have a military responsibility: for the recruiting and training of cadres for a German Red Army (Rosenhaft, 1983: 101).

From 1930 onwards, after the RFB was banned, the RFB was structured in a cadre formation along conspiratorial lines, too complex for it to be unravelled so many years later (Rosenhaft, 1983: 103–104). The operating unit, initially eight, was reduced to five, for the sake of security, cohesion and mobility. Those units were linked to other similar units. Each member had a clearly delineated function: the intelligence expert, an enemies' expert, organization, etc. We know such units existed in Berlin, indeed were formed into 'Ordnerdiesnt' (OD: Marshall-Corps) (Rosenhaft, 1983: 114). I suspect my father learnt how to survive 'underground' in the RFB, skills which would have helped keep him alive when he went underground in 1933.

The battles between the left in general and the Nazis were increasing from around the late 1920s and particularly in the working class districts, taverns and housing estates of Berlin. Though the SA at this point did not discriminate between the SDP and the KPD, KPD/RFB members and those aligned to them on the ground saw the Nazis as their target and became the principal street fighters, not the SPD. The NSDAP was the 'main enemy' in the neighbourhoods which, following the onset of mass unemployment, increasingly came to replace the factory as the actual location of political conflict (Rosenhaft, 1983: 7ff, 18ff, 26). The fighting was increasingly brutal. From 1929 onwards, the SA and KPD members regularly disrupted each other's meetings and 'fought' for control of the taverns, a key meeting place in Berlin working-class community life (Rosenhaft, 1983, passim).

I was to discover that the RFB was a key and very lived in organization, at least in Berlin. (It was apparently not of such importance in Leipzig.) Elfrieda, from Prenzlauerberg, and Rudi, from the red district of Wedding, both emphasized how the Red Front and the SA were involved in daily battles in the streets. Rudi talked about how even people who were in the SPD joined locally, though the cadre was KPD. (One assumes this was unofficial activity, not endorsed by the SPD itself.) Both emphasized also that the Red Front was defensive: the SA would attack their meetings, their demonstrations and any group of 'lefties' they could find. Rudi even said it was safer to travel alone, because you were less likely to get beaten up. He belonged to the Youth Red Front, which, for reasons of security, was divided into groups of eight (Rudi was the leader of his group). Some of them were hotheads, he said, and he would tell them to stay calm, but, if they were attacked, they would defend themselves. Again, without giving a precise date, he talked about how they would send out scouts, sometimes on bikes, to see if the coast was clear; courting couples were also a favoured tactic. The Red Front, in other words, was key to the everyday safety and existence of the left.

Rudi's testimony confirms Rosenhaft's (1983: 105–106) analysis that the KPD leadership did have some real cause for concern: some of the local youth groups and gangs who participated in RFB actions against the SA were attracted by the fight for their neighbourhoods, including the use of weapons, as much as by the RFB's politics, and some were rather too close to the criminal underworld.

Clearly, the RFB cannot be reduced to the KPD, or seen simply as its military adjunct. Again, this became much clearer from the interviews. Rudi led his group of eight and walked a tightrope, or so it seemed to me, between cooling down his hotheads and defending his comrades by whatever means necessary. My impression was that this had little to do with the line of the KPD and far more to do with the reality of the situation and expediency.

Rosenhaft's (1983) research on the KPD's tactics in Berlin addresses the question of how the KPD did respond to the NSDAP on the streets and casts far more light on the role of the RFB than most historians, but she still does not give enough credence to its importance. Rosenhaft's (1983: 101) argument – 'insofar as the RFB had an attraction after 1929, it lay precisely in the romance of conspiracy' – is indicative of a serious underestimation of the RFB's significance. Instead, she emphasizes the role of the KPD itself, arguing that, despite the party's ideological limitations in interpreting the political situation, in practice its response was 'tremendously vibrant and surprisingly responsive to the shifting needs of its actual and potential constituency.' While Rosenhaft is, I suggest, here implicitly referring to the Red Front, nevertheless her comment reveals she is not sufficiently focused on either the changes in Party line or the interplay between Party line and members' activities. LaPorte's focus, on the other hand, allows him to highlight the role of the RFB and the degree to which local circumstances, as in Red Wedding, had created a level of autonomy between members' committed activism against the SA, and the vacillating Party line.

When the Berlin KPD did finally decide that the NSDAP was the 'main enemy', they did not, however, present this as a significant break with the policy of 'social fascism'. Instead, the validity of the policy for rank-and-file activists is explained in terms of a response to the role of the SPD in the Prussian government. Party members' everyday experience with the SA and the SPD-administered police and the welfare state made Communist propaganda concerning a united front extending from the Nazis to the SPD seem credible.

Cross-membership

The Nazis were not simply seen as class enemies. What emerged from my interviews was the – unexpected – importance of drawing people away from the SA (confirmed in LaPorte, 2002). Weber (1982) also emphasizes that the KPD saw the SPD as 'communism's main enemy'. LaPorte observes:

> 'The "united front from below" tactic was merely extended to the Nazis' "misled" supporters among the "working people" and nationalistic propaganda was pumped into the German body politic... The KPD's grass-roots organizations were instructed to win over Nazi support among the lower middle classes and the peasantry: the threat of "Hitler-fascism" was to be overcome by turning its social basis from brown to red…With party propaganda so strongly emphasizing winning over the Mittelstand from the Nazis, the need to recruit among Social Democratic workers was played down. The KPD's local membership was instructed not to "overestimate" the Nazi threat and to avoid making a false distinction between bourgeois democracy and fascism' (LaPorte, 2002, from D. W. Daycock, 1980).[69]

The Berlin interviews cast a fascinating light on the issue of cross-membership. Elfrieda talked about Felix, who was both part of their Communist-aligned writers' group and in the SA, and used to arrive at meetings wearing his uniform. (This had disastrous consequences for the comrades in 1935, as will be seen in Appendix 2.) The KPD, at least on a few occasions, invited SA speakers to their meetings. Rudi provided an eloquent explanation for this policy: the people who joined the SA were workers too, he said. They belonged to the same families, had gone to the same schools, lived in the same streets and were often good friends. This semi-official attempt to draw over workers may have helped legitimate what happened next. Rudi talked of counter-recruitment but noted that most of the traffic was one way, especially after 1933 (his dating) because some Communists were so harassed by the SA and so afraid, that they joined the SA. Hans at one point appeared to suggest that the KPD wanted to appease the SA. People were far more likely to go from the KPD to the SA, than the other way around. The CC's attitude to confronting the NSDAP was erratic and led them at times to criticize the Red Front's emphasis on confronting the Nazis.

The joint picketing during the brief Berlin transport strike of November 1932, including both KPD and SA members, is an acute example of the KPD CC's policy of drawing Nazis over to them. This strike had been called by the KPD and the 'Red Unions' and was not supported by the mainstream unions. It is not clear whether the KPD at an official level endorsed the joint activity. Carr (1982: 77) states that both Thaelmann and Ulbricht in their retrospective accounts failed to mention Nazi participation in the strike. For all that, what happened indicates that at least some members of the KPD did not have an ideological objection to joint activity.

I grew up with the strike. 'Never,' my father told me when I was still quite young, 'stand on a picket line with Nazis.' My mother explained: 'Would you believe it, there were Nazi pickets standing alongside the Communist pickets during the transport strike. The Communists allowed that to happen. Can you believe it?' In contrast, the KPD refused to call out the RFB to help with the Berlin transport strike (Rosenhaft, 1983: 85).

The infamous events of the Berlin strike illustrate the CC's emphasis on the desirability of drawing members of the Nazi movement towards the KPD, rather than attacking them.[70] Carr (1982) refers to Neumann, on the CC's 'left', putting to the 16th Party Congress in June 1930, (in almost the first reference ever to German fascism) that the KPD should try to draw away 'the toiling masses' from fascism. (Ironically, Neumann, though he took the Nazis seriously, saw the SPD as the more dangerous.) In

1931, in Munich, a 'fascist general', and in Berlin, Hitler himself were invited to public debates with KPD leaders (Carr, 1982). Both refused. Carr (1982) sees as one of the most significant examples of the KPD collaborating with the NSDAP against the SPD, the occasion when the KPD finally uncritically backed the plebiscite in 1931 for a new election to unseat the coalition government in Prussia, headed by the Social Democrats; Trotsky too condemned the KPD's participation in this plebiscite, arguing that the KPD had entered into a united front with the Nazis against the Social Democrats (Trotsky, 25 August 1931).

LaPorte (2002, drawing from Weber's *Hauptfeind*) also refers to the KPD 1932 Party Conference whose policy clearly promoted joint activity: 'Joint actions must be carried out with the Nazis' working-class supporters in the factories against cuts in pay and unemployment benefits and against the Papen dictatorship.' Another intriguing illustration, in LaPorte (2002: 371), with implications for Siegi's work, is that at an agitprop conference, it was even suggested that the slogan: 'Anti-Fascist Action', the 1932 CC's official position, should be changed to 'United Action' to avoid deterring Nazi workers.

The KPD's intermittent emphasis on street cells (especially during periods of high unemployment when work-placed cells were less useful), vital in areas such as Wedding (where Rudi lived, and judging from one of Siegi's letters, he at one point also lived), was also tied in with the role of the RFB. LaPorte brings out that left-wing KPD members submerged themselves in the RFB to 'avoid the political paralysis induced by the internal factional struggle' and the Third Period line. Even by 1929, the RFB was 'regarded by the ZK [CC] as a reservoir of potential opposition to the party line.' Indeed, when the RFB was banned after the May events of 1929, Thaelmann's reaction, at the CC on 10 May, was that the KPD no longer considered it appropriate to organize 'non-party' RFB members into the KPD. Instead, the CC created alternative defence organizations, including those which could function during a period of illegality. This was not presented as a response to the rise of the NSDAP, which in 1929 remained on the periphery of the internal Party discussion. The CC's aim was to control the RFB more closely (LaPorte, 2002). Far from the RFB being the KPD's armed wing, it was seen rather more as a wayward teenager.

It is unlikely that Siegi's level of participation in the RFB will ever be known. This is not an organization that its members proclaimed they belonged to. The fact that he was allowed to hold his own gun (if we trust what Lotte said) marked him out as a reliable, long-standing and trusted member. As suggested earlier, the probability is that he represented, and tried to get others to hold to, the Party line (a difficult task, as it kept changing).

Siegi's participation in the RFB suggests that he saw the fight against the Nazis as more of a priority than did the Party. The RFB, as we have seen, was far more committed to taking on the SA than the KPD leadership. For the KPD CC, the SA were just another form of fascist, like the social fascists, and their real task was the overthrow of capitalism – which would stop all forms of fascism anyway. Indeed, I do wonder how Siegi, the man from the KPD, the man with a Bavarian accent and a slightly *haute-bourgeois* manner, related to these turbulent and angry youths, who wanted to take on the SA and defend their homes, their communities and their places of work. Siegi had been at the heart of the earlier Bavarian maelstrom and had witnessed Nazi tactics. My guess is that he felt a profound sympathy with the young Berliner working-class anti-Nazis, though he would also have tried to moderate their more adventurous behaviour. I suspect he suited his role well.

Siegi once told me that before he fled, that is, in the lead up to the Nazis taking power, he could never trust anybody, even people who had been his long-standing friends. Rudi also talked about not trusting anybody at all, even friends and comrades, in noticeably similar terms. 'I would wait in the shadows, where nobody would see me,' he told me, as I listened, captivated and terrified. 'That way I would see whether the man I was meeting (it was always a man) had a tail. I used to wait for hours out of sight just to be sure. But even if he was alone, I could never be sure he could be trusted.' The RFB was an illegal organization from 1929 onwards. It had to be run as far as possible on a disciplined basis. My father adapted to working as a conspirator 'underground'.[71] In the longer run, this method of working probably saved his life.

Berlin Proletarische Freidenker (BPF)

Papers obtained from the *Bundesarchiv* confirm that Siegi was on the committee of the BPF. Significantly, Siegi's membership alone connects the BPF with the RFB.

While there is a level of uncertainty over the exact structure and role of the BPF, it is worth noting that this humanist organization was banned in 1932. While it was banned three years later than the RFB, the government's April 1932 ban under the Emergency Laws of 1932, introduced by Chancellor Brüning, was in theory against paramilitary organizations, which the Freethinkers would not appear to be. Von Papen, the subsequent Chancellor, reversed the ban on the SA and SS when he took over a few months later. But the BPF remained banned. The suspicion has to be that the BPF was seen, not so much as a humanist organization, but as a front for anti-fascist activity and even street fighting; maybe the BPF's involvement with sports clubs closely associated with the KPD (discussed below) fuelled a suspicion that members pursued fitness as much for quasi-military purposes as for its own sake.

The BPF has no real parallel in British society – it developed originally from 'The Union of Freethinkers for cremation', which was founded in the iconic year of 1905, and became the Central Union of German Proletarian Freethinkers in 1908. By 1914, there were 6,400 registered members of the Proletarian Freethinkers (Volker Berghahn, 2005).[72] Both these organizations, particularly the Proletarian Freethinkers, were part of the extensive network of social and cultural organizations linked to the SPD in pre-first-world-war Germany. The two groups merged in 1927, becoming the German Freethinkers' Association in 1930. These groups, which were very popular in a period when the bourgeois left had been discredited, campaigned particularly around the issues of the secularization of elementary schools and, with great effect, for Germans to disaffiliate from their Churches, as well as around typical 'humanist' issues such as rights to divorce and abortion.

An International of Proletarian Freethinkers was formed at a congress in Czechoslovakia but conflict broke out at an international level between the forces associated with the USSR and with the Social Democrats. No doubt associated with the Third Period, in 1930 the pro-Soviet delegations took over from the Social Democrats. Whether the BPF in Germany came under the sway of the Communists at that point or earlier is not clear, though it seems likely that with the Third Period, the KPD leadership would have encouraged some sort of break with the Social Democrats.

Though, at an official level, the BPF had become a part of the Freethinkers' Association in 1930, a letter (discussed below) from Fomferra (a leading member of the KPD) refers to a Proletarian Freethinkers group up till 1933. What may have happened is that there was a 'faction' within the Freethinkers' Association which retained the name of Proletarian Freethinkers, almost certainly made up of KPD members and therefore including Siegi. Or it could be that, from April 1932, when the Freethinkers' Association was banned, the name 'Proletarian Freethinkers' was used for the underground group – after all, the KPD tactic at the time was theoretically that some members had to be prepared for going illegal. From talking to various people and in documents gained from the *Bundersarchiv*, there is evidence that there was a cell within the BPF, certainly in Berlin, which operated illegally, at least from April 1932, which may have been used by Communist Party members operating 'underground'. (It is as yet not clear whether this cell existed prior to April 1932.) It has not been possible to find out how large this shadowy grouping was. But there is another possibility. Hans, a KPD member, was a member of the youth section of the Proletarian Freethinkers in Leipzig and here it was clearly separate from any 'Social Democratic' Freethinkers. So the relationship between the two groups may have varied according to locality and local politics. Bodek (1996: 63)[73] refers to a 'Freethinkers-opposition' – who were once the 'League of Proletarian Freethinkers' – as attending a cultural exhibition, organized by the KPD in 1930. This also suggests the existence of a faction within the League itself, surely Siegi's.

What I do know is that Siegi told me he was the Secretary of the Berlin group of the Freethinkers, indeed, telling me a 'funny' story about taking a tram to bury the Freethinkers' funds, carefully wrapped up, under a tree outside Berlin – and musing, forty years later, whether it would still be there! (I would now surmise that this took place in April 1932.) Maybe Siegi was the secretary of the official branch of the Association, though we do know from Fomferra's letter that he was also a member of the Proletarian 'cell' (see below) and it is therefore also possible that this is what he was referring to. There is no record of the activities of either 'organization', so we can only surmise what Siegi's role involved.

Fomferra (see Appendix 4 for fuller information) was also active in the BPF and we know from his letter that he was at some level responsible for the illegal cell in the BPF between November 1932 and June 1933. We do not know whether this was as the responsible KPD official for the illegal cell or as an 'ordinary' member of the cell. Little is known about Fomferra other than what he tells us in a couple of documents, which he signed, on 14 February 1947, for submission to the SED (the Sozialistische Einheitspartei Deutschlands or the Socialist Unity Party of Germany, the governing party of the German Democratic Republic) (obtained from the *Bundesarchiv*). Based on the list of names of the committee that Fomferra provided the SED, the committee members of the illegal cell were: Walter Weidauer, the secretary until his arrest in March 1933, when he was replaced by Hans Mainz, Walter Jopp (though there is a question mark by his name), Fritz Bischoff and 'Siggi' Moos. (For the 'careers' of these remarkable anti-fascist fighters, see Appendix 4. Siegi/Siggi was the only one to flee, though some others survived.)

So, at the time of his involvement, Siegi seems to have been a member of a committee/cell probably composed of only four people (all men, all youngish). One noticeable feature is that, in so far as there is information, the committee was composed of trusted and long-standing Party comrades: these committee members all held significant positions in the KPD as well as the BPF, many over a long period of time. Again, though the comparison with the other men cannot be conclusive, it does strongly suggest that Siegi had been in the Party for a significant period of time and was a well-recognized cadre.

Siegi is the only comrade in this group that we know was based in Berlin. Walter Weidauer, who had joined the KPD in 1922, and became a city councillor in Zwickau, in 1932, became the 'election leader' of the KPD Proletarian Freethinkers in Saxony. (Arrested soon after the Reichstag fire, he continued his work with the Proletarian Freethinkers after his release some months later.) In 1930, Bischoff was the head of the group of the Proletarian Freethinkers in Hessen, Frankfurt. Indeed, of the four people for whom we have details, two were from Saxony, confirming the strength of the left and the Proletarian Freethinkers there.

Though one is again only dealing in 'maybes', it is possible that Siegi may have been the BPF Secretary before Weidauer, who was its secretary only from November 1932 after the BPF was made illegal. But Weidauer, as we know, was not based in Berlin and it is possible that Fomferra, reporting to the SED after Siegi had left the KPD and Germany, may have preferred to give Weidauer, who by 1948 was the mayor of Dresden, that honour. It is also possible that Siegi actually was the Secretary of the 'parent' body of the Freethinkers, which maybe in Berlin was dominated by the KPD. Perhaps I have remembered it wrong, for he rarely repeated such information, and Siegi said he was the Chair. In any event, he held a position of responsibility and trust in this layer of the movement.

Certainly, Siegi was expressing humanist beliefs: included in his writings for the *Journal for Theatre* (discussed in the next section) were regular attacks on religion, in particular the Catholic Church. In the February 1931 edition, he railed against the Church's oppression of women, and its opposition to abortion and contraception. Siegi took his atheism seriously at this point, even if it was against the form that religion took.

To leap ahead of ourselves briefly, we know that out of the five people Fomferra lists as members of the cell, at least three were arrested in March 1933 (see Appendix 4 for further details). The SS and SA, following the earlier arrests on the night of the Reichstag fire, then swooped on the next level of 'lefties', both political and cultural, in March of 1933. This was more a dreadful game of cat and mouse, however, than were the arrests a few years later – its purpose was to intimidate, not yet to destroy.[74]

Hans linked the Proletarian Freethinkers with sports activities in a way that I have not seen elsewhere. Hans, when interviewed, was insistent on the importance of the *Fichte* sports organizations which were, he suggested, connected to the KPD, and were of some importance. Hans, who was very much into various sporting activities, left the SPD-dominated Free Thinkers, to join the sporting facilities offered by the Proletarian Free Thinkers, because he had felt uncomfortable in the regimented atmosphere of the SPD-dominated FT clubs. He also said that the SPD-dominated Freethinkers were all mouth and no action. He stated he would belong only to a KPD sports organization, not one dominated by the SPD. It appears that because of the dominance in Saxony of the SPD, who were strongly anchored in the subculture of sporting and cultural organizations, the SPD continued to dominate the *Fichte* and Red Sports units, and often to exclude KPD members, whereas in Berlin, the *Fichte* and Red Sports were dominated by the KPD (Copper, 1988).[75]

Siegi's going underground and subsequent flight can be partly understood within the context of his participation in the Freethinkers. Not only had membership of the Freethinkers become illegal, also he was one of only a handful of members of a leading cell. Fomferra's papers help make sense of a piece of family 'folklore': Siegi, according to Lotte, had originally gone to hide at the home of Lotte's very bourgeois aunt, Tante Klara, who took him in on the night of the Reichstag fire and hid him for two weeks. Fomferra's papers reveal that their group was subject to persecution after the Reichstag fire.[76] Siegi, one can surmise, got to hear that the other members of the Freethinkers' cell had been arrested, that the cell had been broken and that he too would be under threat, and this, one can reasonably guess, contributed to his decision to flee Germany.

The importance of left sporting organizations

While there is no evidence that Siegi was involved in a personal capacity with any sporting organizations, he became centrally involved in performances for a *Sports Revue*. Sports organizations in Germany held a place which has no parallel in Britain. Workers' sports associations were first formed in Central Europe in the late nineteenth century as a reaction to the increasing conservatism of the traditional gymnastic societies, and by 1900 the strongest workers' sports organizations were built up in

Germany.

For millions of workers, sport was a vital aspect of the revolutionary movement. The *Fichte* were established in the nineteenth century as a radical alternative to the deeply reactionary sports clubs of the time, aimed at drawing in working-class children and adults and which, like Woodcraft Folk today, also offered a variety of holiday activities. The first world war disrupted organized international workers' activities, but afterwards there was a successful campaign by the Lucerne Sports International (LSI), which was to become the Socialist Workers' Sports International (SWSI) representing the SPD, to relaunch the national workers' sports movement. It is worth paying attention briefly to goals so dissimilar to anything ever associated with sports in the UK. The basis or aims of the movement were proclaimed to be anti-militaristic, to develop as part of a proletarian subculture, to inoculate the workers against bourgeois culture and the bourgeois clubs and educate them in a socialist spirit. The founders of the organization, believing that sport could be revolutionary, wrote that the workers' sports movement was no less important than the political, trade-union and cooperative movements of the working class.

In all countries the sports movement played an important role in the struggle against 'capitalist nationalism and militarism', which pervaded the so-called 'politically neutral' bourgeois sports organizations seen as corrupting working youth. Fritz Wildung, one of the social-democratic ideological leaders of the workers' sports movement, declared that, while capitalism fostered mistrust among people in order to keep workers around the world apart, the LSI would strive to create international brotherhood. To preserve the socialist character of the LSI in the face of the necessary cooperation with bourgeois governments, it was decreed that no one could be a member unless he shared the view that the goals of the organization could only be achieved in a socialist society and no member of an organization associated with the LSI could participate in a bourgeois sports organization.

Sports activities should draw people towards left ideas, towards the importance of cooperation and against the competition which ran through most 'bourgeois' sports. The competitive character of sport aligned itself with the competitive character of capitalism and needed to be challenged. Labour sports supporters, in opposition to 'conventional' sporting activities, wanted to present a new set of ideals for workers through sport: not simply to add sport to the arena in which the working class could oppose the ruling classes, but because physical culture and the body were the foremost aspects of the workers' existence. Since they neither owned, nor could acquire readily, means of production, property or political influence, it was their own bodies that they needed to retain control over (Lehmann, 29 July 2012).[77] Lehmann comments on the significance of proletarian sport in Germany in the 1920s:

> 'The body of the worker is his and her very own physical capital; literally the "engine" that would drive, through work, political participation and cultural demonstration, the progress towards a different social and economic system. The body was both the site where change needed to happen and the expression that would demonstrate collectively this change. The body needed to be improved through better healthcare, safer work, improved diet, standard of housing and, of course, physical exercise; and such a body then could perform, in solidarity with others, the tasks needed to improve the cultural, social and political standing of the working class.'

But, if the worker's body failed, then his ability to hold a job, earn a living wage and keep a reasonable standard of living also failed. As Lehmann eloquently puts it: 'The body becomes the site for repression, alienation and exploitation at work but ...

remains also the site of potential liberation.' There is no obvious equivalent in the UK, unless one goes back to the far narrower and smaller, though largely working class, Clarion Cycling Clubs, when a sports organization was linked to the left political perspective of rejecting the imperative and dominance of money in sports.[78]

Though the Social Democrats saw the political importance of their sporting clubs, the SPD's support in Parliament for war credits against Social Democratic Party policy paved the way for the setting up of separate Communist sports groups from 1917 and the Communist 'Red Sports International', even though the SPD-linked clubs continued to retain by far the larger membership nationally (though not in Berlin).

Red Sports International (RSI) was founded on 23 June 1921 in Moscow. Its mission was 'the creation and amalgamation of revolutionary proletarian sports and gymnastics organizations in all countries of the world and their transformation into support centres for the proletariat in its class struggle.' It was not till 1924 that the Comintern Executive recognized it. Many clubs sympathetic to the Communist movement nevertheless rejoined the Social Democratic ATSB (Arbeiter, Turn und Sportsbund, or the Workers' Gymnastic and Sporting Federation) (Gounot, 2001). The KPD finally modified their position: having previously maintained that involvement in sports activities was petit-bourgeois, the KPD formed a separate faction within the SWSI in 1928.

In 1928, the two workers' sport internationals, the SWSI and the RSI, had over two million members between them (Steinberg, 1978).[79] But the 1920s were marked by increasing hostility and sectarianism between the SPD- and KPD-aligned sporting organizations. Finally, in July 1927, relations between the RSI and LSI broke down completely and the two organizations ceased to even try to have any sort of fraternal relationship (Steinberg, 1978). Indeed, the LSI changed its statutes to be able to exclude members from their clubs for political reasons and even excluded 60,000 of its own members who had played with KPD members. (So Hans may have been pushed out of his SPD-dominated sports club, as well as jumping.) This sectarian position lasted till well after the Nazis took over power.[80]

One of the RSI's main functions, according to Copper, writing in East Germany in 1988, was to have been to offer a home to athletes expelled from the SPD-dominated *Fichte*. The Red Sports groups were supposedly to provide unity in workers' sports. Their aim was to provide working people, especially the young, with the opportunity to participate in healthy physical activity in a positive working-class atmosphere and to avoid 'achievement addiction'. By the late 1920s, the *Fichte* were connected with Red Sports. (For further information on different Workers' Sports Internationals, see Appendix 8.)

As the Third Period approached, the RSI saw its role increasingly to pull working-class youths from the SWSI's clutches (Steinberg, 1978). Condemning the SWSI's claim to political neutrality and perceiving them as sidling up to the bourgeoisie, the RSI put their energies into fighting them. 'Only "Red Sports" is a worker sport,' wrote Ernst Grube (the CC member with responsibility for sports, subsequently murdered in October 1932, quoted in Steinberg). Red Sports was banned in 1933.

All the soccer clubs in the Berlin-Brandenburg regional federation joined the Communist workers' Red Sports organization. The suggestion by Copper (1988) is that about 16 per cent of athletes in Berlin belonged to proletarian sports organizations. (Before we dismiss this as a low number, imagine having a UK sporting club attached to the revolutionary left which 16 per cent of all athletes belonged to!) The little we know about the Red Sports unit (*Rote Sporteinheit*) in Berlin is that Kurt Seibt, who joined the youth KPD in 1924, was its state youth leader from 1930 to1931.

But Kruger (in Kruger and Riordan, 1996)[81] suggests that

workers did not generally do as well in these Red Sports clubs as in the bourgeois clubs – workers who were keen on sports would generally join better equipped clubs, with better trainers. Both Gounot (2001) and Kruger (1996: 15) argue that Red Sports, although its aim was to endow sports with a new political meaning of collective endeavour and class struggle, did not develop a distinctive attitude or spirit to counter the bourgeois character of sports or the SPD sports clubs. Its purpose, to link sports and politics, led to tension, even conflict, between organizers and members as worker sportspersons joined for the sport, personal satisfaction and achievement, rather than the politics and solidarity. The fundamental structural problem of how to integrate individual subjective expression and autonomy into collective performance remained in the KPD-dominated sports groups, as it had in the earlier socialist groups.

LaPorte (2002) also emphasizes the significance of the sporting and cultural clubs, and the sports clubs' political character. He too highlights that here is an example of some limited cross-party membership between the SPD and KPD, but observes that where local Communists belonged to the SPD-dominated sporting and cultural organizations, there was a loosening of their allegiance to the Party line. One illustration is in Saxony, where the KPD-dominated sports organizations expressed a form of non-acceptance of the implications of the Third Period line in 1928 (LaPorte, 2002).[82] LaPorte (2002) argues that these clubs provided a source of identity which helped keep back the Nazi tide.

Though *Fichte* and *Sports Revues* are outside British experience, Siegi clearly understood their pivotal role in resisting fascism. Siegi, on at least a couple of known occasions, wrote for, and was involved in, agitprop political events to be presented to sports and cultural events in Berlin (discussed in the section on Siegi's agitprop activities, one of which was called: 'Die Fichte').

Although Siegi's writings for the *Sports Revue* in 1932 will be fully discussed in the next section, it can be mentioned here that

Siegi's lyrics, which were critical of seeing sports as a refuge in the storm, will have been a response to the character of the Red Sports and *Fichte*, as we shall see, emphasizing the importance of solidarity, not individualism and competition. (Till his death, Siegi would refer to the contradictory nature of sport – both palliative and possible site of resistance to capitalism.) Yet again, what we have here is another link between Siegi's different activities, in this case the Proletarian Freethinkers and his lyrics for the *Sports Revue*, within a socialist network of sporting and cultural organizations and activities which we can only imagine.

Further work on the Freethinkers in the early 1930s at a grass roots level would be useful to establish not just its exact structure but also how far its overlapping membership with the sports club (surprisingly) led it to be categorized as a 'paramilitary organization'. Coming from a 'British' perspective, we lack an understanding of a tradition of a working-class 'cobweb' of political and cultural organizations. But one is left with the impression that the Red Front, the BPF and a variety of sports clubs were closely aligned, probably under a large KPD umbrella but maintaining some levels of autonomy. For example, both the Freethinkers and the Red Front were involved together in the 'Large Press and Cultural Exhibitions in Red Wedding' in March 1930, organized by the KPD (Bodek, 1996). Again, it is Siegi, one assumes not single-handedly, who 'personifies' this cobweb of activities and allegiances.

Agitprop

One of the few things I knew about my father was that he was involved in agitprop theatre. Indeed it provided, as I now realize, a cover of 'respectability' for why he had to flee Germany. He did not need to tell me or remind himself that there had been other causes, which he had ceased to embrace, by the time I was asking him questions about his enforced flight. The story was a simple one. He directed plays for the workers' theatre; my mother was one of the actors. My mother's view of all this, in so far as she said anything, was that the plays and my father's directing really left a lot to be desired.

My first glimpse of light, many years ago, was when my father asked a distant American cousin, Danny, who was, God forbid, visiting East Germany ('Make sure you come back,' my parents hissed at him, while I studied them curiously as if they were mad creatures in a zoo) to bring him back two volumes on the German workers' theatre in the 1920s and 1930s. My father never of course showed me the volumes but Danny told me, knowing that this was a secret, that he had looked Siegi up, and there he was, an important man in the revolutionary theatre in the early 1930s. Danny recently told me that, when he gave Siegi the volumes all those years ago, Siegi said that one of the chapters was all about him. 'I could write a song in the evening and it would be performed across Germany the next day,' my most unboastful father had told Danny, comparing himself, I suspect with good cause, to Brecht and Weill.

Then, one day, many years later, I was going to speak at a memorial gathering to my parents and had idly put my father's name into Google, only to discover to my utter astonishment, that a few of his songs were being produced at that year's Edinburgh festival, with music by Wolpe. I tracked down in Germany an expert on Wolpe who kindly sent me copies of many of my father's songs, and many articles about agitprop theatre. Roll forward another year and I finally got these translated. Much of the next section is based on these articles, written for the *Arbeiterbühne und Film*, and our interpretation of them. (Anybody interested in the fascinating debates about the role of revolutionary theatre should check *Arbeiter Bühne und Film*, edited by Henke and Weber, first published in 1974, which contains all the articles written between June 1930 and June 1931.)[83]

First, it is necessary to situate the organization: *Arbeiter, Bühne und Film* (ABF) within the context of the existing 'revolutionary theatre' in Germany and its relationship to the KPD. According to Weber, in his introduction to 'Arbeiterbühne und Film' (1974), at the beginning of the 1920s, the KPD did not have a perspective on the role of culture in the revolutionary struggle. (Compare that to the heated debates amongst the Bolsheviks.) At the 1st National Educational Congress of the KPD, they were unable to resolve their position, though they did agree on the importance of political theatre as a means of popular propaganda and of winning the broad masses over to class struggle. The leading theoretician was Gertrude Alexander, who disagreed with both Grosz and Heartfield on the one hand, and Piscator on the other. It seems Alexander defended the existing culture, in effect opposing the development of proletarian theatre. She was not open to the notion that, even in a transformative phase, proletarian revolutionary art should be encouraged.

Piscator, the most well-known figure from the early 1920s, took a contrary view. Piscator had first joined the Sparticist League and then the KPD. In 1924, he was already putting on propaganda performances in the pursuit of revolutionary theatre on their behalf. Piscator saw theatre as revolutionary because it was rooted in working-class experience, and as propaganda and agitation to defeat class injustice and build the final triumph of socialism. As far as I can gather, however, he did not have any dealings with ABF.

In the mid 1920s, Reimann favoured the development of a revolutionary theatre programme to ideologically strengthen proletarian theatre troupes and to turn them into the centres of class struggle. He wanted them to revolutionize workers in the fight against the ideological influence of Social Democratic fascists. At this point, the emphasis was very much on Greek choruses, directed to the 'community', not to the class, with its usual backward looking ideology, both of which came in for much later critique.

By 1926, the KPD's Youth Organization had founded a troupe

under Maxim Valentins, which encouraged other agitprop groups. By the time of the 11th Party Congress, the KPD had changed its mind and decided not to boycott the movement, agitprop groups and the ABF, but to join it. Agitprop should have a propaganda function. They agreed that agitprop groups should be centrally organized. Cultural areas were to be encouraged to combat imperialism.

This change of line by the KPD had profound political consequences for the control of the ABF. The ABF had originally been established in 1913 and been under the influence of the Social Democrats. However, in 1928, the 10th Congress of the *Arbeiterbühne und Film* (associated with the Arbeiter-Theater-Bundes/ATB: the Association of the Worker-Theatre) brought victory to the Berliners and the 'young guard' (Weber, 1974) for the ATB, causing the old Social Democratic leadership to step back. The Berlin group, presumably Siegi's grouping, was under KPD influence.

The Berlin district in the KPD had put in intensive preparation to show the delegates what a left-wing troupe could achieve. Troupes like Red Blouses put on new forms of plays, which emphasized the possibility and importance of propaganda. Pieck was elected President of the IAITB (Internationale Arbeiter-Theater-Bundes: the International Workers' Theatre), and Bela Belaze the artistic leader (Weber, 1974), both KPD. The Berlin group also introduced many well-known and impressive dramatists and theoreticians, such as Piscator and Friedrich Wolfe, and also a booklet by Pieck himself.

The umbrella organization, the DTLB, was also now 'taken over' by the Berlin/ KPD groupings. The congress proclaimed that the DTLB, essentially under Social Democratic control, should be renamed the ATBD (Arbeiter-Theater-Bund Deutschlands: the German Workers' Theatre Association). The ATBD was to be a national organization of workers and agitprop theatres/troupes, with the function of directing the activities of the agitprop troupes. (How far this was the actual case, will be discussed below.) The ATBD was to be responsible for the publication of the ABF, should join the international theatre movement and should have an agitational function.

The KPD's control of the organization was reinforced by the 1929 National Conference of the ABF, which gave a unanimous confidence vote to the KPD position originally adopted in 1928. The debate then, and again at the 1930 11th Congress, was around whether the role of revolutionary theatre was to put on popular, but revisionist, rubbish or to back the need for centralization and a revolutionary perspective. Pieck stated that politically independent troupes were threatening to split the movement. The KPD line was carried by 200:50. The 11th Congress also added a couple of film pages to the ATB publication and agreed to go for articles which were less abstract and more to do with real issues of concern to the class.

In 1930, the Social Democratic core left and formed their own troupes, yet some of the articles from 1930 reveal how far there was still a tussle between the more open church of the old Social Democratic stalwarts and the far more disciplined approach presented by Siegi. Bodek wrote the following to me (2010):

> 'Now, here's where my memory kicks in. I believe that before *Arbeiter und Film* began publishing, it existed as a journal with a title (I think) like *Arbeiterbühne*, which was an SPD organ. When it became *Arbeiter und Film*, it was completely Communist. The ATB was also, after 1930, completely Communist. Social Democrats had their own theatre league... In short, the Communists took over the organization. This was part of the suicidal split on the Left, which certainly helped the right take power.'[84]

It is at this point, in 1930, it is safe to surmise, that Siegi becomes the editor and chief theorist. Indeed, according to the website *wolpe.org*, 'Moos was editor of *Arbeiterbühne und Film* [Workers' Stage and Screen], the organ of the ATBD (Workers' Theatre League of Germany).' *Arbeiterbühne und Film* was one of the key sources for agitprop troupes from 1930 to 1933. Indeed, it was probably the single most important thing that agitprop players read (besides the *Rote Fahne*, the KPD's official newspaper) (personal email from Bodek, 2010). My father's songs would have been spread all over Germany, I presume by means of the ABF.

But before we look at Siegi's precise role, it is worth highlighting how ambiguous and controversial the relationship between the agitprop troupes and the KPD actually was. While this is a matter of historical interest, it also has relevance to my father's story. Formally the KPD had a guiding, if not vetting, role in terms of line and content (Bodek, 1996: 68). The troupes were supposed to submit their scripts for their political acceptability to the ATBD, and also to the new 'Red Union', the RGO (Revolutionare Gewerkschafts Opposition: Revolutionary Union Opposition) and to party factory cells (Bodek, 1996). But how far the KPD was in control is open to debate. It seems likely that in practice, even by 1930 (Bodek, 1996), the troupes, even if in theory under the thumb of the KPD, in practice maintained a healthy independence, partly rooted in their own lived or learnt working-class experiences and the high levels of participation of working-class audiences, especially its youth, in the performances. This gave rise to the accusation that the troupes grossly overestimated their own importance in the class struggle and there were (largely unsuccessful) attempts by the KPD to rein them in as late as 1930 (Bodek, 1996).

These debates and struggles for control were not of marginal significance – agitprop groups were very popular during the 1920s and early 1930s, particularly in working-class Berlin (Bodek, 1996: 55–78). The ATBD alone had 300 affiliated troupes, with about 4,000 members (*Rote Fahne*, 12 March 1930, from Bodek, 1996). In 1931, there were 28 troupes just in Berlin, with about 500 members (Bodek, 1996). The troupes were generally small: between six and twenty members, young, amateur, drawn mostly from the working class and working-class districts, and dressed simply but distinctively (Bodek, 1996: 65). They generally played in the internal courtyards of Berlin's working-class districts, at factory, party and similar meetings. Indeed, one of Bodek's themes is the similar characteristics of the 'real' working-class youth cliques and the agitprop troupes.

The importance of the troupes' political role is illustrated by three examples (Bodek, 1996: 64, 65). The first (Bodek, 1996: 65) is when 20 Berlin agitprop troupes with around 500 members performed 180 times in two weeks during the 130,000 strong metal workers' strike in Berlin in 1931. 100 of those performances were before striking workers. (My mother, most unusually, almost wept in 1981 when nearly 1 million West German metal workers went on strike for the first time since 1931, 50 years later and 48 years after the unions were smashed. 'Today,' she told me, 'it is worth living.') The second example of the troupes' role is that, during the September 1930 election (when the NSDAP only gained just over 14.6 per cent of the Berlin vote), the Red Wedding troupe appeared in the courtyards of Wedding (the best known of the Berlin working-class militant areas), campaigning for a KPD vote (Bodek, 1996).

The final example, which also raises broader issues, is from the 'Large Press and Cultural Exhibitions in Red Wedding' in March 1930, organized by the KPD. Of interest is the presence of so many different separate but intertwining organizations under the KPD umbrella, including the Freethinkers and the *Rote Front*. One of the many agitprop groups, 'Curve Left', performed. The RFB, already outlawed, provided a brass band (in the 1950s and 1960s, my father went on to love the miners' brass bands which trumpeted in the Durham Miners' Gala Day march). This proliferation of cultural/ideological organizations was a feature of the German mass working-class movement, so different from anything we in the UK have ever experienced. Siegi, as we know, was a member of agitprop, Freethinkers and RF groups, and he would not have been the only one.

Thus the 1920s and the early 1930s can be seen as a period when there was intense debate about the role of revolutionary theatre and its relationship to the Party. Siegi's involvement in agitprop and his articles have to be understood within this context. In the debates about traditional versus popular theatre, he appears to have taken a broadly 'neither one side, nor the other' position. Siegi is quoted in Weber's introduction to *Arbeiterbühne und Film* (1974) as stating:

> 'What the class struggle at the present moment requires [is]...that what we have to put on the stage has to be constructed in such a way that the worker recognizes what has to be done today in order to reach the final goal: the fall of the capitalist societal order and the construction of the proletariat dictatorship. (...) Now the need is to mobilize the working class against the tyranny of class justice, against anti-Soviet incitement, against already existing or coming bans of revolutionary organizations, against reactionary culture, against arming for war, against the young plan and cutting wages and against sackings, against the existing societal order (...) the need is to stop the fascist murders. On the basis of the thesis formulated at the 6th World Congress of the Comintern, Moos here made a connection: "that all single issue struggles (...) can only lead to a proletarian revolution in a roundabout way" which he contrasted with the necessity for struggle of the revolutionary working class against the economic and political offensive of monopoly capital and against fascism to construct the dictatorship of the proletariat.'

Siegi was on the editorial board of *Arbeiterbühne und Film*, indeed, by the end of the short period for which we have these pamphlets

(1930–1931), is writing the lead articles and can be seen as its editor. Why this is such a short period has not been established. The journal itself appears to cease publication in 1932. Was it that the Party told Siegi to put his efforts elsewhere and the paper then ceased publication? Was it that Siegi himself could not abide the party dictates? Bodek (1996: 69) suggests the emphasis on subordination to work cells and the party became more intense. Or is that that there is some other reason why the journal's publication ceased, maybe because it fell under one or other law, so that, as with the *Rote Fahne*, it became illegal to publish it? Whatever the answer, we only have a short run, all of which fell clearly into the Third Period.

The extent of the KPD takeover and the underlying tensions is interestingly revealed in an article in *Arbeiterbühne und Film* by one of the old Social Democratic leadership, Bernhard: 'Our opponents' (September 1930: 7, 149). Bernhard was explicitly commenting on Siegi's earlier and significant articles and role. Bernhard acknowledges that there has been opposition within the workers' theatre movement to the position Siegi represented. He stated that 'those coming from the right wanted to carry on sleeping, under the guise of favouring unity and keeping everybody happy.' He argues that it was the movement's failure under the Social Democratic leadership to fight against this tendency earlier, which allowed them to retain and build an opposition to the new position. So, there was an acquiescence in expansion for its own sake in the 1920s, which let in working-class amateur theatre, including people without politics, who just wanted to put on their plays and use the available resources of the ANF. They continued with their performances, which had a broad populist appeal and were entertaining, but had little politics and less connection with the class struggle. So the organization ended up making political compromises and generally went too far down the united front road. Bernhard suggests that, after the youth faction took over, the old guard drifted even further towards populist productions but that Siegi's position, he believes, of a turn towards the class, was the correct one. The Berlin KPD group, of whom Siegi was a leading member, can clearly be seen to have won!

What Siegi's writing is noted for in this period is, however, not so much his 'line' as his interesting attempt to apply political principles to agitprop theatre. The articles are of interest in terms of how the Third Period line is interpreted in terms of its application to agitprop. It will be suggested moreover that limited elements of dissension are discernible. The articles will principally be considered chronologically.

The first article we have is from 1929, therefore towards the beginning of the KPD dominance of the magazine/organization and also almost at the start of the Third Period. Siegi's position, interestingly, is that the prime fight is against the Nazis, not the Social Democrats (also Thaelmann's line at the time), a position, as already examined, that was certainly not the Party line.

A theme that appears in the article, which will reoccur frequently, is that the theatre needs to emphasize the political, and not go in for the easy laugh, for example, the capitalist with his cigar, the priest with a fat stomach. The task is to emphasize the role of the capitalist, the manager, not to present a stereotype. That is too populist and not sufficiently agitational.

In 1930, the Committee of the ATBD produces a call to all members of the Association of Workers in the Theatre. It is worth considering it and the subsequent article by Siegi in some detail, both to understand the contours of the general position which Siegi is taking and writing within, and to give expression to a fairly representative Third Period perspective, albeit directed to the role of theatre.

The ATBD statement of 1930 presents the line that the social fascists are the Social Democratic representatives of workers who compromise with the existing system, not the workers themselves. The social fascists split the working class and its organizations, and therefore act on behalf of the bourgeoisie and must be resisted. Moreover, in relation to the role of theatre, the Social Democratic leaders destroy the cultural organizations of the working class and the revolutionary organizations of the proletariat. 'But we will defeat them, in the path of the new revolutionary class struggle.'

Siegi Moos follows this with a lead article which 'applies' this 'line' to the specific purpose, form and content of workers' theatre. The workers' theatre must appeal to a united working class. Workers' theatre must fight to bring theatre to as high a stage as possible and free it from all 'rubbish'. In bourgeois theatre, each scene ends happily, for example with a kiss, but workers' theatre needs to end with a workers' salute. Happy endings need to be used sparingly because they becalm the workers. The worker sees on stage victories against capitalism when he knows capitalism is still in power. So the play becomes empty rather than real, and leaves the audience dissatisfied. Workers need to be shown the tasks ahead, to stir them up.

The theatre needs to display a revolutionary situation accurately, including the need to use weapons for the victorious storming by the working class. Then the 'audience' will swap the stage for the real fight and take the message into the dynamic of the class struggle and the struggle for the proletarian dictatorship.

The readers of the magazine are reminded of the importance of mobilizing the working class against anti-Sovietism as well as against the programme of dismissals and wage cuts, associated with the austerity Young report, which had recently been introduced. (No wonder my father wanted to forget some of this!)

The indifferent, found amongst Social Democratic and Christian workers' organizations, must be won over to the class struggle. Siegi elaborates at some length on how, though one must understand and respect belief, Christian workers can be pulled over by revealing to them the corruption of their leaders, not by showing the priest as a semi-idiotic clown. That will not reveal the dangers of the Church.

He calls for a fight against the bourgeois press and the importance of a revolutionary press. Only the revolutionary press represents the interests of workers. A worker who gets a subscription to the revolutionary press is a victory against the fascist thugs, though we also need workers' fists. We need to show that mass action can stop dismissals. That is the way that female workers will become involved in active class struggle. Significantly, he argues that they must try to get trusted revolutionaries and their people into posts in works councils, as shop stewards and trade union officials. To win over male and female workers, the theatre needs to reveal that workers can defeat the fascists with their fists. Then we will get a 'happy end'. The audience become agitators in line with what they have seen on the stage. Lovely endings do not turn the audience into agitators (a position that has been debated from that time to this). Enjoyment needs to be only a side-effect. Agitation must be alive.

This can be achieved through content, not from dramatic tricks. If the Church, bourgeois press or democracy are represented simply as idiots, as servants of capitalism, as jesters and whores, this is enjoyment, not agitation. This is farce and will not win over an audience that is not already revolutionary, indeed could rather repel them. Satire, which is different from farce, convinces workers in part through presenting a factual analysis and explanation of, for example, the lies of the bourgeois press, the attacks on the working class or on the USSR, and the rise of the Nazis. The Church must be shown as exploiters, as in league with the law. The fascist murderers must be stopped. The task of the revolutionary is to tear up the tissue of lies produced by capitalism. 'Our enemies are not clowns but enemies. We need proper weapons not toys. Our troops must be fighting troops. Our words must be arrows.'

Siegi develops on his theme in a subsequent article, published in July 1930 (Vol 6, February 1930, p 2 in the original, *Arbeiterbühne und Film*, p 36, ANF Committee statement called 'Revolutionary Theatre'). He states that the principles of revolutionary theatre are still not clear. He has three principal concerns. First, he considers the limitations of the non-revolutionary left theatre. To be revolutionary the theatre must reveal the causes of proletarian misery as class society, not just display that misery. To be revolutionary, the theatre must show a revolutionary solution, the proletariat as a class that is both oppressed and fighting to abolish the existing social order and introduce a new social order. The theatre is only revolutionary art if the persons on stage or screen are real representatives of their class. So showing prosecutors, factory managers or doctors as compassionate is out. They must be shown as hypocrites or as meaningless exceptions, who are far more dangerous than their brutal colleagues, and are the exceptions which reveal the true nature of class contradictions. To show a doctor or judge who has revolutionary views only makes sense if we want to show to the intellectuals their common interests. Only when the proletariat and the wider audience form a unified whole can we create something healthy and unified – the revolutionary theatre. In the framework of bourgeois commercial theatre, these conditions cannot be provided. The revolutionary theatre remains the task of revolutionary theatre.

Secondly, as in the article we have already considered, Siegi is critical of the idea that the revolutionary theatre is there to entertain. He introduces two examples from the history of bourgeois theatre which demonstrate the possibility of its having a revolutionary effect – *The Marriage of Figaro*, performed in the revolutionary days of 1789, and *Die Stumme der Porcini*, in the August days of 1830. Here, the effect was so great that, afterwards, the audience demonstrated through the streets, destroyed an enemy publishing house and burnt the houses of the Minister of Justice, Director of Police and hated journalists. Siegi adds that the free time of the proletarian actor is taken up with rehearsals, performances, and political education. He is a true functionary of the working class because workers' theatre is not entertainment, but living effective agitation for class struggle.

Finally, he looks at revolutionary theatre as party theatre. We want, he writes, to publicize the writings of Marx, Engels and Bebel on the stage by showing them in current conditions. He quotes Bebel: 'If I, as a Social Democrat, join an association with the Bourgeoisie, I bet 1000:1 that it is not the Social Democrat who is the victor but the bourgeois parties and we are the losers...Party comrades must be aware that the leaders of the party do not damage the party.' (Given the range of possible quotes at his disposal, one might wonder why Siegi, presciently, chose this one.) 'The representatives of both a monarchy or of the bourgeoisie form class societies, which maintain a state which perpetuates the class domination of the bourgeoisie.'

Then he approvingly quotes Engels: 'Between capitalist and communist societies is the period of revolutionary change, of one into the other. This equals a politically temporary period, the state of which can be nothing but the revolutionary dictatorship of the proletariat.' Finally, he returns to Marx's most famous statement: 'The proletariat have nothing to lose but their chains.' He concludes: 'We have the duty to use these teachings in creating our performances. The political basis of our plays must be what Marx and Engels said and the continuation of their thoughts. Workers' theatre is not entertainment. We want revolutionary theatre, which can only be realized and must be reached by the workers' theatre.'

One other article from 1930 is worth highlighting, published in the issue of November 1930, and simply called 'Material about...'. The broad position in Siegi's article, as in the articles above, even though their purpose is to discuss the nature of revolutionary theatre, is that there have been too many concessions to the Social Democrats; their critique of capitalism has become too loose, allowing left workers to 'fudge' their allegiances, and therefore letting them off the hook of following the revolutionary path (so to speak!). The Social Democrats do not take on the bourgeoisie or address the real problems. The article evokes the idea of the 'united front from below', expressing the importance of relating to a wide audience, but not at the cost of political purity.

In this same issue, there is a committee statement which is headed: 'For the Unity of Workers Cultural organizations', suggesting that some sort of split or dissension is being addressed, though we can only guess at what that was. While the Central Committee statement talks of the danger of the social fascists, Siegi's article noticeably does not use this term. Though this has to be speculation, is the absence of the label 'social fascist' because he had doubts about this approach or because he is presenting essentially the same idea in a more subtle form? We cannot now know. It is tempting to expect Siegi to be more sensitive to the threat of real fascism, because of his experiences of the SA in Munich, which the comrades from Berlin and the North of Germany had not experienced. But at this point, even if his emphasis is not quite 'on the line', and despite his professed opinion that the Nazis are the enemy more than the Social Democrats, his writing does appear to target the Social Democrats.[85]

Because of the rapidly changing political situation, it is worth, at least briefly, considering the March 1931 issue (No 3) of *Arbeiterbühne und Film*. The lead article, 'The political position and situation of the ATB', is by Siegi, indicating that he is now recognized as the lead theoretician, and the paper's editor. His article as usual condemns the Social Democrats for being all words and no action, while the crisis of capitalism intensifies. It calls for further development of the role of revolutionary theatre. But significantly, it also calls for the need to build a mass opposition to the growing threat of the Nazis, a slight but suggestive shifting in position from earlier.

This brief overview of Siegi's analysis of the link between the political situation and revolutionary theatre concludes with a telling quote from the March 1931 article about the role of revolutionary theatre:

> 'Is the workers' theatre armed for the tasks ahead? Are our weapons sharpened? Our art will create, in a focused way, decisive connections between the class struggle and its environment which is decisive for the class struggle and it will activate the class for the daily struggle. In this, it will not just address the intellect, but chooses to address the emotions. Did we achieve this for example in the chasing out of capitalism by the workers as a stage happy ending? No. In this chase, we have formed in a concentrated manner, the emotional relations of the workers to the class enemy and we have managed an appropriate effect... The fatter the tummy.., the bigger the cigar of the capitalist, the easier the effect but the less the political value.'

While Siegi appears to be largely reiterating the classic Third Period position of a 'united front from below', what is significant about much of these articles is his attempt to apply it to theatre and to argue that the 'soft' and more cartoonish approach of some 'left' theatre does not bring out enough the politics that divide them from the Social Democrats and fails to lead to political action.

What is also interesting about Siegi's articles, which is not explored here, is how far his analysis of the agitprop is situated in his analysis of capitalism in crisis. Even then, Siegi was adept at digging out figures and analysing how the class system was impoverishing the many to the advantage of the few. His articles damning capitalism then remind their readers of the urgency of organizing against it. (See, for example, his article from February

1931, to be found in Appendix 1.)

Finally, with the power of hindsight, it is worth observing how early on Siegi shows a concern with maintaining 'standards', rather than opting for easy entertainment, a position that, arguably, later on in his life, will develop into an élitist condemnation of popular art and populism in general. (This will be considered more fully in the section on Siegi's writing of the 1940s and 1950s. However, to introduce briefly one personal anecdote from the 1950s: he refused a television in our house until the satirical *That was the week that was* miraculously was broadcast in 1962, previously having having told me, 'Television rots the mind.')

There is a very different final article by Siegi that takes the form of a report from the National Congress of Culture (*Reich Kulturkongress*) from April 1931, which reveals not only the 'cobweb' of organizations but also the level of repression they were working under. (As stated earlier, it is not possible to know whether this is the last article Siegi wrote or the last to be presently available.) Siegi writes that, at the Congress of Culture, there were representatives from every part of the cultural movement: literature, sculpture, music, song, the press, revolutionary theatre, film, radio and more. One group represented was the Red Trade Union opposition. Significantly, the article highlights the role of the National Conference of the Freethinkers, which had taken place just prior to the Congress. The Congress, the article states, was encouraged to work with and within this 'movement'.

Here is further evidence for the close association between the Freethinkers and the agitprop organizations. Indeed, the Congress of Culture is another manifestation of the cobweb nature of the many different organizations surrounding the KPD, and of a left-wing mass movement. Its civil organizations are woven loosely together, though, by 1931, the dominant discourse and, indeed, dominant control is by the KPD. But this dominance is not of a small political grouping, as we think of the British Communist Party, even in its heyday in the 1920s, but represents a leadership, maybe even an organic leadership, of a living and large mass movement. The workers' theatre was one part of this mass movement.

But Siegi's article also describes the attempts to close down the Conference. Siegi berates the Social Democratic leadership, in particular in the person of Fleiszner, the Social Democratic President of Leipzig, for condemning the Freethinkers' material and drawings, as well as the photos and texts from the agitprop groups. Fleiszner had obtained an injunction to close down the exhibition and confiscate the exhibits, as it was not a 'cultural' show. While no evidence has come to light on this, if we assume that what is described here is essentially what occurred, it indicates how difficult, even dangerous, it was to organize culturally and politically in the last years of the Weimar Republic, and how far the repression enforced by at least some of the Social Democrat leadership paved the way for the Nazis. It also helps an understanding of the main speech delivered by Herman Dunker, a leading member of the KPD, who asked, Siegi tells us: 'How do we forge a united front of working people against cultural fascism?'

Siegi's combination of political activism with the use of lyrics, song and theatre was not unusual amongst revolutionary circles in Germany. The revolutionary left, in other words, had a level of synergy or penetration into cultural activities in the Weimar years. Harry Wilde, a friend of Siegi's, of whom more anon, worked with Piscator and was a member of the KPD from early in the 1920s. Johannes Becker, an acquaintance or friend of Wilde's, born in 1891, and who had lived in Munich when young, had been a German expressionist poet and a member of the KPD from 1923. Theodaor Plievier, born in 1892, a friend of Becker's, was another German writer and revolutionary, who would, after the end of the war, become a leading cultural figure in Germany.

So Siegi's use of poetic stories to further revolutionary ends was familiar at the time in the east, then from 1948, in West Germany.

Alles an der Roten Start. Music by Stefan Wolpe, lyrics by Siegi Moos

It was not till I was well into writing this biography that two events occurred, both connected to Siegi's association with Stefan Wolpe. Composer Stefan Wolpe was one of the leading voices in the stand against fascism in Germany during the Weimar Republic and close to the KPD, though probably never a member. Alongside his contemporaries, such as Ernst Krenek, Vladimir Vogel and Kurt Weill, he dedicated himself to creating agitprop songs and music for workers' choruses. Wolpe's songs and music were performed in a variety of Communist-affiliated organizations, such as the ATBD/AITB and numerous agitprop groups and, as with Hanns Eisler, the songs that Wolpe orchestrated became some of the most popular of the time, especially in Berlin.[86]

Wolpe and Siegi must have met in the left-wing world of agitprop. I discovered this connection by accident when Wolpe's *Muziektheater Transparant* was due to be performed for the first time in decades at the Edinburgh Festival 2008, including, to my amazement, the orchestration of one of Siegi's songs. Wolpe's star is again, after 80 years, apparently in the ascendant.

This is my loose translation of Siegi's words, with help from Thomas Phleps:

Do you have sorrow?

Do you have sorrow, do you have worries,
Will Lehmann refuse you further credit:
With us you will find a more beautiful world!
Three hours of forgetfulness for so little money,
Oh for how long have you craved this!

With us there is laughter, with us there are tears.

Refrain:

Come, come and get a ticket!
What we offer is first class!
Come in, come in, come in!
The theatre will be your heaven!

Better than Kintop and better than hooch,
The theatre gives you a happy high.
As long as you have a few pennies, don't give up!
The stars of the stage will beguile you too!
Just for you, are our gifts,
And here you can also get education and new horizons.

Refrain

Our theatre also has morality,
Robbery and murder or the pain of love,
Never damages the authority of the state.
We respect the order which now exists
We offer you the best of what is good,
Only happy hours, serious minutes.

Refrain[87]

Other lyrics by Siegi and set by Wolpe are listed in the *Bibliographie der deutschen Arbeiterliedblätter* 1844–1945 (Bibliography of German Workers' Songs).[88] Siegi was working with Wolpe. Wolpe and Siegi's collaboration indicates that Siegi had a sufficient reputation from earlier – but now unfindable – work. It is improbable that someone of Wolpe's stature would have worked with Siegi otherwise. But this script will probably be, sadly, one of a few illustrations of Siegi's work that can now be retrieved or definitively known about.[89] My father never mentioned his work with Wolpe – though he did tell me he knew and liked Eisler.

Phleps, the editor of the Wolpe score and the transcript, highlights that the *Sports Revue, Alles an der Roten Start* from 1932, which Siegi worked on with Wolpe, has received far less publicity than Wolpe's earlier work. (Phleps also questions why Wolpe has generally not received more attention, compared to, for example, Weill and Eisler. Though again only conjecture, there would appear to have been factional 'ins' and 'outs' even amongst the left-leaning musicians in these vital pre-Nazi years, perhaps one factor in my father's subsequent anonymity.) The temporary banning of *Rote Fahne,* the KPD paper that would normally have given publicity to the *Sports Revue* at the exact time that the *Sports Revue* was put on, Phleps suggests, is one key cause, and also provides one reason why I too found it impossible to get information about this work.

The purpose of the *Sports Revue,* Phleps states, was to give support to the election campaign of the KPD leader, Thaelmann,[90] further evidence that Wolpe was also at the time close to the KPD. The fate of the *Sports Revue* illustrates both the political climate in 1932 and the – to us today – extraordinary influence of left ideas. The *Sports Revue,* which was planned for 14 February 1932, was to include a wide variety of acts, from brass bands, choirs, a variety of sports activities through to Wolpe's *Alles an der Roten Start.* Wolpe composed the music, which was supposed to be easily understood by the masses. Siegi wrote many of the lyrics. Wolpe apparently directed the rehearsals with enthusiasm. Central to the *Sports Revue* organization was *der Fichte* (discussed earlier).

We can learn something more of the *Revue* from references to it in *Rote Fahne* and other Communist-leaning press before the actual performance. For example, on 31January 1932, *Rote Fahne* comments approvingly that there is a new initiative by the Red Sports group, a group which had close ties with the Berlin working class, and whose performances had been sell outs. Its task, we are told, is propaganda for the united front. (Beware interpreting this as meaning a united front with the Social Democratic leadership – it is not. This is a call for joint action with their membership only.) The *Revue* is mentioned regularly from then on until the *Rote Fahne* is repeatedly banned: on 9 February, 11February, etc. *Berlin am Montag* (another KPD-dominated paper), on 9 February 1932, stated that the most important current problems in sport would be dealt with in the *Revue*. And there was much else besides.

But the *Revue* ran into many difficulties, not just with the police and the SDP (who ran Berlin) but also with the KPD. (Sadly, Phleps does not go into detail about the cause of the disagreement between the *Revue* and the KPD.) However, the police clearly took exception to the *Revue*. *Rote Fahne* on 14 February, presumably published before it was banned but before the performance of the *Revue*, reported that there had been a new attack on the Revolutionary Sports people and that, because of the censorship board implemented under the new emergency legislation, the police had announced that day at 11.30am that they were putting *Alles an der Roten Start* under surveillance and threatened to put an immediate stop to the performance should any scenes be performed. What appears to have caused the police particular disquiet was a film, banned by the film censors, that was to be shown during the intervals and which was seen as affecting the 'present State in a negative manner' – though it was composed of publicly available clips.

The *Revue* was to take place in the International Sports Palace.[91] According to the two reviews in existence, the *Revue* did not finish because the police did stop it. Right at the beginning, there was an announcement from the stage that the Police President did not like the *Revue*'s line on the USSR and had classified this event as a political rally and it was therefore under surveillance. According to *Die Welt am Abend*, the person announcing this said, 'Our answer is to vote for Thaelmann for Vice President,' and everybody cheered and clapped.[92]

The police kept to their word. Again, according to *Die Welte am Abend* of 15 February 1932, towards the end of the show, when Siegi's song, 'All Warmongers cry for war', was being performed to tremendous applause, there was an announcement from the stage that the Troupe had been banned and that the *Revue* had to stop. The curtain was drawn back to reveal one police officer and a plain clothes officer walking across the stage, the actors and other participants marching behind them. The stage was soon full of police. Loud singing erupted during Siegi's song, 'Strengthen your muscles', and amidst an enormous amount of noise and excitement, a large Red Flag was pulled across the stage which stated 'For a Red United Front. Vote for Thaelmann'. Apparently, it was an amazing scene, which concluded by the dignified singing of the 'Internationale'. The paper reported that Wolpe's music was not always well chosen, but that the songs were great, especially 'Steel our Muscles'. The Red Sports people, who presumably had been interviewed, stated that in spite of everything, 'We cannot be stopped.'

This tale of 'cat and mouse' gives a sense of how difficult and threatening it was to be working in agitprop at this time, even though it is almost a year before the Nazis take power. What it also confirms is the earlier analysis of the close tie between Red Sport and Siegi's role, in this case as a lyricist, in agitprop.

To give a brief overview of the three characters in *Alles an der Roten Start*: Walter Vogel, a lowly white collar worker is often hungry and unrealistically strives for importance but, thwarted, ends up turning to sport. Marie Schmidt, a factory worker aged 20, produces commodities but remains poor. Anton Schmidt is unemployed because he has been rationalized out of the productive process and, after a long struggle, meets up with the

Red Sports group. Through life and the struggle, the actors demonstrate how revolutionary sports people can be victorious. It ended, or would have ended, with the demand for a Red United Front and a vote for Thaelmann.

Below are three lyrics from the performance by Siegi, although the notes on *Alles an der Roten Start* state that Siegi wrote four 'lieder' but it is not completely clear which the fourth one is. Even without a good knowledge of German, the rhythm and rhyming of these 'poems' are clear. Despite the absence of *Rote Fahne,* the following three lyrics have all been taken from the press reviews on *Alles an der Roten Start* and suggest how widely these poems will have been read and spread, possibly more so than Wolpe's musical score, which would not have been reproduced or understood so easily in print.

All out for the Red Start by Siegfried Moos (translated by Irene Fick)

Marie Schmidt was 20 then.
Every day she worked all day.
She produced commodities,
Yet she remained in poverty.
As she learns from watching films,
Marie lives – she waits and waits
For the miracle to come.
Success comes with her start!

Walter Vogel was a small
Employee in a company.
Almost famished he lives by
His fantasy of being grand.
If promotion doesn't come,
Sport is used as substitute.

Always start on Red! [93]

This is Sport by Siegfried Moos (translated by Irene Fick)

I
This is the sport of the ruling class,
This is the essence of capitalism:
Each person breaks with the masses,
Or a person pulls away from the masses
And pursues his search for profit.
And if it means forfeiting life,
That won't stop him; he must succeed.

II
1. Capital is fearful of the thoughts
Of those that toil for famine wages.
To distract the oppressed from the struggle
Hear the radio, press: Look at the sporting aces!
2. But not enough: the profiteers
Of capital, not satisfied with this distraction, say
In order to forget your class, you must
Use sport to prepare for our war.

III
1. The sportsmen call: do not be silent!
Attention now: No need to wait!
Stop kowtowing.
Now attention! Go! Wait no longer.
Hone your muscles! Focus your eyes!
Sharpen your brains! Work your lungs!
We must be fit for our struggle,
Right until we reach our goal.
2. Recruit today to strike tomorrow.
Today we struggle and discuss.

No one will stop us, we will not be hushed,
Red sportspeople on the march.
Hone your muscles!...
3. Red sportsmen fight for all,
For the causes of their class
Unforgiving against all those
Who oppose the broad masses.
Hone your muscles!...
4. Solidarity of sportsmen
of all countries, of all races.
Solidarity of sportsmen
For the final battle of the classes.
Hone your muscles!...

IV
Red sportsmen don't believe that
Sport alone can liberate.
Then join the red fighting front
To be soldiers of the class struggle.
Hone your body, recruit in word and deed;
Always prepared – march into struggle 'Red Sport'.[94]

From Berlin: *Arbeitersportverlag* (1932)

Fichte in the Große Schauspielhaus (Great/Grand Theatre) by Siegfried Moos (translated by Irene Fick)

Hone your muscles! Focus your eyes!
Sharpen your brains! Work your lungs!
They must be fit for the struggle,
Right until we reach our goal![95]

Sportsmen call, not silenced by Siegfried Moos (translated by Irene Fick)

The sportsmen call: do not be silent!
Attention now: no need to wait!
Stop bending over backwards.
Now attention! Go! Wait no longer.
Hone your muscles! Focus your eyes!
Sharpen your brains! Work your lungs!
We must be fit for our struggle,
Right until we reach our goal.[96]

The plot of *Alles an der Roten Start* reads like ghastly social realist fare, but, performed partly in song, with its strong beat, and set to Wolpe's highly modern and supposedly accessible score, it may have galvanized its audience to support the KPD candidate and it certainly upset the police and Social Democratic administration.

It is not difficult to see how it fits with Siegi's theoretical exhortations to relate to the issues of the everyday (which indeed still resonate) and to avoid a bourgeois style of romantic happy ending, but there is, for all that, what appears to be a caricature quality to the characters and the plot. And there is little doubt that the overall message here, which Siegi must have gone along with, was an uncritical support for the KPD and the USSR.

The day before the Revue, the *Rote Fahne* was banned by the police for 15 days, not only indicative of the political climate but also meaning that the Communist paper with the largest circulation was not in a position to review the *Revue* of the previous day. Nor was the *Revue* mentioned in the Social Democratic papers. However, one or two Communist or sympathetic papers did comment on the *Revue* afterwards, reporting that it had been well attended, a gigantic success with around 4,000 people attending. Siegi's 'The Sport of the Ruling Class', 'Steel the Muscles' (particularly admired) and one other of his songs were specifically mentioned. The songs' themes, according to this review, centred on the role and function of sport, rejecting the reformist view of freeing yourself through sport, as sport cannot free the oppressed and exploited, and holding that the bourgeois sports movement is anti-revolutionary. The songs also rejected the warmongers who organized for and profited from war. The songs, we are told, were political but without descending into merely being popular revolutionary songs and without the sentimentality of bourgeois music.

This is one of the only examples we have of Siegi's actual work in agitprop but it is unlikely to have been the first or the last. My guess is that he also worked independently of Wolpe but that this work has all been lost. Indeed, my mother's story that she had originally met Siegi when he was directing a workers' agitprop group in which she was acting, bears out the existence of his work in other now forgotten troupes. It was probably far more impromptu, organized in taverns and workers' halls, and never aiming for, or receiving, the publicity of work done in association with Wolpe.

I remember my father's story that, shortly before the night of the Reichstag fire (and how I now wish I had been listening more carefully), he had been directing a play when the whole stage was occupied by the SA. Siegi pulled up the curtain and the last the audience saw were the SA men chasing the actors around the stage. My father presented this as seizing a small victory from the jaws of a terrible defeat. Theatre used as a part of revolutionary struggle is rare in Britain. But Siegi represented a position, far from unique at the time, that political opposition could be mobilized through the use of theatre, agitprop and song.

It is impossible to know Siegi's exact role during the vital years 1930–1933. No KPD Berlin minutes from the time have been found – and probably no longer exist[97] – so it has not proved possible to establish Siegi's role in the Party itself. While clearly not one of the Party leadership, he appears to have had a leadership role in some of the more cultural organizations that circled around the KPD. Moreover, he embodied a link between at least four of these: the Red Front, the Proletarian Freethinkers, the 'revolutionary theatre' and its journal, and some left sports organizations. This kind of coordinating role would alone have given him a strategic influence, and is indicative that he was a trusted Party man.

It may be that I want to create a distance between my father and the Party that did not exist, but my impression is that there are hints that he was ambivalent about identifying too closely with some of the KPD positions – his consistent failure to use the concept of 'social fascist' in any of his extensive writings when that term was much in fashion, the emphasis on the Nazis being the main enemy, connected with his work in the Red Front, all suggest he was not always 'on line'. Crucially, his involvement with the Red Front suggests he was, at a minimum, able and willing to ride out the swings in the line of the KPD leadership towards the Red Front. And, although, to varying degrees, all maintained their Third Period positions, the interviews with the Berlin 3 suggest Siegi was not alone in his critical, though loyal, approach. Siegi's involvement in different working-class organizations, the BPF and the youthful Red Front, is likely to have reinforced for him the importance of the anti-Nazi fight and helped him keep a critical distance from all-out hackery.

The India connection

One small and intriguing puzzle remains from this period. In the India files in the British Library, there is a report: 'Negotiations between Jehangir Vakil with Russian Oil Products Co.' (ROP), dated 1932, which centres on the creation of a new Russian company to negotiate with the Indians over supplying India with oil, instead of alternative companies, both Russian and American. (See Appendix 7 for details of ROP, and MI5's suspicions about it.)

These negotiations involved trips to Europe where the Russian and Indian representatives met. One leading figure in this world was the Indian, J. Vakil, who was in touch with Saklatvala (famous as the first British Communist MP, first elected in 1922), who introduced him to Brenner, 'probably an Austrian'. Then the document states: 'And it seems that Vakil and one Moos returned to London via Vienna (the latter seems to have received his orders from the company in India).'

Saklatvala, who will reappear in Siegi's story, was born in Bombay and came to the UK in 1905. A regular delegate to Independent Labour Party (ILP) Conferences, he joined the CP in the early 1920s.[98] (The source here is Saklatvala's daughter's biography on the web, 2008, which no longer exists.) Saklatvala maintained a passionate involvement in the anti-imperialist and class struggles in India, even being banned from visiting by the Home Office in the late 1920s! In 1927, the League against Imperialism was launched by Münzenberg, a German KPD member, here acting for the Comintern. Fenner Brockway, a leading ILP member, was the League's first International Chair, but the ILP disapproved because of the League's Communist links. James Maxton (another significant figure in Siegi's life) subsequently replaced Brockway as Chair.[99] In this overlapping world of politics and people, Saklatvala also visited Berlin in 1931 addressing KPD meetings (Pennybacker, 2009).[100] Maybe there he encountered Siegi, who was already involved in Indian matters.

How to make sense of Siegi's links with India? Firstly, it can only be surmised that 'Moos' is Siegi but this seems highly likely. Moos is not a common name in Germany and even less so in Austria. The name is Swiss. Also Siegi possessed a rare, and useful, combination of skills. He had some (limited) managerial banking experience, had worked, even if in a subordinate position, for a highly successful vintner business in Bavaria, was able to speak some English and, crucially, we know was a leading and apparently trusted activist in Berlin at that time.

If we assume it is him, what does one make of this information? What seems likely is that Siegi was seen as a safe pair of hands by the Berlin KPD leadership, one who also knew something about western business practices (an expertise, one assumes, not held by many in the KPD), and someone who had never appeared on any security radar and therefore would be more able to gain easy entry into the UK or elsewhere. Moreover, even if his English was limited, he could therefore communicate relatively easily with Indian business people. From the USSR's perspective, trade with India was beneficial both for commercial purposes (the USSR economy was in crisis) and in terms of the political influence it offered. We also know that after the first world war, a variety of Indian activists with Comintern affiliations operated out of Berlin (Pennybacker, 2009).

As the Indian papers make very clear, the British government maintained a close eye on all things Indian in the early 1930s (and beyond). India was not referred to as 'the jewel in the crown' for nothing. The Home Office (144/17917, HO: 'Activities of ROP in India', 10 January 1933) kept files on ROP and assumed that its trip to India (by Bauer) at the end of 1930 (which did not apparently involve Siegi) was to arrange for the sale of Russian oil. They were also aware that Vakil and Joshi visited Moscow in Bauer's company during 1931, which they assumed was for similar purposes. Why the UK Indian Service was so interested is not stated but is certainly, at least in part, because they suspected that such business dealings could also be fronts for Communist activities. That the Comintern's contacts with India were located in Berlin will in part be due to the keen level of the UK HO's surveillance on Indian affairs.

Siegi will almost certainly have been part of a negotiating team. His political and economic expertise and his mention in the India office files lend credence to his playing a significant role. That role, one can presume, included negotiation with Jehangir Vakil on behalf of ROP, providing managerial expertise, keeping an eye on the books, or/and as a political overseer for Russian Oil and the Comintern. If we trust the UK India Office minutes, which refer to Moos 'receiving his orders from the company in India', Siegi was acting in some manner on behalf of the Indian buyers during the negotiations in London. Siegi's activities were probably rewarded through the Comintern, providing a small source of income to the KPD.

This analysis is given credence by the similar, and better known, activities of Willy Münzenberg.[101] Münzenberg, who already had much practice dealing with Comintern monies, also negotiated with a rival Indian company on behalf of the (nationalized) Russian oil companies and the Comintern. Indeed, the UK India office appears to think that the Russians were playing 'divide and rule' games with different Indian companies. Münzenberg was a key figure in the KPD and the Comintern and the owner of the German papers *Welt am Abend, Berlin am Morgen* and *Arbeiter-Illustrierte* (among others). The British kept an eye on Münzenberg. Münzenberg had launched the World League against Imperialism (1926–1929), which campaigned, among other things, for Indian independence and which supported the Indian Communist Party.[102] A HO document (HO144/17917, 7 December 1932) states that they have definite information that a financial – but 'hidden' – link existed between W. Münzenberg and ROP, lending support to the hypothesis that the ROP did transfer monies to German comrades.

Siegi managed, yet again, to stay under the surveillance radar. His MI5 file either is not available or has been destroyed but evidently he was admitted as a refugee to this country in 1934, so, one assumes, was not 'spotted' in his earlier trip to the UK in 1931 or 1932. (Though not germane here, while Siegi's role could be seen as acting in the interests of Russia – or at least one fraction there – it shows up how vague are the parameters of the concept of 'spy'. Siegi was acting in the interests of the USSR/India in these dealings and distributing 'foreign' monies to the German comrades.)

Siegi's knowledge of, and involvement with, Indian matters is also evident in his writing for the AITB Journal. In the issue of March 1931, No 3, there is an article, signed by Siegi, that goes into a high level of detail, rhetorical in tone, about the Indian opposition to British imperialism, which would not be known through casual interest. He excoriates the giving of honours to those in positions of responsibility: '82 members of the police force were honoured for their heroism...60,000 political prisoners are languishing in Indian prisons...The police President of Bombay and of Punjab who have hundreds of lives on their conscience were awarded with hereditary titles.....Prison directors...lead judges...all honoured. Archbishops and missionaries honoured....'

When in Durham in the late 1940s and early 1950s, Siegi gave a series of lectures for the BBC on 'Gandhi and the spinning wheel', again suggesting a deep knowledge of Indian affairs. He argued, as I remember it (but I was still very young), for combining the modern with the old. (Unfortunately the recording no longer seems to be available.) I took listening to my father's voice coming out of the wireless for granted and it was not till writing this biography, that I became curious as to how he became an expert in this area, indeed invited by the BBC to give a series of talks. Now I guess that his involvement in Indian affairs in the early 1930s gave him a lasting interest.[103] Strangely, there were no notes or records of these lectures in his voluminous papers which I later cleared and sorted. So, despite his willingness to stick his head above the parapet and be broadcast, his desire to keep the KPD part of his past completely hidden must have won out.

Siegi's India link may also be connected to his coming to Britain a few years later. He had visited Britain as part of the Comintern/India dealings and may well have made contacts, for example with Maxton, that would prove useful.

Going underground in Berlin

My father told me the 'story' of the night Hitler completed the deals that made him Chancellor on 30 January. Siegi went out that night thinking that Berlin would rise in revolt. But neither the KPD nor the SPD called a counter-demonstration. Did Siegi hope that Red Wedding would rise, that the RFB roots in the working class and the youth gangs would somehow mobilize a mass counter-demonstration? Instead, he was left as a bystander, watching as the candle-lit procession of the SA 'spontaneously' marched past. There was no protest. It must have broken his heart.

Margaret Dewar (1989), a member of the KPD in Berlin at this time, confirms Siegi's take on that night. She writes that there were no protests called either by the SPD or the KPD, 'yet everybody had expected some action: a demonstration, a strike. But nothing happened. Not one demo, not one strike. The Communist press came out with the slogans: "The worst the better" and, "After Hitler, it will be us".'[104]

Siegi was, I suspect, not quite on the Party line. After all, why otherwise did he come out on the night of 30 January, when the Party had not issued a call to do so? This was surely more than curiosity. It reflects, I suggest, his greater awareness of the real threat the Nazis posed. Moreover, as argued earlier, Siegi's involvement in the RFB, however much he was the Party man in the RFB, also is likely to have led him into some conflict with the Party. His articles for the ATB also ploughed their own furrow. My guess is that Siegi was already developing private criticisms of the Party line.

Rosenhaft (1983) notes that many middle ranking KPD officers opposed the KPD decision not to call a counter-demonstration. I can hear my father's voice now. 'Now or never,' I hear him argue. His defeat was the first time he seriously questioned his membership of the KPD. But I am only guessing.

The story of 30 January curled its way into my emotional

entrails. I still wonder what went wrong that night. How did Berlin – unlike Vienna in 1934 and unlike Barcelona – allow the Nazis to walk in and occupy its streets without any resistance? Indeed, there were demonstrations in Stuttgart, in Frankfurt and in some cities in the Ruhr and Rhineland, and strikes in Hamburg and other northern ports the following day, but not coordinated and not sustained, and crucially, not in Berlin (Merson, 1986).

After Hitler gained power, 'only one member of the ten man Politburo [Hermann Remmele]...is known to have urged an attempt to draw the workers into armed struggle in [pre-25 April] 1933 in order to prevent the new government from consolidating its power' (Merson 1986).[105] Just how wrong the KPD got it is shown by Pieck's stating on 6 February, days after Hitler assumed the Chancellorship: 'We are by no means pessimistic.'

There are different ways of looking at the failure of the Berlin working class to rise, some already discussed. The KPD's own explanation was that at the time of the January elections and soon afterwards, they lacked the industrial strength, the political allies or the paramilitary preparedness to take on the Nazis (Merson, 1986). Moreover, the KPD was no longer confident they could direct their membership, never mind a larger periphery. Their lurches of line and Third Period sectarianism had fatally caught up with them.

To return to an earlier analysis, a further ambivalence, which blinded the KPD to the deathly anti-working class nature of the Nazis as opposed to the Nazis' usefulness to the 'establishment', was whether their primary task was to build the working class for revolution or to specifically counter Nazism. Their (vacillating) emphasis, previously explored, was that by smashing capitalism, fascism would also be destroyed.

Another factor in the failure to oppose the Nazi takeover was that the KPD's recent vacillations on whether to work with or against the SA may well have confused some of its members, especially given that the KPD was not initially banned after Hitler became Chancellor (indeed, not immediately after the Reichstag fire). Moreover, the KPD had, except when under extreme rank and file pressure, generally not supported, either as strategy or tactic, the use of force against the SA. This position was also partly a result of their other intermittent tendency not to want to put off the SPD, and partly a result of the KPD's growing parliamentary orientation.

Though here is not the place to develop on this, many historians argue that the crucial failure to resist Hitler's becoming Chancellor and the Nazi takeover, which marked the end of any real possibility of legal resistance to the Nazis, had its roots ten years earlier, back in the 1920s, in the failed insurrections of 1919 and 1923, and the subsequent unresolved divisions between the different warring factions in the KPD.

Over the coming months, the KPD reiterated that the Nazis were running into their final crisis (wrong), that the SPD leadership were bankrupt (wrong – though almost all the SPD notably failed to resist the Nazis in Parliament or elsewhere), and that this would open the doors to proletarian revolution (wrong). It seems only Thaelmann of the main leadership showed even a glimmering of understanding, referring, on 7 February, to the fight against fascism being different from the goal of proletarian revolution (Merson 1986). Thaelmann was arrested a few weeks later and this idea also disappears.

The Nazis' accession to power marked the final and lethal product of the rift between the KPD and SDP. Though this book emphasizes the role of the KPD and the Third Period, because its concern is with Siegi, the SPD were as culpable for the failure to cooperate as the KPD (and did a good deal less on the ground). The working class – in the unions, cultural organizations, and localities –was fatally split.

'So, why did you continue to resist the Nazis?' I remember asking my father, who was already old, mystified that he had chosen to take on an irresistible force and to risk his life doing so. 'You never know,' he had replied, and I remember, for a moment, he had looked as if he were a young man again.

Siegi did not go into hiding until the night of the Reichstag fire.[106] There was an interlude of a month between Hitler becoming Chancellor and the Reichstag fire. He and Lotte, by then married (in preparation for flight, she told me – see Appendix 9), had talked about whether to flee. 'I told him,' she informed me one day when doing the ironing, with clarity in her voice, which there was no misunderstanding, 'that we knew all was lost before Hitler became Chancellor. So I told him I was leaving for Paris with or without him.' I do not doubt her. She wished to save his life, she said. But she did not appreciate, she also said, that the Nazis would stay in power. And her version also neglects Siegi's commitments as a Party man. My father did not want to flee: 'The working class have no hiding place,' he told me. (I still wonder whether he ever recovered from his 'betrayal'.) For a frozen month, the two stayed put.

One month after Hitler assumed the Chancellorship and a few days before the March elections, on the night of the Reichstag fire, 27 February 1933, the man from the corner shop who sold Siegi and Lotte their milk, banged at the door of their flat and woke them up in the early hours of the morning. He wanted to warn them. (As it was told to me, the man was not somebody they particularly knew, but one might question that.) Siegi, who I suspect, would have prepared, escaped just before the Gestapo came knocking. He went, my mother told me not long before her death, to a highly respectable cousin of her mother's who lived near her parents, and who (amazingly) agreed to hide her wayward nephew-in-law. Siegi hid there for two weeks, not able to go out. Lotte did not even dare contact him there for fear of leading the SA or Gestapo to him. She was not to see him again for a very long time.[107]

As Lotte told Richard and me, the Gestapo picked her up in

March, probably hoping she could (and would) give them a lead to her husband. She was taken to a detention centre, which she told us she thought was in the Brandenburg area of Berlin and which later became a camp, and there was questioned.[108] She claims she knew nothing and from what she told me, she did not know what had happened to Siegi. But I have no doubt she would not have given anything away. The Gestapo, having failed to discover Siegi's whereabouts, released Lotte soon afterwards.

The next few paragraphs will consider more generally the period immediately after 30 January. The RBF bravely continued with their local fights with the SA in the streets and housing estates, though these were growing ever fiercer (Merson, 1986). Rudi's testimony bore witness to the RFB members' bravery during this period. Many of the RFB leadership were later picked up and murdered for their resistance to the SA prior to January 1933.

Although the KPD as a party was not at first banned, the Gestapo arrested what they could find of their leadership, and many of the KPD meetings in the pre-election period up to 5 March were banned. (The Gestapo was formally set up by Goering in April 1933 as the 'secret' wing of the police.) Within these limits and the daily harassment – and worse – by the SA in left areas, the KPD were able to campaign for the elections on 5 March. Indeed Merson (1986) argues that the appearance of being able to maintain legal activities further blinded the KPD to the threat the Nazis posed and to the importance of building the underground.

It is now academically and politically accepted (even taken for granted) that the combination of the election of 30 January1933 and the Reichstag fire four weeks later, marked the division between some sort of democratic –even if autocratically dominated –regime, and fascism. But read about the KPD at the time and you find this was not the case – listen to the accounts of the Berlin 3, and again, it is clear that this watershed moment of history was not recognized at the time. Nor are they alone. This will be discussed further when considering why Siegi did recognize the disaster and its personal implications. But to quote Carr (1982): 'It was only in retrospect that Hitler's appointment as Chancellor on January 30 1933 was seen as the decisive day in his ascent to power.'

Only three members of the Cabinet were Nazis (Carr, 1982), the rest nationalist. 'The first reaction of Pravda was to hail Hindenburg, the representative of monopoly capital, as the most important man in the new government.' Extraordinarily, even in January 1933, Pieck (later leader of East Germany) was still declaring that the SPD was the enemy. And in February 1933, Manuilsky was still damning the Social Democrats. Nevertheless, at the beginning of February, at a secret conference (posing as a meeting of a sports club), attended by about 40 delegates and addressed by Thaelmann, the KPD did put out a call to Social Democratic workers for a common struggle against fascism, all too late and all ignored.[109]

The election results on 5 March, less than a week after the Reichstag fire, appeared to show that the KPD vote, given the level of repression, had held up remarkably well. Around 5 million people maintained their allegiance and voted for the KPD – 12.3 per cent of the total vote, compared to the roughly 30 per cent in the previous November election. But beware using this vote as an indication that the Communists had not yet been defeated, as some still do – if ever there was an indictment of trusting in the power of the ballot box, the March elections surely must be it. The day after the election on 5 March, the KPD was declared illegal and, on 9 March, its parliamentary mandates were cancelled (Merson, 1986).

Then began a reign of terror designed to smash the KPD once and for all. The SA set out to exact their revenge for past blows, essentially unfettered by any police or legal apparatus, though certainly unofficially condoned (Merson, 1986). Many

Communists, particularly the activists, who were not arrested, went underground after February 1933, but many, especially the rank and file members, who hoped to disappear into the working-class areas where their friends and comrades might hide them, were picked up: these areas were already infiltrated by police and Gestapo agents (Palmier, 2006). From 28 February onwards, for about the next two years, strict controls were imposed, with the primary purpose of arresting Communists and Communist sympathizers, though stopping Jews was also important (Palmier 2004).

On the night of the Fire and the days that followed, 1,500 Communists were arrested in Berlin alone and about 10,000 in Germany as a whole. Palmier (2006), although his focus is not on the KPD, suggests that the fire took the KPD leadership by surprise. Most of their functionaries, even if not the top leadership, were arrested. 'The wave of arrested that followed the Reichstag fire decimated the hierarchy of the KPD cadres in a single night... Those functionaries who escaped often had no further precise orders'(Palmier, 2006). We will never know how far Siegi acted independently when he went underground, how far he was under Party directions.

Among those seized, were a high proportion of middle ranking functionaries as well as some full time regional officers (Merson, 1986). The top leadership and some of the key regional figures escaped (except Thaelmann who was probably betrayed and was finally murdered). In the few weeks after Hitler had become Chancellor, the KPD's top leadership finally started to live and work clandestinely (Merson, 1986).

Too late, on 28 February, the KPD's CC issued an appeal to the three main trade-union federations, that is, not just the Red Federation, and to the SPD. It called for a united response of 'strikes, mass strikes, general strike' (Merson). The SPD leadership ignored it, although there were some local attempts at coordination, such as at Leipzig and Stettin (Merson 1986).

Between 30 January and the Reichstag fire, it was still possible for anti-Nazis to exit Germany legally and without significant risk (Palmier, 2006). Indeed, a very few leading members of the KPD and significant literary figures did get out in this brief 'window' of one month. But not Siegi. He remained, whether because of political instructions or a deep reticence to leave his own country, we cannot know.

In the dark hours of the early morning of 28 February, as my father went into hiding and saved his life, most comrades did not know about, or did not appreciate the significance of, the Fire. 'Many were dragged from their beds or seized at their place of work before they had realized the full significance of the Fire or received any political guidance about it, and were taken into "protective custody"' (Merson, 1986). Indeed, in my interview with Rudi in particular but also the other two Berliners, my impression was that the significance of the Reichstag fire as the final break with democracy – even though the Weimar Republic had become autocratic and repressive – is still not fully acknowledged.

Around 53,000 people altogether left Germany in 1933, including many German intellectuals and musicians, among them Richard Tauber, Max Wertheimer, Cassirer, and Erich Fromm. Like Brecht and Weill, Einstein was out of the country and decided never to return. Later, Klemperer, Janacek, Freud, Bloch and Adorno all escaped. But there was also a wide mix of political anti-fascists, from Conservatives to Communists (though very few Social Democrats) (Palmier, 2006). 37,000 of those who left were defined as Jews: some who saw the writing on the wall and had the money to get out, and many who were actively anti-Nazi (Palmier, 2006). There was no 'typical refugee'(Palmier, 2006).

Siegi was in one sense lucky: still relatively young at 29, he was fit, had no children or possessions and, as will be explored later, had a generous and loving uncle. He had experienced illegal and clandestine work through the RFB. Moreover, he would have made contacts across Germany not only through his theatre work but also through the different networks of which he was a part. In comparison, most of the KPD were older than Siegi; many had families and homes, were less experienced in illegal work and, crucially, could not support themselves without paid work – going underground becomes far more difficult in such circumstances. It was clear from interviewing the Berlin 3 that none of them, nor most of their friends, ever considered leaving Germany.

Given what we know from the various 'official' police documents dated 1937, the police/SA knew about Siegi's involvement in the KPD, the Red Front and the Proletarian Freethinkers. He would not have stood a chance. My mother's arrest bears testimony to that. From the same documents, we know that the 'library' of Communist literature which my father told me he had hidden under the floorboards of their flat was also found and seized. (That would have upset him enormously, had he known.) Indeed, the SA tore apart many homes in their search for illegal typewriters and duplicating machines, and hidden caches of anti-Nazi literature as well as wreaking revenge on some of the working-class areas which had stood up to them in the past (Merson 1986).

I had been brought up to know that the Reichstag fire was a Nazi plot, a position which was – and still is – contentious. Then, in the early 1980s, my father drew my attention to a snippet in the *Guardian* newspaper. It had been established, it read, that the Reichstag fire was not started by Van der Lubbe, the man, loosely associated with the Communist Party who was accused by the Nazis of having started the fire. 'You see,' he told me, 'it takes fifty years, but, in the end, the truth comes out.' He went on, 'I knew that the Fire provided them with the excuse for a surprise attack on the opposition,' (though he meant the KPD). I'm left suspecting that Siegi – and almost certainly Lotte too – had anticipated that the Nazis would stage some such event and had been prepared.

There is a question which cannot be answered: why did Siegi decide to flee at all? As already mentioned, none of the Berlin 3 considered flight. Indeed, my impression was that they would have seen flight as betrayal, though it must be remembered that they failed to recognize that the Nazis' coming to power and the Reichstag fire marked a fundamental break with the 'democracy' of the Weimar Republic. Siegi, too, saw himself as a fighter for the working class. Leaving the fight would have been close to desertion. We know that he was in a better position to leave than many, but this is not sufficient to explain why he did leave.

We already know (Merson, 1986) that it was only quite significant figures in the KPD who went underground on the night of the Reichstag fire. As already suggested, it is possible that initially Siegi only 'went underground'; that the initial decision was for Siegi to get out of Berlin where he was known but to lie low elsewhere in Germany, to await a fightback or the Nazis' collapse. Maybe it was only when all the other members of his Freethinkers' cell were arrested, that Siegi realized that, if he wanted to survive, he had to leave Germany.

Or maybe the decision of the KPD from the start was for Siegi to leave Germany. It is possible that the KPD instructed him to leave, or at least had made it clear that he could be useful abroad. Sonnenberg (in private correspondence) emphasizes the necessity for KPD members to be instructed to leave if they wished to stay with the Party: a subcommittee of the CC took these decisions. Given that Siegi had already been used in the negotiations over supplying Russian oil to India, had journalistic and organizational skills and could speak both some French and English, the CC subcommittee could well have seen him as a suitable candidate to help build an exile organization or network. Hobsbawm (2002) testifies to the degree to which comrades in this period would accept the Party's decision as unquestionable commands. The Party had the first claim in their lives. Whatever it ordered, would be obeyed.[110] So perhaps the Party ordered Siegi abroad.

But maybe Siegi approached the KPD. We know that Lotte, whose political acumen should never be underestimated, had said she was going to Paris with or without him. This would have encouraged Siegi to leave. What we do know is that, in the UK, Siegi became the secretary of the KPD exile group with KPD approval. This suggests he was, whatever the exact reasons he left, acting 'on line' as late as 1934.

German police records reveal Siegi's role in the RFB and KPD, that he was on the EC of the Proletarian Freethinkers and very active in the agitprop movement. His application to come to the UK in 1933–1934 (in the MI5 documents) reads: 'Wanted by the Gestapo.' Siegi got out, but I suspect that he never quite forgave himself for his survival when so many stayed and died.

Escape from Germany

It is not possible to disentangle family myth from the political imperatives my father was under. The story as told to me by my father was that he was wanted for his theatre work (a 'smoke-screen' he created as much for himself as for me, I suspect). He had had to walk across Germany because he could not catch a train or buses because he would most likely be caught that way. He told me that at least some of the railway officials had Nazi sympathies. This is confirmed by Palmier (2006). As he walked, he lived by grazing the fields – having been brought up on a farm, or so he implied, he knew how to survive on the land's produce. He then planned to get out by swimming the Rhine near Basle, but when he discovered that there were Gestapo on the French side, turned and walked north to Saarland. There he caught the 'right' train, as the French and the Gestapo checked alternate trains.[111] This was the family story, told, often with some wrath against my mother's sister, whose suggestion it had been, or so the story went, for him to swim the Rhine.

My father never mentioned that he first lay low for a couple of weeks after the fire or explained why he chose a route that took him across almost the breadth of Germany. But there is logic to his route. He had family and contacts around Bavaria and Baden Wurtenburg, where he had spent the first 24 years of his life and where he had probably been some sort of activist up till1928, only five years earlier. Even if he was unlikely to have wanted to put his close family at risk, he may have chosen to go south, or been sent by the Party, because of his local knowledge of the area.[112] But Siegi would have rapidly realized that he was far from invisible – a Berlin intellectual, even if safely in a city such as Munich or Augsbug, rather than walking along countryside lanes and through small villages, neither sounds nor looks like a Bavarian bourgeois or farmer. When he also realized that there was no way out across the river, he headed back up to Saarland.

Siegi was not alone in heading south. Again, Palmier (2006) confirms that some of the people who went underground immediately after Hitler became Chancellor and again after the Reichstag fire, headed to Bavaria. They mistakenly hoped that Bavaria, so jealous of its independence, would stand up to the Nazis, which the State Government was promising to do. Indeed, Bavaria was the last 'anti-Nazi' stronghold in Germany, holding on to its own regional government until 9 March, when, without any resistance at all, they resigned. But it had given some of the exiles one month's grace in the free air of Bavaria before the Nazis unleashed their terror (Palmier, 2006).[113]

After the fall of the Bavarian government, those who were underground there had to flee for their lives again, generally to Switzerland and Saarland (Palmier, 2006).[114] I once asked my father why he hadn't headed for Switzerland, rather than Saarland and France – the obvious place as he had relatives there, or so he had told me (although no living relatives have ever materialized!). The impression he gave me was that he, correctly, did not trust that he would not be handed back to Germany either by the Swiss border guards or the police. Indeed, the Swiss were to become notorious for turning back refugees from Germany. Palmier (2006) tells us that there were German frontier guards on the German side of the frontier to Saarland; some anti-fascists made use of clandestine crossing points from Germany to reach Saarland, crossing the border at night, or disguised as local climbers as the area is mountainous, or with local assistance. Siegi headed for Saarland. It may well have had a political draw for him: the KPD already had established a clandestine press and organization centre there (explored later). Moreover, Siegi had the relative advantage of being acquainted with mountain walking, as he had spent some of his childhood in a mountainous area, getting to school in some winters on skis, he told me.

In general, the trajectory via Saarland to Paris was a 'normal' escape route for many KPD members (U.Sonnenberg, in private correspondence). Some wanted to support the struggle against the affiliation of the Saarland and for some the aim was to build the new KPD headquarters for western Europe in Paris. For example, Münzenberg was instructed to go to Paris in order to rebuild the headquarters for Agitprop and his different organizations. (In fact, in 1935, when Saarland was about to fall under Nazi rule, and the League of Nations withdrew payment for their upkeep, 7,000 members of the underground/exiles then fled to Paris (Palmier, 2006).)

Altogether, it took Siegi seven to eight months between disappearing from his and Lotte's flat in Auguststrasse and reappearing in Paris around August (according to MI5 records). By the presumably straighter route of modern 'A' roads and motorways, it is 596 miles/962kilometres from Berlin to Bern, then about 225 miles/360 kilometres from Bern to Saarbrucken. So the overall distance covered was probably roughly 800 miles/1,300 kilometres. If he was averaging eight miles a day, and, improbably, walking every day, the journey would have taken him a hundred days, a little over three months.

How Siegi survived for so long on the road, dodging the Gestapo and SA and always fearful of casual or deliberate betrayal, will never be known. What was he living off? He may have been given a personal 'contact map' of comrades (presumably with false names), part of the 'underground', who could offer him a floor and food. He certainly would have had a network of contacts from his different zones of previous political activity but would he want to put these people at risk – or indeed would he have trusted them enough to knock at their doors? Maybe he had been tasked with trying to organize the Communist resistance underground. Maybe the Party paid him in some form. On the rare occasions he referred to his 'walk to freedom', what I sensed all those years later was how isolated and afraid he had been.

Siegi did tell me something of his 'walk' across Germany and explained to me how a cobbler had saved his life. The soles of his shoes had completely worn out and he had no choice but to have them repaired. He was walking through small towns and villages, not through larger towns, and went into the local cobbler's. Apparently, not a word was exchanged. My father told me he was terrified the cobbler would give him away as soon as he was out of the shop and get himself a few 'brownie' (or SS) points, even a reward; my father had walked on fearing imminent arrest. But nothing happened. He saw the cobbler's cooperation as an act of silent solidarity, and it seemed to give my father a hope in humankind.

Theoretically, the KPD had built up an underground organization. One effect of 1 May 1929 was that the KPD became more aware of the importance of building for probable illegality (Rosenhaft, 1983).[115] But, as already mentioned, the KPD, despite its nominal acceptance of the Comintern's instructions to build a parallel illegal organization, had not done too well. Merson (1986) claims that the underground unit of the KPD had become little more than an intelligence-gathering body. Of course, there is now new evidence, referred to earlier, that the CC had acquired its own paramilitary defence unit (Marpe), but this was not of use to its membership and its absence from most historical records, including Merson (1986), suggests that it was not only clandestine but also ineffective. Nevertheless, the KPD, by the end of 1932 (in other words only a couple of months before Hitler became Chancellor), did introduce some preparations for semi-illegal work, such as setting up clandestine quarters and contacts, directing clandestine work as well as arranging for alternative presses in Germany and abroad (Merson, 1986).[116]

But in general, preparations for illegality seem to have been more policy than practice. Even after Hitler became Chancellor in January 1933, it seems the KPD Central Committee in their first illegal meeting on 7 February, did no more than make the usual gestures towards the importance of illegal work, without any sign of increased urgency or real commitment (Rosenhaft, 1983). Indeed, the evidence suggests (based on my parents' memories, sources from Rosenhaft, 1983, evidence from the Berlin 3 and key documentation from Fomferra) that the KPD were not fully prepared in 1933, with too many brave comrades getting picked up within months of the Nazis getting into power.

This absence of an effective underground network is all the more noteworthy given how many of the organizations broadly associated with the KPD had become illegal well before 1933, such as the Freethinkers, the Red Front, that the KPD's associated papers, for example *Rote Fahne*, were regularly banned as were events such as the *Sports Revue*. Indeed, the Red Front's cadres, who were mostly KPD, had been working under clandestine conditions since 1929, which Rudi testified to. Nevertheless, one interpretation of Siegi's (and Reimann's, another comrade at the time) flight from Germany is that there was enough of an underground organization to allow him to walk his way across Germany.

At the end of March 1933, the Politburo (finally) decided that the presence of almost all its members in Germany had become too dangerous. From autumn 1933, the leadership of the KPD were almost all in exile and the Politburo was based in Paris, at least up till 1935, when they moved on to Moscow and Prague (Merson, 1986). By March 1933, my father was already in hiding and had left Tanta Klara's by the end of March, so may not have heard of the KPD's decisions. But it is also possible that my mother mis-remembered or never really knew the exact length of time that Siegi hid at Tante Klara's and that, in reality, Siegi only set off at the end of March, not mid-March, after the Politburo's decision to send many of its leading cadres abroad.

After the KPD leadership appreciated the necessity of preparing for illegality, it divided itself into two sections – a Home or Internal leadership, based in Berlin, and an External leadership, led by Pieck, based in Paris, a structure that had taken effect by May (Merson, 1986). The External leadership was responsible for émigrés. John Scher, who had been close to Thaelmann, was initially the key to organizing underground work and contact for émigrés. We can surmise that Siegi would have at some level been under his 'guidance'. But Scher, who was the only member of the Party leadership to stay in Germany, was arrested in November 1933 – just after Siegi had finally got out to France – and was murdered in February 1934 (Merson, 1986; Palmier, 2006).

In June 1933, the Internal and External sections coordinated that the KPD papers should be printed and then distributed by the External leadership from abroad (Merson, 1986). The External leadership, now moved to Paris, became responsible for the crucial publication of the Party's paper, *Die Rote Fahne*,and other materials for the underground, as well as making arrangements for people and publicity to be smuggled in and out of

Germany (Merson, 1986). It can be no more than conjecture but it is possible that Siegi was 'sent' to Paris to help to organize all this. Organizing the presses for the distribution of illegal leaflets and pamphlets, a crucial part of the resistance, had become extremely dangerous and difficult.

At the same time, the KPD were forced to move their printing headquarters from Berlin to Saarland in 1933. Significantly, the Technical Branch, first based in Berlin, which then moved to Saarbrucken, carried out printing operations, though it apparently developed a controversial level of autonomy (Merson, 1986). It is not clear where *Die Rote Fahne* was actually published, as Merson (1986) has it being published in both the Saarland (whose organizational structure, Merson describes as 'complicated') and Paris. From mid-March, *Rote Fahne* was produced two or three times a month in Saarbrucken, though, understandably, by 1934, this had gone down to about once a month (Merson, 1986). (Again, here is not the place to explore this, but it should be noted that the KPD members in the local workplaces and communities bravely produced a torrent of papers, dependent for their national news and theoretical analysis on receiving the Party paper.)

In mid-spring, the Gestapo, although they theoretically had no powers in Saarland, broke up the printing organization (Merson, 1986: 117). All operations had to be moved on, largely, and remarkably, to Düsseldorf, Solingen and, later, Cologne, but they were all broken up in 1935. Between 1933 and 1935, 50,000–60,000 copies were illicitly published per run, from a variety of presses (Merson, 1986). After 1935, the difficulties became even greater.

My father was lucky to have got safely into Saarland and not to have been caught. Given that Saarbrucken provided a KPD clandestine centre, as detailed above, there is the real possibility that he headed there because instructed to and because he could help with Party work.[117] Also he could be helped across the frontier into France. At some point, Siegi got out using the local workers' train which ran into Forbach, the train which he claimed was checked in turn by the Gestapo and the French police. He had, he said, no way of knowing when he got onto the train if he would get off it in the hands of the Gestapo. I presume, but without any evidence, that the underground in Saarbrucken had furnished him with sufficient forged papers (and French francs) to try to get him through the different possible checks into France. Siegi kept the ticket, which I now possess. He told me that when he got off the train and saw a policeman, he had to stop himself from running. Do not draw attention to yourself, he had thought. And then he remembered that he was in France and free.

It is noticeable – but could be coincidence – that the two places we know Siegi ends up in, Saarbrucken and Paris, have printing presses. Presumably, his central involvement in the earlier production and publication of the ATB would have given him significant hands-on experience of writing articles, working printers and organizing the production of literature. Indeed, the fact that my father never mentioned Saarbrucken to me gave me the impression that the train which ran into France came out of Germany, implying that his involvement in Saarbrucken was political and clandestine. It could not be talked about even many decades later.

Across the border in France, Siegi caught a train and arrived to Lotte's welcome in Paris. One of Lotte's few stories, always told with exultation, was that one day, on intuition alone, she had gone down to the Gare de l'Est. She had not heard from Siegi since the night of the Reichstag fire. And there he was, strolling along the platform, having just alighted from a train.

Stay in Paris

Lotte had arrived in Paris in April. She had got official papers from the police and had caught a real train. She told me she nevertheless dressed up for the occasion, wearing a sombre tweed suit and carrying a bunch of funereal flowers. She arrived in Paris not knowing anybody but with a contact with a man who ran a small textile plant, who offered her a job as a *bobineuse*.[118] She got herself a flat in a working-class tower block somewhere behind Montmartre. The name escapes me but the block was called after one of the Communist heroes, so presumably she got the flat through a political network.

Always brilliant at languages, Lotte could converse fairly easily at work and elsewhere. Somehow, she read the political tea leaves: she spotted the rise in xenophobia and anti-Semitism, and decided the tea leaves were not propitious. (The extreme right was indeed getting ever stronger.) Very soon after she and Siegi were reunited, Lotte left alone for England. Based on MI5 documentation, Siegi arrived a mere month later. Lotte insisted it was not safe to stay in France and that, anyway, she wanted to study economics at the LSE.

Paris was a common destination for the early political refugees, who saw it as far closer to their cultural and geographical home than London (Pennybacker, 2009). According to Reiter (2011), Paris in the mid-1930s was apparently the place where the political debates took place to pull together the fragmented left. Around 25,000 entered France soon after the Nazi seizure of power, 85 per cent of them Jews (Pennybacker, 2009). (3,000 Central European Social Democrats and 3,500 Communists got to France before Daladier introduced internment. Half a million subsequently fled Spain.) Pennybacker (2009) argues moreover that there was also a strong movement in support of the refugees, which allowed them some breathing space. A variety of left groups and support organizations, even including some on the left of the Catholic Church, agitated for refugee rights. Also, the French-based aid agencies were far more political than in the UK, because the left were, from early on, far more willing to work with each other than was the case in the

UK. Moreover, their emphasis was far more than here on the political, not the 'Jewish' refugees.

So why did Siegi not stay longer in Paris? It is not possible now to understand the balance of all the different possible factors. I have found no personal or official correspondence or any relevant sources covering this period. Does Siegi again not leave with Lotte because of his commitments to Party work? Were they finding resuming their relationship difficult? As explored later, their relationship did not go well in London and the brevity of this re-encounter in Paris may well be an early indication of things going wrong.

On the other hand, was Siegi aiming for London all along and simply needed that extra time to get together the relevant documents to gain access to the UK? Perhaps he needed Lotte to be in the UK, where she had relatives who had moved here at the beginning of the twentieth century, before he had the right to come over to join his wife. Maybe the ultra-right's rapid increase in popularity and influence in France meant that Siegi could no longer obtain a residence permit, and that was why he had to move on.

But it is not just that Siegi stayed, but that Lotte left. Lotte, who never would be told what to do by anybody, wanted to go to the LSE. Maybe she also despaired of having a relationship with Siegi in which she would be his first commitment. Lotte used to insist that she had saved my father's life twice, once in the flight from Germany, then in the leaving of France. This suggests that Siegi had serious other commitments in France. Lotte certainly believed that without her, Siegi would have remained in Paris – and not survived.

Indeed, there is the further question as to why Siegi did subsequently go to London. Factors external to Siegi's (and Lotte's) own desires will have undoubtedly affected their decisions. Paris was increasingly seen by the KPD as unsafe politically and was moreover a long and complicated way from the German frontier for smuggling in papers. The KPD leadership in exile in Paris all moved on within about a year. Siegi was too well known to be sent back into Germany and not important enough – or perhaps not willing to desert Lotte – to be sent on to somewhere like Prague.

The rise of the ultra-right was a major factor in Siegi and Lotte's decision to get out of France. Siegi's departure in February would have been made more pressing by the mobilization of the ultra-right in Paris. (Unfortunately, the exact date Siegi left France is unknown.) On 6 February 1934, there were fascist riots in Paris, which confronted French troops, with twelve dead, and which some on the left saw as an attempt at a fascist coup. On 9 February, a strike was called by the French Communists, resulting in violent clashes, especially in the working-class suburb of St Denis, with five dead. On 12 February, the successful call for a general strike led to the Socialist and Communist marches merging in Paris. This marked the effective end of the Third Period: a position of cooperation with the Socialists became the dominant position by mid-1934 (following a bitter internecine battle within the French Communist party).

It has been credibly argued that the divisions associated with the anti-Semitism of the Dreyfus affair (ironically a distant relative of Siegi's, or so he told me) had a long running effect on France. French anti-Semitism became exceptionally entangled with anti-capitalist sentiment, though it receded temporarily after the end of the first world war. But the depression years re-opened xenophobic attitudes, particularly in the liberal professions, and particularly as a result of the influx of German anti-Nazi refugees from 1933: about 25,000 in 1933 alone, a far larger number than arrived altogether in the UK till after Kristallnacht (Caron, 2005).[119] Within weeks, local businesses, doctors and other professionals in Paris and elsewhere were complaining bitterly about foreign competition, a position strongly laced with anti-Semitism. In 1933, when the French government enacted liberal provisions for German refugee students to complete their university degrees in France, these tensions were further exacerbated. Already in 1933, Parliament had passed a law that limited the practice of medicine to French citizens, and in 1934 and 1935, it passed additional laws that barred even naturalized immigrants from becoming a doctor for five to ten years following their naturalization.[120] McMeeken (2003)[121] also quotes Münzenberg in spring 1934, stating he was exhausted because of the police surveillance. Münzenberg was using Paris as a base to get the printed word relatively easily into Germany (Pennybacker, 2009).[122] Even if surveillance was likely to be more intense in Münzenberg's case, the level of surveillance and repression experienced by many of the Communist refugees, such as Siegi, was generally acute. Siegi would have been aware of the racist, xenophobic climate and been under police surveillance. He may well also have been unable to find a job, although my suspicion is that he was working for, and being paid in some manner, through a section of the Communist network.

A clue may lie in the similar path followed by Reimann.[123] He also first escaped from Germany to Paris and then went onto London (Hrebeniak, *Guardian* obituary, 1 March 2005), where he pops up in the KPD exile group in London, along with Siegi. The obituary stated: 'He soon discovered that the radical political circles that had always engaged him now lay across the English Channel.' In London, there was a KPD exile group and for Siegi, too, its existence may have been a motivating factor. But we may again be observing the hidden hand of the KPD, directing their cadres from Paris to London to protect them from the increasing right-wing popular and political hostility in France. Maybe, as Reimann was also an 'intellectual' type, it indicates that the External section of the KPD had decided to keep their 'organic intellectuals' safe in London.

Yet Siegi was unusual in ending up in the UK. Though the figures are contested, it has been suggested that only about 12

'Communists' were given the temporary right to stay in the UK in these early years. These figures come from a later East German source but, even if an underestimate, the number is unlikely to exceed 100. Certainly, most German political refugees did not aim for the UK. 9,000 had arrived in France by 1936; another 5,000 went to fight in the Spanish Civil War. As late as 1940, only 5,000 had arrived in Britain, and many of them had come via France, like Siegi, or from Spain (Reiter, 2011).[124] The total numbers of all refugees who had arrived in the UK before Kristallnacht in 1938 was only about 10,000. These early – and mostly known anti-Nazi – German exiles are too often made invisible by the far larger exodus after Kristallnacht (but this is an issue outside the scope of this book).

Many of the decisions about where to try to settle must have been emotionally and politically difficult for Siegi. London, reputedly wreathed in mist and smog, was far more on the edge of the world than Paris, especially before the days of fast trains and the tunnel, requiring crossing the Channel on a ferry. London, unlike Paris, was not a European city. Paris, unlike London, had a political tradition that embraced a revolutionary left. Moreover, unlike Lotte, Siegi did not have relatives in, or real ties to, the UK; nor did he, like Lotte, have a burning desire to attend the LSE.

But neither Siegi nor Lotte expected the UK to become their home. Neither of them appreciated that they had become exiles for the rest of their lives. Neither of them understood that by the time the Nazi regime finally collapsed, they would never want to walk on German soil again.

Lotte told me she thought the Nazis were such an idiotic bunch, they wouldn't last. How could the established German ruling class, or at least significant fractions of it, allow the upstart Nazis to remain in power? She saw the Nazis as incompetent, and had expected that the political class and military would soon dump them, a view more associated with the left SPD than the

KPD, with their emphasis on a popular revolt. It seems likely that Siegi will have held a less rosy view than these perspectives suggest.

Reducing Siegi's life in these four turbulent years to the details of KPD policy and the intricacies of the where and when, can obscure the meaning of such exile. My father had lost what for him made up his life: his political activities, a close connection to a political organization, and his comrades from the Red Front, the RFB and agitprop. He had failed to prevent Germany falling under the Nazi boot. He lost almost all his family, whom he was never to see again and who were mostly murdered. His relationship with his wife was profoundly damaged. Those four years framed him and, though my father tended towards an optimism of the spirit, the scars were clear to see for the remaining 50-odd years of his life.

Endnotes

62. 1 May also revealed the gulf between the KPD's statements and propaganda, and its reluctance to organize; it was a portent of what was to come. After 1 May, KPD's leaflets in the Saxon factories called for the arming of the proletariat and urged workers to demonstrate against Zoergiebel's 'social fascist police terror', but it is clear that the CC had no intention of calling for a May Uprising (LaPorte, 2002: 271). They did call for a protest strike but 'in Berlin itself the strike call was only taken up by a handful of building sites, a sweet meats factory and a few cigarette factories' (LaPorte, 2002).
63. A subsequent leader, Willi Leow, fled to the USSR after the Reichstag fire and was judicially murdered there (Palmier, 2006).
64. Unusually, in 1927, the strength of the left-wing opposition in the KPD is revealed when a KPD membership meeting in Wurzen, West Saxony, voted to adopt a resolution in

support of Trotsky and Zinoviev and expressed hostility to any move to expel them from the party. The chairman of the local RFB, Munkelt, stated that, 'It would be outrageous to expel Trotsky and Zinoviev ...[because] there would also be expulsions in the KPD for representing a different point of view' (LaPorte, 2002). Again the RFB was criticized for 'lacking discipline': 'It [the RFB] had carried out a leftist political line throughout the period [even] when the "moderate" united front had been official party policy.'

65. Drawn from W. Kaas, 'Die soziale Struktur der KPD', in *Die kommunistische Internationale*, IX (19) (9 May 1928).
66. Merson, *Communist Resistance in Nazi Germany*.
67. The KPD CC did set up its own military police. It gave orders in autumn 1930 to form a small illegal self-defence organization of the party, made up of groups of ten, some of them with *handfeuerwaffen* (handguns), who underwent training, theoretically and in practice. Only the leader of the group knew who owned a weapon. They had to guard the leaders and the party houses and were strictly controlled by the CC. Not stated in this source, is the suspicion that the Red Front must have been seen as too far outside Party discipline and too volatile to be trusted with this task. I owe this footnote entirely to the kindness of Harald Marpe, Berlin, who found the following in *Revolutionäre militärpolitik gegen faschistische gefahr* (revolutionary military policy against fascist danger), an East German book of 1982.
68. Drawn from archives quoted in T. Weingarten, *Stalin und der Aufsteig Hitlers* (1970).
69. Daycock, *The KPD and the NSDAP: A Study in the Relationship between the Poltical Extremes in Weimar Germany 1923–1933* (Ph. D. thesis, LSE, 1980).
70. LaPorte (2002) highlights the ineffectiveness of this policy in relation to Saxony. There was not one Nazi delegate to the Regional Saxony Conference in 1931. LaPorte also uses the

Nazi-led strike in the Leipzig textile factory, Tittel and Kruger, in 1932, to illustrate the extent to which the KPD wanted to appeal to Nazi workers. When the strike broke out in late October there were only four Communists in the factory, compared to 76 Nazi workers. The district KPD leadership instructed the KPD factory group to act jointly with the Nazis at strike meetings and on the picket line, using 'ideological discussion' to win them over.

71. Peterson tells a very similar story though he is referring to events immediately after the Reichstag fire.
72. Volker Berghahn, *Europe in the Era of Two World Wars: From Militarism and Genocide to Civil Society, 1900–1950* (English translation, 2005).
73. Bodek, 'The Not so Golden 20s: everyday life and Communist Agitprop in Weimar-era Berlin' (*Journal of Social History*, Vol 30, No 1, 55–78, 1996).
74. Lotte once said that she had been arrested and kept briefly, one can assume, during this same swoop. The details were unfortunately thin. She cannot, however, have been held for long. She then received a notice that library books were overdue and had to be returned immediately. 'I was no fool,' she told me. 'I wasn't going to fall into that trap.' Genuinely unwell, after Siegi had disappeared, she went to stay, and hide, with an aunt in the country. She seems to have known who to apply to for the necessary papers, telling me that some of the police remained Social Democrats. She dressed up for the train journey as if she were going to a funeral, carrying a wreath of flowers, to decrease any chance of being questioned or arrested. Unlike Siegi, she travelled on a German passport, with the appropriate papers, probably leaving Germany in April 1933 for Paris. She said she thought she would be returning within a few years. It was not to be. She was never to see her mother or sister again.

75. Copper, *Workers and athletes against fascism. The struggle for Community sporting red units in Leipzig from 1933 to 1935.*
76. Fomferra himself was arrested in March 1933, 'for a separate matter', in this case by the SA, with the whole of his family, although he was released after fourteen hours, and survived.
77. Lehmann, talk on *The Worker Olympics*, 29 July 2012 at Tate Modern, London.
78. There is also no comparison in terms of support. In Germany, the Workers' Cycling Association in 1929 had a membership of 320,000 and maintained a bicycle cooperative factory!
79. Steinberg, D.: 'The Workers' Sport Internationals 1920–28', in *Journal of Contemporary History*, Vol. 13, No. 2, Special Issue: 'Workers' Culture'.
80. By 1930, the SPD-dominated sports organization encouraged joint activities with the Stahlhelm, which were to soon join the SA. After the Nazis took over, the SPD sports leadership even informed the Nazis that they were as anti-Communist as the Nazis and that the organization was willing to subordinate itself to a strong, that is, Nazi, national leadership in sport. It called on its members to refrain from politics (Kruger, 1996).
81. Kruger, 'The German way of Worker Sport', in A. Kruger and J. Riordan (eds.) *The Story of Worker Sport*.
82. LaPorte's (2002) analysis of the switch from 'red' to 'brown' in Saxony is telling and gives far greater prominence to cultural and sporting organizations than normal. LaPorte refers to F. Walter's 'Sachsen – ein Stammland der Sozialdemokratie?', in *PVS* 32 (2) (1991), a study of Saxony which argued that the primary obstacle in the path of the Nazis' electoral rise was not the percentage of workers or the scale of unemployment, but the 'milieu' of cultural and sporting organizations (plus the attachment of workers to

their parties). Walter indicates that where the 'milieu' of left-dominated sports clubs was strongest, the SPD was most stable and the vote held up at the polls against the Nazis.

83. Weber: *Arbeiter Bühne und Film.*
84. The importance of some of these agitprop groups is also revealed in Len Crome's *Unbroken.* In the four weeks preceding the 1930 Reichstag elections, 19 Berlin agitprop groups gave 650 performances in halls, courtyards, factories and in the open air.
85. Siegi is, however, taking a pro-USSR position in his writings at this point, even though even here, he is emphasizing – even optimistic about – the possibility of working with the SPD (though note the absence of reference to the SPD's leadership). Siegi's articles in full are included in Appendix 1. See for example, his article from February 1931. Just to highlight his 'line' in early 1931, here is an extract:

'How dare such people (fascists, church etc) argue against the USSR. Here the incredible is coming true. They need 2m new workers. Compare this to the 50m unemployed in USA. The 5 year plan has been realized in 4 years. What an impressive achievement in the land of the proletariat dictatorship and the laws of Bolshevism "which destroy everything". Capitalism is conscious of the danger hence its feverish war preparations and the oppression of the revolutionary proletariat by means of fascism (sic). Our task is to start mass struggle against fascism...The election to the works Councils [in March] gives us a new opportunity to measure our revolutionary struggle against the opposition. We can witness now in the wider circles of the SPD a strong honest opposition against its politics, a strong need for unity against fascism. Never was the situation as favourable as today to build this front. It is up to us to use this situation with all our strength. It is not yet too late.'

86. Wolpe's music is not easily pigeon-holed, with styles ranging from jazz, folk and ethnic influences, to *sprechgesang* and complex composition, evocative of a very particular place and time in history. He was forced to flee Berlin in March 1933, a short while after Siegi, making use of his Romanian passport, and eventually settling in New York after a time in Israel. Once in the US, he moved away from his left affiliations.

87. 'Haben Sie Kummer' in the original German (by Siegfried Moos)

Haben sie Kummer, haben sie Sorgen,
Will Ihnen Lehmann nichts mehr borgen:
Bei uns finden Sie eine schönere Welt!
Drei Stunden Vergessen für wenig Geld,
Nach dem Sie sich, ach, schon so lange sehnen!
Bei uns gibt es Lachen, bei uns gibt es Tränen.
Immer ran, immer ran an die Kasse!
Unsre Ware ist prima Klasse!
Kommen Sie rein, kommen Sie rein, kommen Sie rein!
Das Theater soll Ihnen Ihr Himmel sein!
Besser als Kintopp, besser als Fusel
Gibt das Theater sel'gen Dusel.
Mit wenig Moneten verzagen Sie nie!
Die Bühnenstars begeistern auch Sie!
Gerade für Sie sind doch unsere Gaben.
Auch Bildung können Sie bei uns haben!
Immer ran, immer ran an die Kasse!
Unsre Ware ist prima Klasse!
Kommen Sie rein, kommen Sie rein, kommen Sie rein!
Das Theater soll Ihnen Ihr Himmel sein!
Unser Theater hat auch Moral,
Raubmord und Totschlag, Liebesqual,

Verletzt nie die staatliche Autorität.
Wir achten die Ordnung, die jetzt besteht.
Wir bieten Ihnen das Beste vom Guten.
Nur heitere Stunden, ernste Minuten:
Immer ran, immer ran an die Kasse!
Unsre Ware ist prima Klasse!
Kommen Sie rein, kommen Sie rein, kommen Sie rein!
Das Theater soll Ihnen Ihr Himmel sein!

88. I owe my thanks to Arnt Nitschke, Thomas Phleps and Peermusic for the publication in 2011 of a score by Stefan Wolpe from 1929 and 1932, which includes both Siegi's accompanying lyrics for the 1932 work, and copious notes on the *Sports Revue* and other activities Siegi was involved in. It is both a cause for rejoicing and a mark of a terrible cultural (and personal) loss and disjuncture that, after 80 years, this work has finally reappeared in the public domain and I want to here express my gratitude for Phleps' and Nitschke's endless work in bringing this about. Prior to my receiving this publication, I had thought it impossible to find out anything more about this period of Siegi's work.
89. One of the stories my father did tell me was how he hid his documents under the floor boards where he and Lotte lived in Auguststrasse. These could well have included his lyrics and poetry. But the SA pulled up all the floorboards and ransacked what lay beneath. Anything that Siegi had not hidden, I gather, my mother's sister, Kate, burned after Siegi and Lotte had fled. Her explanation was that she was safer that way but my parents never forgave her.
90. This was far from unique. *Das Rote Sprachrohr* (Red Megaphone), apparently the most popular agitprop group and led by the famous Vallentin, regularly performed at large demonstrations and meetings before or after Thaelmann spoke (Crome, 1988).

91. The *Großes Schauspielhaus*, originally designed for Max Reinhardt, reopened in 1919, and contained seating for 3,500 people. Max Reinhardt wanted to attract a working-class audience. The Nazis took over the theatre in 1933 and changed the name to The Theatre of the People. In 1988, it was condemned and demolished.

92. *Die Welte am Abend* had originally been established in 1922 by Münzenberg, then head of the propaganda section of the KPD, though it seems to have had a more cultural viewpoint than *Die Rote Fahne*. It was closed down in September 1933 and its editor arrested.

93. 'lles an den roten Start!'

Marie Schmidt war 20 Jahre
zur Fabrik sie täglich ging
und sie schaffte täglich Ware,
doch sie blieb ein armes Ding.
Wie sie es im Film gesehen,
lebt Marie und wartet, harrt,
bis das Wunder wird geschehen.
Zum Erfolg beginnt ihr Start!

Walter Vogel war ein kleiner
Angestellter im Konzern,
Ausgehungert lebt er seiner
Illusion vom großen Herrn.
Kommt er im Beruf nicht weiter
sucht er sich Ersatz beim Sport,

Al[l]es an den roten Start!

94. 'Das ist der Sport' by Siegfried Moos (from Berlin: *Arbeitersportverlag* (1932))

I
Das ist der Sport der herrschenden Klasse,
das ist des Kapitalismus Sinn:
Der Einzelne löst sich von der Masse,
steigt empor zu eigenem Gewinn.
Und büßt er auch das Leben ein,
er will, er muß erfolgreich sein!

II
1. Gefährlich wird dem Kapital das Denken
der Massen, die für Hungerlöhne fronen.
Vom Kampf der Unterdrückten abzulenken
schreit Radio, Presse: Seht, die Sportkanonen!
2. Doch nicht genügt es den Profitinteressen
des Kapitals, die Massen abzulenken –
du sollst, wenn deine Klasse du vergessen,
im Amateursport in die Kriegsfront schwenken.

III
1. Sportler rufen: Nicht geschwiegen!
Achtung! Achtung! Nicht gewartet!
Sollt nicht mehr die Rücken biegen.
Jetzt heißt's Achtung! Los! Gestartet!
Stählt die Muskeln! Schärft die Augen!
Schärft die Hirne! Übt die Lungen!
Müssen gut zum Kämpfen taugen,
Bis wir unser Ziel errungen.
Müssen gut zum Kämpfen taugen,
Bis wir unser Ziel errungen.
2. Heute werben, morgen streiken.
Heute kämpfen, diskutieren.
Keiner bringt uns mehr zum Schweigen,
Rote Sportler aufmarschieren.
Stählt die Muskeln!…

3. Rote Sportler kämpft für alle,
Für die Sache seiner Klasse.

PCH

Unversöhnlich gegen alle,
Die ein Feind der breiten Masse.
Stählt die Muskeln!...
4. Solidarität der Sportler
Aller Länder, aller Rassen.
Solidarität der Sportler
Im Entscheidungskampf der Klassen.
Stählt die Muskeln!...

IV
Rote Sportler glauben nicht daran,
daß der Sport allein befreien kann.
Reihn sich in die rote Kampffront ein,
wollen Klassenkampfsoldaten sein.
Stählt den Körper, werbt durch Tat und Wort;
stets bereit zum Kampf marschiert "Rot Sport"!

95. From: Berlin: *Arbeitersportverlag* (1932)

'Fichte im Großen Schauspielhaus'

Stählt die Muskeln! Schärft die Augen!
Schärft die Hirne! Uebt die Lungen!
Müssen gut zu kämpfen [!] taugen,
Bis wir unser Ziel errungen!
(Aus der Roten Revue.)

96. 'Sportler rufen, Nicht geschwiegen' by Siegfried Moos

Sportler rufen: Nicht geschwiegen!
Achtung, Achtung, nicht gewartet!
Sollt nicht mehr die Rücken biegen.
Jetzt heißt's: Achtung! Los! Gestartet!
Stählt die Muskeln, schärft die Augen,
Schärft die Hirne, übt die Lungen,
Müssen gut zum Kämpfen taugen,
Bis wir unser Ziel errungen.

97. I gather that many of the KPD records were destroyed in Allied bombing. Some records may have been sent to the USSR and disappeared into the Moscow archives. But these records were not something many in the post-war German Communist Party would have wanted found after January/February 1933!
98. A 'centrist' organization, the Independent Labour Party, always to the left of the Labour Party with a belief in combining parliamentary and extra-parliamentary methods to bring in socialism, was in a state of decline at this point, having walked out of the Labour Party in protest against the policies of the 1929–1931 MacDonald government.
99. During the first period of the League Against Imperialism, individuals such as Jawaharlal Nehru (later India's first Prime minister), representing the Indian National Congress, whose participation Saklatvala opposed, Indonesian nationalist Mohammad Hatta, Mexican painter Diego Rivera, author Upton Sinclair, and Professor Albert Einstein (acting as Honorary President), were all active in the League (Peterson, 2009).
100. Pennybacker: *From Scottsboro to Munich. Race and Political Culture in 1930s Britain.*
101. Münzenberg, a hate figure on the right, was a pivotal figure and deserves to be better known on the left. Based in Berlin, a member of the Reichstag representing the KPD, he

successfully established and raised millions in aid for the Soviet Union through the Workers' International Relief (Red Aid). He became a leading figure in the Comintern. After 1933, he fled to France and broke with the KPD/Comintern over the Soviet/Hitler pact of 1939 (not easy for somebody whose life had been the Communist movement). His premature and mysterious death in 1940 is often suspected to have been the result of another Stalinist killing. (The Soviets certainly did not publicize him after his death.) The chances of he and Siegi knowing each other at least as comrades are great – both were activists in the Berlin KPD, and subsequently fled to and lived in Paris, and both dealt with India. Nevertheless, my instinct is that Siegi did not approve of him – Münzenberg is described as having a nice taste in suits and enjoying the high life. I remember my father studying Derek Hatton, the Militant leader of Liverpool council in the 1970s, and declaring (correctly) that this man was not to be trusted because he was too keen on the cut of his suit.

102. It was banned by the British in the late 1920s; in fact, the British government banned the LAI from even meeting in London in 1929, and Münzenberg planned to convene the meeting in Cologne – except that many delegates were arrested before they ever got there. Indeed, according to Brinson and Dove (2014), there had been regular contact between the Metropolitan Police Special Branch and the Prussian Secret Police during the 1920s and into the 1930s including about the League against Imperialism. There had been shared discussions as to whether Communists, including Münzenberg, should be admitted to the UK.

103. Siegi may have met Nehru who visited his daughter in Oxford in 1938, where she was studying. Nehru, a man of the left, who was actively pro-Indian independence, and supported the Republicans in Spain without being pro-

Communist, might well have interested Siegi.

104. Dewar, *The Quiet Revolutionary.* Dewar continues, significantly, that after the Reichstag fire, the KPD in Berlin became inactive and demoralized, although a small nucleus did continue with underground work, usually at a terrible personal cost. Moreover, the KPD was so unprepared that they regularly put their members at risk from arrest, as the interview with Elfrieda also testified.
105. Remmele, accused of ultra-leftism, was ousted from the Politburo on 25 April 1933, and sent to the USSR, where like, so many German comrades, including Neumann, he was 'purged' (Merson, 1986).
106. D .N. Pritt (in *From Right to Left*) calls the Reichstag fire 'perhaps the most important [world] event between 1917 and 1939.' Pritt was part of an unofficial investigation by a group of European lawyers to investigate the cause of the Reichstag fire, which was held in England and inevitably had to overcome many legalistic hurdles. Pritt rejected the argument, still popularly held, that it was the Communists who had started the fire and instead pointed out that the group who immediately benefited from the fire were the Nazis in the elections five days later. The fire started at between 30 and 40 points in the tunnel under the Reichstag, which precludes it being one man's (van Lubbe's) work. Moreover, given the level of guards patrolling the Reichstag and that access to the tunnel was through Goering's residence, Pritt is unambiguous in pointing the finger at the Nazis as the planners and culprits. The conclusions of this unofficial enquiry are not universally accepted, even on the left. (Münzenberg was also involved in this unofficial enquiry and this was the stated reason the UK refused him admittance.)
107. Jan Peterson's *Our Street* (2009) is a unique 'novel' about these days in a street in Brandenburg in 1933, written at the

time, and, with great difficulty, smuggled out of Germany. He too highlighted the absence of a left presence on the night Hitler became Chancellor, apart from some heroic but futile leafleting outside a factory for a general strike. Peterson documents the savagery with which the SA and police attacked the left in the following months. On the night of the Reichstag fire, one comrade fled, others were arrested. The talk amongst the comrades was that they would overthrow Hitler soon. Peterson himself amazingly survived after escaping from Germany in 1934, to end up living in East Germany.

108. Maybe the detention centre was at, what was in August 1933 to become, the Brandenburg-Görden concentration camp which housed, and murdered, political (and later T4/'euthanasia') prisoners (including Lotte's sister, Annamarie). Neither of my parents ever gave details.

109. By 1935, at the Brussels Conference, held in Moscow, two years after the Nazis had taken power, Pieck appears to have accepted that he had been wrong and called for 'a united front of the deed' to liberate the working class (Harald Marpe; Ian Birchall). The fascist demonstrations in Paris in early 1934 were fundamental in causing a change of Comintern line (personal letter from Ian Birchall). However, as modern day defendants of the Third Period line will remind us, the call for a united front was not new (Ian Birchall). It may well be that, by 1935, it was circumstances, rather than Pieck's opinions, that had changed.

110. If the Party ordered you to give up your lover or spouse, you did so. Hobsbawm gives the example of the KPD ordering Margaret Mynatt to go to England from Paris to help organize the German exiles. She obeyed, leaving behind the love of her life.

111. There are some question marks over my father's version of events. Were the Gestapo on the French side of the River

Rhine? And were the Gestapo allowed to check alternate trains running from Saarbrucken in the Saarland to Forbach in France? Theoretically, this was not possible. Saarland was at the time under a League of Nations mandate, in practice under French military occupation. But on the rare occasions Siegi referred to this escape, his fear, all those years later, was palpable and I believe him over any official records which suggest the Gestapo were not allowed into Saarland.

112. Josef Wagner, whom Siegi could well have known from his time in Bavaria, maintained an underground KPD network from Augsburg. He appears again in 1935 as a key leader in Paris for the Saar territory (Merson, 1986). A long-standing member of the KPD, Wagner was a member of both the Bavarian Parliament and the Augsburg City Council. Arrested by the Gestapo on 28 April 1933, released, then later re-arrested, he was later to escape to the USSR, only to die of TB.
113. Palmier, 1996, from *The Spokesman Review*, May 10, 1933, Google.com/newspapers.
114. After the Treaty of Versailles, Saarland, which had been a part of Germany, was put under a French/British League of Nations' mandate from 1920 to 1935. Its coal fields were ceded to France. Both were a cause of great disaffection in Germany, and not just on the right. Siegi was one of many political refugees who sought refuge there after early 1933 and they campaigned strongly for the continuation of the mandate. But Saarland was to fall back under the control of the Reich in 1935, following a plebiscite there. Its record under Nazism did not distinguish it favourably. Weber, in his study of German Communists, refers to Paul Lorenz, who had represented the KPD in the regional government, and who, thrown out of the KPD in 1934, supported the Nazis – a trajectory which may be illustrative.
115. Since 1921–1922, the KPD, like all CPs, had been theoreti-

cally committed by the Comintern's 21 Conditions to develop and maintain an illegal structure. Moreover, the events of 1918–1919 and of 1923 would have left some sort of legacy about the need for underground work, though there is no definitive evidence on this.

116. In Berlin alone, 5,000 members continued to carry on the struggle in illegal and often highly dangerous conditions (Merson, 1986). Even by 1936–1937, clandestine groups in Berlin were sufficiently numerous to be divided into seven districts. There were six local Siemens factories where there were illegal KPD cells and an illicit KPD paper, *Lautsprechen*, which was distributed and discussed! (Merson, 1986). The heroism of many of its members in the years between March 1933 and 1936 is remarkable and, often, heart-breaking.

117. Münzenberg, whose adventures often appear to parallel Siegi's but with the advantages of privilege, also fled on the night of the Reichstag fire, escaping as the police raided his flat early in the morning (as they did at Siegi's). Münzenberg also aimed for the Saarland but, unlike Siegi, he had use of his own chauffeur-driven car. Nevertheless, he too had to be smuggled across the German/Saar border. There he made contact with French Communists who provided him with papers so that he could 'legally' enter France (McMeekin, 2003). He and Siegi would have probably come across each other in Saarbrucken. Münzenberg also then travelled onto Paris, where, with existing international contacts and reputation, he was welcomed, indeed granted a special residence visa, on condition he did not intervene in French politics. In fact, he set up a variety of front organizations (one, once again, with Einstein as its Honorary President). Ellen Wilkinson, ex- (and soon to be again) Labour MP, also arrived in Saarbrucken in June 1933, by when Siegi could well have arrived there, to help provide support for the political exiles on behalf of the UK Relief Committee

(Pennybacker, 2009). Who is to know whether Siegi met her there, or even came away with the mistaken impression of a swell of left grass-roots support in the UK for the Communist refugees?

118. Lotte used to tell me how, over the short period she worked there, from around April to November, the woollen thread that was being woven on the frame started to break more frequently because it was of poorer quality, and how she had difficulty keeping up with the 'girls' whose experience meant they could knot the ends together quickly and keep the shuttle flying.
119. Caron, *The Path to Vichy: Antisemitism in France in the 1930s.*
120. After Siegi had left, there were increasing demands, often successful, for further restrictions of refugees and, increasingly, specifically of Jews. The second major theme of anti-Semitism in the 1930s, Caron (2005) argues, was the identification of Jews with the political left. Anti-foreign sentiment was transmogrified into an attack on all Jews, French as well as 'foreign'. Anti-Semitism became almost respectable, even though laws were always framed as being against the foreigner, not the Jew.
121. McMeekin, *The Red Millionaire: A Political Biography of Willi Münzenberg.*
122. Münzenberg, like Siegi later in the UK, seems to have remained fairly remote from the French Communist Party (PCF). But, unlike Siegi, Münzenberg, McMeekin (2003) argues, retained an unambiguously 'social fascist' position towards the Social Democrats into spring 1934, much longer than the PCF.
123. Born Hans Steinicke, to a Berlin-Jewish bourgeois family, Hans adopted Reimann as a pen-name when he started to write for the KPD newspaper in about 1925. In 1923, he had joined the Youth league. From 1923 to 1927, he studied economics at Berlin university. In 1931, he was a member of

the Central Committee and editor in chief (Weber says 'an' editor, suggesting there may have been others) of *Die Rote Fahne* (writing a controversial article about the key role of the unemployed). According to Weber, he became an independent writer in 1930. In 1932, he allegedly belonged to the group that wanted to replace Stalin with Buckarin and led a resistance group made up of KPD and SPD dissidents.

124. Reiter, 'Political Exiles and Exile Politics in Britain', in *Political Exile and Exile Politics in Britain after 1933*.

Part 2

In exile in Britain

Chapter 6

1934–1938 The first years of exile

Introduction

This second part of Siegi's biography looks principally at how this man who had been a committed revolutionary slowly came to terms with living in a relative political backwater against a background of the 'betrayal' of his socialist values by the USSR. The period between the mid-1930s and the late 1950s was moreover not a propitious time for revolutionaries in the UK and were even harder if you were a foreigner.[125] This is an attempt to show how Siegi tried to adjust to this new reality.

As discussed, Siegi was one of a mere handful of political exiles to aim for and gain entry into the UK. Pennybacker (2009) estimates that only about 200 German Communists arrived in the UK. Very few anti-Nazi émigrés thought of settling in the UK in 1933 (Palmier, 2006). Britain was suffering from high unemployment and it was difficult to get a permit to work. Moreover, immigration authorities could forbid refugees suspected of Communist sympathies, even though this was against the law. Palmier (2006) states that immigration authorities made every effort to keep out Communist activists. This helps to explain the very limited number of anti-fascists who successfully sought refuge in the UK between 1933 and 1938. Indeed, Palmier suggests that the UK was not generally seen as attractive by German anti-fascists in terms of somewhere to carry on the struggle. Most other European countries in 1933 would have seemed more culturally familiar. The few political activists who settled here in 1933 were more likely to be Liberals, Catholics, Conservatives and Social Democrats (Palmier, 2006).

The first refugees from Germany to the UK are often subsumed or overlooked because of their lesser number – and probably because they were less obvious 'victims'. Most refugees arrived here after the 1938 pogrom/Kristallnacht. Although the Immigration authority's figures are unreliable, they suggest that, between March 1933 and October 1934, only 4,000 refugees, almost all German, had arrived here (London, 2000). The exact numbers are not known: not everybody came straight from Germany so would not necessarily appear as a German refugee. Moreover, British immigration /the Home Office did not have a classification for political refugees or even, more generally, refugees: everybody who arrived here entered as one form or another of alien.

This initial influx comprised predominantly, not political activists, but an assortment of scientists and academics, the 'literati' , mostly in theatre and cinema, and the representatives of the 'liberal bourgeoisie', including the more far-sighted industrialists – so largely drawn from a 'respectable' and potentially highly employable middle class, and many, though certainly not all, Jewish (Palmier, 2006). Even by 1937, there were only 4,500 refugees in the UK (Palmier, 2006).

Examples of writers or journalists who came to the UK are: Rudolph Olden[126], Otto Lehmann-Russbueldt [127] and Alfred Kerr.[128] The most well-known and influential was the playwright and revolutionary leader, Ernst Toller, whose time in the UK is considered below. As opposed to Siegi's more interventionist inclinations, most of these men largely wanted to influence public opinion by getting the ear of influential public figures (Furness, 1995), but the British were generally not responsive to these foreign émigrés' exhortations. These principled exiles were not just taking on the predominant attitude of appeasement, expressed clearly by sections of the British ruling class also rooted in the anti-militaristic left, but also, like Siegi, running the real risk of deportation from the UK for engaging in 'political activities'.

Indeed, MI5 were particularly suspicious of political refugees from Germany, an interest out of all proportion to their numbers, and a consequence of their historic concerns with German spies and Communist agitators (Brinson and Dove, 2014).[129] There were even discussions between MI5 and the Prussian Secret Police about German Communists and whether German Communists should be admitted to the UK. Brinson and Dove argue that MI5 had received details of a list of German political refugees' activities in the years up to 1933. The political refugees, Communists but also Social Democrats or from a more broadly aligned or non-aligned left spectrum, who generally arrived in the UK in 1933 and 1934, were very different from the post-1938 pogrom Jewish refugees, even when the political refugees were themselves, in a Nazi, even if not always self-identifying, sense, Jewish. Unlike many Jewish refugees, the vast majority of the refugees who retained an alignment with the KPD (and its other European equivalents) intended to return to rebuild their countries of origin, preferably within a socialist framework, and indeed started to make plans while still in the UK. Siegi's rupture with the KPD also meant he was unlikely to want to return, which makes his trajectory all the more unusual.

From 1938, the government's policy towards the refugees became increasingly restrictive, even more so than the earlier 1933–1937 period when Siegi and Lotte were struggling to remain on this island. Not just Kristallnacht in Germany, but also the Austrian Anschluss and the invasion of Czechoslovakia (soon to be followed by the invasion of Poland), caused a considerable increase in the numbers wanting to flee for their lives and seek refuge in the UK, numbers which now included many families, not all respectably middle class, who may have required far more public monies. The rate of expulsions from the UK also quickens from 1938 with terrible results for too many of those expelled (London, 2000).

The UK government was very reluctant to admit all refugees from Nazism. By the 1930s the tradition of granting asylum to refugees had been put on the political back burner, despite continuing humanitarian appeals.[130] After the 1938 pogrom, the leaders of the Jewish community (initially the Jewish Temporary Shelter, then the Jewish Refugee Committee), leaders of an established and 'integrated' Jewish community, reached an agreement with the government that they would allow in some refugees, in exchange for guaranteeing that they would bear any costs of settlement. They became deeply involved in helping limit the numbers given permission to be admitted (London, 2000b).

There was no legal obligation on the government to admit refugees and, indeed, the government emphasized the policy of transit, not settlement, for refugees, in a country considered to be overcrowded and which had mass unemployment. Nevertheless, until 1938 and the increasing number of exiles following Kristallnacht/1938 pogrom, relatively few refugees were turned back or expelled, though they were offered only temporary admittance, had to undergo regular applications to remain here and had severe restrictions on their rights to work. These early exiles found it almost impossible to obtain a work permit – only a few were favoured, and they were generally the best connected. The most common sources of employment were the BBC and the universities (Palmier, 2006).

We don't know why Siegi came here.[131] It's too easy to assume that because he did, this was inevitable. It cannot be ruled out that the Party directed him here.[132] According to his son, it appears likely that Jürgen Kuczynski came to the UK because he was instructed to do so. Siegi's India connections from only a couple of years earlier might have led the KPD to want him to build on his existing contacts. Or, as previously suggested, the Party may have wanted to protect their 'intellectuals', given that much of mainland Europe was looking increasingly unsafe. Or was Lotte being here Siegi's main concern? Maybe the imperatives coincided. I suspect both Siegi and Lotte realized that the UK was going to be the safest place to be, having understood far sooner than most the nature of Nazism and the balance of international forces. After all, they were only going to be in the UK till Nazism collapsed or was destroyed.

Siegi arrived in London in February 1934 and left for Oxford in 1938. 1938 is significant also because, by then, he had left the KPD. These four years are crucial to chart the shifts in Siegi's political development. The rest of this chapter will be divided into four sections. Firstly, Siegi's political life, in particular his participation in the Communist exile group, will be examined. Then Siegi's search for jobs and his legal insecurity as a refugee will be looked at. Intertwined with Siegi's changing of allegiances is Lotte's complicated trajectory. Siegi's disengagement with the USSR and the KPD/CP will therefore be examined, along with his difficult personal life.

Background

From MI5 papers, we know that Siegi arrived in Folkestone either on 13 July 1934 or, more likely, in February 1934 (the records are not consistent). He had arrived in Paris, according to MI5 records, in August 1933. He had gone underground in Berlin at the end of February 1933, so it had taken him almost exactly a year before he arrived in London.

My mother arrived in the UK around four months before Siegi. But she had family in the UK, a most anglicized aunt in Hove, who ran a bed and breakfast, and who agreed to officially provide Lotte with accommodation. Lotte writes about her arrival here in a couple of her stories. She tells of the generosity of the Immigration Officer, who, knowingly, did not ask too many questions. He did not, for example, ask her too closely about how much money she had. (A few pounds, my mother told me, also emphasizing quite how hard it had been for her so save this small amount of money from her work as a *bobineuse.*) Lotte wrote that she slipped away from her aunt's after the first night, after her aunt had told her, 'We don't want troublemakers here.'

Whether Lotte really preferred to be in London, penniless and friendless, is questionable; what seems more likely is that she suffered her aunt for just long enough to make some contacts in London. The aunt had served her function. Siegi, with a wife safely on British shores, would probably have had an easier time of getting in himself.

There were a variety of organizations in the UK, in particular the British-German Relief Committee.[133] The committee was supported by a roll call of the radical literati and socialists, including Havelock Ellis, Harry Pollitt, Sylvia Pankhurst, Isabel Brown, and Ellen Wilkinson (who earlier appeared in Saarland) and Saklatvala, whom we earlier encountered in the India connection.[134] Of particular relevance to Siegi is the support of Brockway and Maxton. Most of the many Jewish organizations and Jewish exile support groups in the UK, however, wanted as little as possible to do with the left refugee groups (Pennybacker, 2009).[135]

A meeting organized by the Relief Committee in May 1933 was attended by around 2,500 people, including Toller and a variety of British literati, for example Bertrand Russell, Wilkinson, Saklatvala, and Maxton, though some in the Labour Party tried to prevent any association with 'Communists and Trotskyists' (Pennybacker, 2006). Other meetings were to follow, at which, amongst others, Wilkinson spoke – against the Labour Party line – on her work in Saarland. Toller, whom we last met manning the barricades in Munich and being sent off to prison, now has reappeared – as an ILP contact.[136] (Toller provides another possible conduit between Siegi and Maxton. My father spoke of him with noticeable warmth.) Toller, who had a well-deserved literary reputation by 1933, provided the link between the ILP and an illegal network of assistance for the German underground (Pennybacker, 2009). As Dove and Lamb (1995) argue, Toller was more successful in alerting the English to the dangers of Nazism than any of the other exiles.

It was far from easy to get into this country (even if it now boasts of how generously it took in poor fleeing Jews), especially if the refugee was political, even worse a Communist.[137] Siegi required sponsorship. He told me that he got into the UK because the ILP MP, Maxton, sponsored him.[138] Getting an MP's sponsorship was difficult and Siegi was not after all a prominent figure like Toller; indeed Siegi seems to have specialized in remaining invisible. Any explanation has to be conjecture. My mother appears to have had some sort of ILP contacts – she told me she had attended, at least, one ILP camp/summer school. (The ILP did not restrict their summer schools and camps to a cadre or members, though the schools were held in August (from G. Cohen's personal communication) so not at the right time, in either 1933 or 1934, for Lotte to approach Maxton to gain his support for Siegi.) But her attendance suggests she was at least on the margins of the ILP or knew somebody who was attached to it. The mother I knew would not have hesitated to go up to Maxton at one of the many meetings or gatherings he attended during this period, especially as Maxton was highly approachable.[139]

Lotte may also have been in touch with Mr Wood. My hunch (or maybe a scrap of memory) is that Lotte made contact with Mr Wood when she first arrived here through a refugee organization. But this contact could well have been reinforced through the ILP network. Ronald Wood was an active Labour member (indeed he became leader of the long-deceased London County Council), who, according to MI5 notes, was an ardent Communist – which he was not. But he was on the left of the Labour Party, and might well have passed through the ILP first. One of the first places Lotte and Siege, once again reunited, went to stay in London was at the Woods', which, if I remember it right, was in Richmond. The Woods were to support Lotte and Siegi from early on in their repeated and exhausting attempts not to be thrown out of the country and became long-standing family friends.[140] Another ILP route to Maxton could have also been via Toller.

It is also possible that Siegi's earlier Indian links had put him in contact with Saklatvala (see earlier for details), no longer an MP, but who had been involved in the India-Russia oil nexus and who had close links with Maxton, via the International League against Imperialism and Parliament (both elected in 1922).

But there is also a possibility that the Münzenberg-Maxton link from the League against Imperialism also lay behind the Maxton sponsorship. Münzenberg, as discussed in the India section above, was also involved in the Russia-India negotiations and would almost certainly have known Siegi while they were both in Berlin. Münzenberg also fled to Paris, indeed via Saarland, so the probability is that Siegi and Münzenberg would have met in one or other place. But the likelihood of a Maxton-Münzenberg link providing the critical conduit has to be balanced against the known tension between the KPD/CP and the ILP by the early 1930s. Maxton, representing an ILP line towards the Stalinists, may not have been on especially friendly terms with a member of the KPD.[141] But in a personal communication, Gidon Cohen wrote:

> 'For what it is worth I wouldn't have thought that the opposing factions (even of a virulent kind) would prevent sponsorship. The ILP's political outlook was much more ecumenical than the Communists – and given his [Maxton's] personality I don't think the factional issue would have mattered greatly to Maxton with respect to such 'human' matters. At the same time Münzenberg would have been aware that Maxton's position as an MP was of considerable value in this regard.'[142]

Thanks to Siegi and Lotte's political contacts, Siegi was one of the lucky few to gain access to the UK.

It is in line with Maxton's general approach to the issue of German exiles that he was willing to sponsor Siegi. Maxton took the issue of German exiles seriously enough to raise the matter in the House of Commons. As early as 16 November 1933, he asked of the Home Secretary: 'Is the Right Honourable Gentleman putting any difficulties in the way of Germans landing here – difficulties that would not apply to the nationals of any other country?' While he got the inevitable denial, it can be assumed that Maxton suspected that what he was asking about was indeed the case – and he therefore must have received information to that effect, maybe from the British German Relief Committee (see endnote 133) that he supported, maybe from individual casework, maybe both. The exact date of Maxton's question raises a further speculation. Siegi had arrived in Paris, Lotte in London, and, though it is only conjecture, I wonder whether Maxton had already been approached about sponsoring Siegi.

But the anti-refugee context of Maxton's question is revealed by the more general tone of the Commons debate. The subsequent question during the same debate was from Lord Stone: 'Was the Home Secretary satisfied that no British professional men or skilled workers were being deprived of their livelihood through the competition of *political* refugees?' (My emphasis.) So, though the number of political refugees was unlikely to have been more than a couple of dozen by November 1933, a scare was already being stirred up about their taking jobs.

There were subsequent questions about Jewish German refugees. I give an extract from the speech of Mr Gilmore at some length to give a taste of official thinking of the time and the difficulties faced by 'aliens' such as Siegi. The Home secretary, Mr Gilmore, who had succeeded Samuel as the Tory Home Secretary in the second Coalition Government, stated:

> 'Any foreigner seeking admission to this country is required under the Aliens Order 1920, to satisfy the immigration officer that he is in a position to support himself and his dependants and, if he is desirous of entering the service of an employer in

> the United Kingdom, leave to land cannot be granted to him unless he is in possession of a permit issued to his prospective employer by the Minister of Labour. If an immigration officer thinks fit, he may, in granting leave to land, attach a time condition limiting the alien's stay in the country. ... An alien who is given leave to land as a visitor is not at liberty to take up employment or otherwise establish himself in this country without my consent. On any application which is made to me, my practice is to consult my right honourable friend the Minister of Labour. While the Government has every desire to accord sympathetic and liberal treatment to persons who have been obliged through force of circumstances to leave Germany and have been admitted to this country as visitors, the policy of the Government, as announced on several occasions, is to give first consideration to the interests of our own people and no consent to employment is given unless it is clear that no displacement of British subjects will result...'

Gilmour ended up by saying, 'I am fully satisfied that the system of immigration control is adequate to secure that undesirable aliens, whether or not they represent themselves to be refugees, are not admitted to this country.' (*HC Deb.,* 16 November 1933, vol 281 cc1094–5) Asked persistently about numbers of German political and Jewish refugees entering the UK, Gilmour did not appear to have the answer. Maxton was unusual in his proclaimed sympathies towards the exiles in the House of Commons.

We know very little about what Siegi did when he first got here. Thanks to Home Office papers, we know that he was a student at the LSE in 1934. The Home Office was watching both him and Lotte, and opening their mail from 12 March 1934 – this occurring very soon after Siegi's arrival here, and possibly precipitated by his arrival. Judging from the files, one can assume this was because they were suspected of having

'Communist sympathies'. Even at this point, MI5 appear to be more suspicious of Lotte than of Siegi, who they thought was a bone fide student. Both of them were already being watched. In 1934, Lotte obtained a few hours' teaching in a language school but I have not found evidence of any other source of income for their first couple of years in London. Siegi received monthly a tiny, but I suspect crucial, handout from his beloved uncle, Hermann, in Munich. Forbidden to work, in these early months, Lotte and Siegi must have lived largely on thin air.[143]

1934–1937 Siegi's political life: the KPD group in exile

Siegi joined the KPD group in exile. It must have seemed like a safe port to shelter in during a life-threatening storm, where he could share a political language, indeed the very language he spoke, with comrades who had endured similar perils to himself and would understand what he had gone through and who he had become.

A document obtained from the *Bundesarchiv* stated that Siegi 'was put in by us as group leader [of the KPD exile group], the only active and willing comrade.' This certainly suggests he was under some form of 'instruction'. The group's membership, again drawn from the *Bundesarchiv* list, is illustrious. It comprised, or at least included: Guenther Reimann (for details, see endnote 123), Rosa Leviné-Meyer, her son Genja Leviné, her stepson Rudi Meyer, Ernst Meyer (known as Ernst Hermann Meyer, presumably to distinguish him from Rosa's former partner), a musician/music critic and his unnamed wife (Ilse Meyer), Lucia Moholy (a well-known Bauhaus photographer and partner of Theodore Neubauer, who was to become a major Communist resistance hero), Edith Bone, Lisa Cocker, Egon Schulenburg, Max Berger, Heinero Cassirer, Paul Berliner, Hans Eisler and his wife, Lou Jolesch ('temporarily'), the unnamed daughter of the CP academic Professor Kuczynski, Gerhard Friedlander (son of Ruth Fischer and Paul Friedlander), and Siegfried Moos.

Significantly, MI5 files also confirm Siegi as a member of this exile group between 1934 and 1937. But the exact date of the list is clearly significant, if for no other reason than to show when Siegi became active in the exiled KPD group. This is difficult to pin down, however. The dating of the list can be limited to the period Gunter Reimann was in the UK: he could not have arrived in the UK until late 1934 and he left again for the USA probably around late 1937 (from Michael Hrebeniak's obituary, *Guardian* 1 March 2005). Hans Eisler's presence here also confirms this rough time line. Eisler, famous as a left-wing musician and associate of Brecht – and a friend of Siegi's – had the good fortune to be performing in Vienna at the time when Hitler was appointed Chancellor. Instead of returning to Germany, he visited many European cities, including London (and Spain to support the International Brigades), finally settling in the USA in 1938.

A closer look at this roll-call of German comrades suggests one reason why Siegi may have been favoured in the 1934–1936 period. Information on the membership of the London group of KPD exiles is again drawn from the *Bundesarchiv*. Rosa Leviné was seen as associated with the right opposition (and was seen by Lotte as 'poisonous'). Moholy was a 'creative' and possibly only a nominal party member. Edith Bone was a functionary of the British Communist Party so maybe was not seen as suitable. (The Comintern's position was that the exile group should avoid contact with the British CP.) Cassirer was a student as, probably, was Kuczynski's daughter, who is listed as 'youth' or 'student'. Two people are listed as 'going to be isolated' – Lisa Cocker on the request of 'Paris', and Schulenberg on the request of 'Claus'. Max Berger was to lose all his functions, that is, was to be removed, and was subject to a Party investigation. Gerhard Friedlander is noted as wanting to be involved but under the influence of Fischer and Maslow, that is, politically unsound .

Ernst Hermann Meyer is the one exception to this list of

'unsuitables', but his exact role is open to debate. His participation in the group outlasted Siegi's and, in one analysis (detailed below), appears to supplant Siegi.[144] Leske (1983) states that Meyer provided the leadership within the group, though the date and Leske's sources are not clear, casting some doubts over her analysis. (The reasons to question this analysis are developed below.) She has Meyer, that is, not Kuczynski (or Moos), as providing the political leadership for the KPD exile group in the UK and being the contact person with Paris, an unusual analysis. It is possible – but seems unlikely – that Meyer had this latter role and that, because of its importance, Leske generalized from this. Meyer, who was able to travel in a way Siegi could not, may have provided the, or at least one, international link with the KPD Paris exile network, while Siegi, in the first two or so years the exile group existed, remained the 'org' man in London. But there is the other very real possibility, judging from Kuczynski's memoir and from a conversation with Kuczynski's son, that it was Kuczynski who travelled regularly between London and the KPD HQ in Paris. The overall impression is of a discordant organization, made up of people who were used to swimming in a large pool, now jockeying for political position in a very small bowl.

Siegi and Lotte also knew Edith Bone (née Edith Hajós). We know this courtesy of the notes on Lotte's interrogation in Holloway, held by MI5.[145] Siegi, too, must have been on personal terms with Edith in 1934. The contact was of great interest to MI5 who posted two policemen outside Bone's flat, no doubt increasing Siegi and Lotte's sense of insecurity and paranoia. Indeed, the files suggest that Siegi and Lotte's relationship was of crucial interest to MI5. We now know, but one assumes Lotte (and Siegi) did not know, that Edith Bone was a spy-master for, and not just a functionary of, the Communist Party.

Lotte protests that the link was no more than her and Siegi's use of her bath as they lived nearby and their bath, which they shared with the other tenants in the house, was unbearably dirty. Lotte also stated that she did some photographic work for Edith, as this was a shared interest.[146] (Lotte had trained as a photographer in Berlin.) Edith Bone introduced Lotte to Edith Tudor-Hart. Hart lived in Lawn Road, as did Lotte (though not Siegi) – MI5 was well aware that one block of flats at the bottom of Lawn Road was a centre of left and Communist exiles, some of whom, such as Edith Tudor-Hart, MI5 perceived, accurately, as spies for the USSR.[147] MI5 files also suggest that Lotte met her friend, Brian Goold-Verschoyles here, of which more anon. Two security men observed the comings and goings: whether Lotte's contact with Edith was as casual as Lotte suggests in her interrogation or whether there were grounds for MI5's suspicions, may now never be cleared up.

Günter Reimann's (1904–2005) history also has interesting parallels to Siegi's. He too walked out of Germany – it is worth observing who has to walk and who is still politically able (and can afford) to catch a train. Arriving in London in 1934 when he joined the exile group, he too left the KPD very early (though the exact date is under contention – see endnote 123 for more details on this interesting figure). Significantly, he was one of the people whom the Home Office threatened with deportation for indulging (maybe) in political activities, no doubt increasing the level of fear amongst this tiny refugee community.

No history of this little group of political exiles can omit the Kuczynski clan. Robert René Kuczynski (1876–1947), a well known economist, listed as a member of the exile group, has long been thought never to have been a member of the KPD, but it now appears that he was. Again, Siegi and Robert almost certainly knew each other. Robert had studied at the Universities of Munich and Berlin. In 1933, Robert Kuczynski left Germany for the UK. A statistician, like Siegi, he was employed at the LSE and later became an adviser for the British Colonial Office.[148]

The list of KPD exile members includes a reference to one

student 'child' of Robert but it has not been possible to establish which one as all were in one way or another connected with the KPD, though most probably it was Sonia (from personal conversation with another daughter, Renata Simpson, January 2010).

Jürgen Kuczynski (1904–1997), Robert's son, is of particular interest, as he became the head of the KPD émigré organization (Childs' obituary in the *Independent*, 13August 1997, KV2/1871, and Jürgen's son). Although he arrived in London in late 1936 and is therefore not on this list, he took over the leadership of the exile group from Siegi and, according to his son and Brinson and Dove (2014), took as frequent trips as was possible to meet the External leadership of the KPD In Paris.[149] According to Childs, Jürgen studied economics at Berlin university, and after a stretch in the USA, joined the KPD in 1930, working as the economics editor of the main KPD paper, *Die Rote Fahne*, until it was banned by the Nazis in 1933. Unlike Siegi, Jürgen remained in Germany until 1936 as part of the Communist underground. His departure for London was, according to his son, probably a result of being directed to do so by the KPD leadership. In his biography, Jürgen dismisses the KPD exile group in a matter of sentences as essentially a group of disorganized intellectuals, dilettantes and student types.[150]

One small but corroborative piece of evidence, culled from MI5 files (KV2/12410) from 1935, is an anonymous letter, listing five members of the KPD exile group as 'Communist agents and agitators for the KPD', including Siegi Moos. The source is unknown and its main interest is that this level of detail indicates that another of the exile group was giving MI5 information. Siegi would have expected this, I suspect, but, if this surmise gets near to the truth, it is indicative of the level of division and suspicion amongst these 'comrades'. Nevertheless, if we assume the information is reliable, some time in 1935, the total (presumably active) membership of this group had reduced to five!

There are, however, two other separate lists. In *Exil*, part of a series of books on the different countries the political exiles ended up in, written under the aegis (and ideological influence) of the GDR, an almost completely different list is provided (the source of the following information is not given): Johann Fladwug, Meyer (the only name as in the first list), Louisa Neumann, Wittkowski and Kuczynski (not yet in the UK when the first list was drawn up), seen as the leading cadre of the group. The absence of a date, the different composition of the list, and the absence of Siegi's name lead to the supposition that this list comes from later, probably 1937 or 1938. *Exil* also states that there were only a dozen German Communists by 1938, and most of those from bourgeois, Jewish backgrounds. Only in 1939, did the size of the group grow, it states. Moreover, it states explicitly that the exile group took their leadership from the Central Committee of the KPD in Paris. They have Kuczynski, not Meyer, meeting there with Ulbricht, Dahlem, Gerhardt Eisler and Paul Merker, who had specific responsibility for the UK.

But there is a third separate list of members of the KPD exile group from 1937 by Leske. Siegi's name is again not on it. The only overlap between the original list and this one is Meyer and the only overlap between the *Exil* list, immediately above, and this list, are Meyer and Kuczynski. The source of Leske's list of party members is not referenced, so we can't know how reliable it is. Brought out in 1983 in Berlin, East Germany, it has to be read and understood within the limits of that context. Besides Jürgen Kuczynski and Meyer, the other members, according to Leske, are Luise Dornemann, Ruth Edwards, Heinz Kammitzer, Margaret Mynatt, Jan Petersen, Hans Siebert and Grete Vittkowski, Hermann Duncker,*[151] Johann Fladung,* and Jan Petersen (*labelled as 'outcasts'). Also listed are Alfred Meusel and his wife, though they are stated as not being Party members.

A letter from Ilse Meyer, dated 30 September 1993, confirms they (undefined) founded a KPD group in exile in 1934 with about twelve members.[152] Ilse Meyer is not included in this list but was included, even though only as a 'wife', in the KPD list.[153] The KPD exile group liaison with the UKCP was Margaret Mynatt (included in this list but not the KPD list), whose father was British and who therefore possessed British nationality.[154]

Siegfried Moos is not on either of the two later lists, whether because he had stood down by the time the lists were drawn up, or had been asked to leave his leadership post, presumably to make way for Jürgen, the more senior figure in the Party, in late 1936 or early 1937. But significantly Siegi is not even listed as a member. Had he left completely or has he been written out of history?

But the puzzle is greater than that. While we know that at least some of those on the original list left for the USA and that three were already labelled as 'outcasts', how does one explain that, when so few KPD members were arriving in the UK, the later list is almost completely different? Arguably, the difference between 1934 and 1937 could be explained by people dropping, or being thrown, out. But there is no easy explanation for the differences in the two lists which theoretically relate to the same period, except that, by 1937, membership had become a loose affair – or that one or both sources are inaccurate.

How is one to interpret that Siegi does not appear in Jürgen's autobiography, the *Exil* list, or Leske's study? One possibility is that the list and comments from the *Bundesarchiv* are inaccurate. But this seems exceedingly unlikely. It was, after all, a contemporary list, drawn up at the time, and crucially confirmed by MI5. More likely, Siegi was subsequently 'cut out' because he left the KPD, possibly doubly damned because – and this is only guesswork – he did not just fade away but gave voice to dissident and heretical views. We now know how comrades who left Communist Parties or indeed were seen 'merely' as oppositionists by the Stalinist apparatus, were airbrushed out of history.[155]

One has to question what Leske's sources were and their reliability and look at the motivation behind this historiography – both Meyer and Jürgen survived and returned to East Germany and both, in different forms, became its heroes. Siegi certainly did not. Even as late as the early 1980s when Leske's Ph.D. thesis was being written, the Stalinist bureaucracy, in this case in the form of the East Germany Institute for Marxism-Leninism, maintained its hold on what constituted legitimate memories of the past, even, I suggest, in so minor a matter as who led the KPD group in exile in London between 1934 and 1936/7!

Yet Leske's thesis does give some information, even if from a limited view, of the exile group's activities in the 1934–1936/7 period, though its concerns are clearly more with the later part of this period. (This may be because of the sources available to, or sought out by, her.)[156] It presents a view of a Party undivided theoretically and organizationally, which we know not to be the case. Indeed, the rapid turnover of people just revealed, indicates a level of disaffection, which, I suggest, is not just due to comrades 'dropping out'.

Leske (1983) acknowledges that there is an absence of material about KPD exile groups in the period between 1934 and 1945. She does however state that very few Communists were able to come to the UK in 1933, with a maximum membership in the group of 15 up till 1938, and then made up almost entirely of intellectuals and Jews. The London exile group was very loose, Leske emphasizes. Moreover, and this is borne out by other research, it was very difficult for KPD members to be open about their political affiliations in the UK, and even more their KPD membership, for fear of not being admitted in the first place, or of being excluded from the UK. This inevitably made any political work very difficult.

Apparently, one task for this group was to make contacts with UK journalists, though on an individual basis. Leske states that the first political activity was in spring 1934 but she does not elaborate on what this work was or who was responsible for it (though it seems reasonable to suggest it was Siegi, as this is the point he arrived in London and presumably became involved).

Leske also confirms that it was the Paris KPD leadership that had responsibility for exile groups. Here, she claims, Meyer met with Paul Merker, who had specific responsibility for British exiles.[157] According to Leske, from 1936, both Meyer and Jürgen Kuczynski met with Ulbricht, Dalem, Gerhardt Eisler and Paul Mercher from the KPD CC in Paris.

The purpose of the KPD exile group, Leske suggests, was to work with anti-fascist émigrés, although Leske does not provide a date for this. This was more difficult than it sounds because of the refugees' fear of being deported by the British State. (Indeed, arguably, British intelligence – who wished to build up internal opposition within Germany to destabilize it – could have made far fuller use of the KPD group with their contacts in Germany, rather than pushing them into the political shadowland.) Others worried because of the possibility of retribution against relatives left in Germany. Others dropped out of politics. She does make clear that, by 1936, the position of the exile group was for 'united front' work, as directed by the Paris Commission. But it seems as if here, as elsewhere, the exiled Social Democrats were not willing to collaborate. Leske, possibly accurately, sees the SPD and all the other left émigré organizations as essentially inactive. There was one exception: *Neue Beginnen*, though by then a splinter group of the SPD, was willing to work alongside the KPD comrades. Regular educational meetings were held under Hermann Dunker who was in the UK till 1937. The lessons of the 1935 Brussels Conference (for a united front) and the later Bern Conference of 1939 were presented.

From 1936, a 'near-party' was established for sympathizers, which also held educational meetings, led by Hans Kamnitzer, a young anti-fascist. This information helps makes sense of one of Lotte's statements in her interrogation in Holloway when she said, disparagingly, that she had nothing to do with the inner or outer groups. This level of detail on her part does however suggest that she, and therefore probably Siegi, were still in one way or another in touch with the KPD at this point. This inner/outer distinction suggests the exile group were maintaining, at least in a formal sense, the Leninist tradition; the outer meetings were the united front. [158] It may also help explain the differences in lists for around 1937. Some time between 1936 and 1937, Siegi leaves the exile group. My guess, elaborated on later, is that it was early 1937.

What happened in the exile group after Siegi left is not fundamental to this story but is worth mentioning briefly. Although again Leske does not provide dates, she states that the tasks of the exile group became to send propaganda into Germany and to propagandize in Britain. It is not possible to know when this shift from building within the émigré group to these much broader horizons took place, but most probably after Siegi's departure. At some point, though again this is not dated, the group wanted to publish their own newsletter to be sent to the press and government agencies, as well as the German émigré community. Meyer was to be responsible. (Given Siegi's lengthy experience with writing for and producing left journals in Germany, this choice by the leadership, assuming Leske is accurate on this point, certainly suggests that Siegi was either no longer trusted or no longer available.) Remarkably, Paul Robeson saves the impending financial crisis with a gift of £500 and a statement of solidarity (Robeson was a regular on our wind-up gramophone in my parents' house). So, *Germany Today* was born, to be renamed *Inside Germany* in 1939 (confirmed in Ilse Meyer's letter). The first editor was Ilse Meyer. The effect of the Nazi invasion of Czechoslovakia was to dramatically increase the size of the group to 400 people (from around 15!), which alone made for a need for a new strategy.

A different view on the exile group is however presented by Merson (1986). Though he does not refer specifically to the

London group, unlike Leske, he does give a sense of the debates going on generally in émigré circles around 1934. He argues that the Third Period line was fizzling out after a decision by the KPD Central Committee in July 1934, though a majority of the Politburo still supported an ultra-leftist position. Pieck and Ulbricht were the only ones to support the Popular Front line. In August and September 1934, Pieck and Ulbricht actually published articles arguing for the importance of approaching the SPD groups with a view to common action around broadly based demands. The positive response of some of the left- wing members of the SPD EC, who nevertheless insisted there should be no set conditions, caused a major divergence of opinion amongst the KPD, which Merson (1986) argues threatened to split the party. The commission of the EC of the Comintern intervened on 27 October, coming down heavily for Ulbricht and Pieck. Apparently, these serious disagreements almost featured in the émigré press, though Merson does not elaborate on what that means (Merson, 1986).It is only in October 1935, at the KPD's Brussels Conference, that there is a clear call for united action between the workers' parties (Palmier, 2006). Rather later on, in 1936, Merson (1986) tells us of the People's Front movement among German exiles centred on Paris, which Palmier bears out – one can infer that this position probably also surfaced in London, even though issues around the Popular Front were not so pressing here as in France or Spain. We shall not go into the details of these debates because there is no lead as to Siegi's position, or indeed what was discussed in the UK, though we can be sure that Siegi would have been involved.

Again, Lotte's testimony to her interrogators in Holloway prison affords us a brief glimpse of the nature of this group of KPD exiles and one of the reasons for Siegi's departure. As already explained, Lotte's testimony, has to be understood within the context in which it was given – an MI5 interrogation. Her description of the group was that it was loose, made up as much by ex-KPD members as members – ex-members because they had not gained permission from the Party before leaving Germany, some of whom were consequently expelled. (This bears out that Siegi had had permission to leave.) Lotte told her interrogators that the purpose of the group was to bring down fascism, not to bring down democracy. Interrogated during the period of the Hitler-Stalin pact, Lotte was making clear that she at least believed in democracy. She also stated that the group was fairly inconsequential – but she is being interviewed in 1940, so one needs to read this comment in that light. The example she gives of discussion in the group was their objecting to the USSR sending tractors to Germany, something most stalwart Stalinists as well as non-Stalinists could agree to disagree with, as she would well have known! She assures her interrogators, though we cannot know the truth of this, that this group were not part of her or Siegi's network of friends.

Lotte's testimony suggests Siegi left in 1937. She left, she explains, because of Brian (see subsequent section) and also because of events in Barcelona (the shooting of the POUM, the Partido Obrero de Unificación Marxista, by Stalinist forces). Though she does not explicitly state why, she writes that Siegi also left then, leaving open the interpretation that these were two of the core reasons for him also.

So it seems unlikely that Jürgen Kuczynski's taking over the group in late 1936 was in itself the reason for Siegi's leaving the group, though it probably did not help. Lotte only returned from the USSR with her tales of what was really happening there in September 1936 and it would have taken Siegi a few months to consider the implications of what she was telling him. Brian 'disappears' only in 1937. My guestimate is that Siegi left the KPD and the exile group in early 1937, before the other two lists were drawn up. In August 1937, Siegi writes to Lotte, who is in France looking for a trace of Brian, a heart-breaking letter, stating that he can now only live for her, as his past beliefs have been destroyed. Clearly by then, Siegi had left.

My parents brought me up in an atmosphere of never-ending suspicion. This can be better understood given how afraid they were of being betrayed. A feature of life amongst these small émigré groups of Communists and other 'lefties' was the fear of informers. Thanks to the researches by Brinson (1998) and Dove (2011), frequently based on now open MI5 files, we have new evidence about this. One example of an MI5 agent in the early/mid-1930s is Claud W. Sykes. As files recently released by the Security Service confirm, Sykes was charged with penetrating German refugee circles in London (Dove, 2011). MI5's operations centred on the surveillance of 'communists and suspected communists', a task which assumed great importance for MI5 after January 1933 (Dove, 2011). Indeed, members of the German exile group, such as Otten, were themselves turned into 'watchers' by and for the Security Service though remaining one of the 'watched' (Dove, 2011). Another sort of informer was Wesemann, a former Social Democrat and editor of *Vorwarts*, and himself a refugee, who informed on the German exiles, non-Communist and Communist, Jewish and non-Jewish to the Gestapo[159] (Brinson, 1998). Fear of informants can only have acerbated Siegi's (and Lotte's) fear of being politically involved, and any incipient fear of other 'comrades'. Siegi had learnt in Berlin never to trust his comrades, a tendency which his experiences here can only have reinforced.

Siegi's leaving of the exile group and the KPD represented a fundamental turning point in his life. His time in this grouplet was already not a happy one. Given much of the left's tendency to pacifism and the right's to appeasement, one can guess how difficult it must have been for many of these highly politicized refugees from Nazi Germany, like Siegi, to be able only to watch as events in the UK unfolded. Indeed, I imagine my father's frustration and despair at discovering that the nearest thing to his previous politically engaged life was to be had in this small, fractious and ultimately ineffective exile group. But leaving the group marked a break with what his life had until then been about. The political nature of the USSR, the show trials, Brian's disappearance and the role of the 'Communist' forces in Spain will all have contributed to his departure.

It is intriguing to look for signs of dissidence in his pre-UK 'career' to assess whether he had earlier misgivings about the KPD. Certainly, he seems to have been a trusted Party comrade during his Berlin days, when many members, as we already know, either drifted away, left because of political differences, or were pushed out. Yet, as suggested earlier, while they should not be overstated, differences in emphasis between his position and that of the Party do appear in Siegi's 1929–1933 days: in his earlier writings on agitprop, where he appears to distance himself slightly from the sectarianism of the Third Period, or in his deep involvement in the Red Front. They represented the first glimmerings of a dissidence which, given the totality of circumstances, ended up with this final rift with the KPD.

It would, I suggest, have been more surprising if he had stayed in. In the tiny faction-ridden exile group, he would have had a forced knowledge of the impact of Stalinist bureaucracy as it increasingly turned on its old comrades ('ate its own children'). Siegi had after all collected the papers from the left and right opposition while still in Berlin, not a sign he did not support the Centre, but that he was interested in the debates and had a critical awareness of the issues.[160] He, more than many, will have followed what was happening in the USSR in 1936 and 1937 and the persecution (and sometimes state murder) of dissidents and loyal Bolsheviks. In addition, if he shared Lotte's support for POUM, he would have been critical of the Communists for failing the Spanish Republicans as well as turning on the POUM.[161] Nevertheless, to break with the Communist movement after he had dedicated the past ten years to its cause must have turned his world upside down, especially when he did so alone.

The effect on Siegi of leaving would have been personally as well as politically profound. For Siegi to leave this group, however fractious it might have been, must have been to tear his last link with the struggle and with his comrades, who, however much he disagreed politically with some of them, would have shared some emotional understanding of the highs and lows of resistance to the Nazis and of being a political refugee. It must have torn him to bits. I do not think he ever recovered from this loss of his past self, though he, far more than my mother, held on to an eternally optimistic view of the world.

An unlikely corroboration comes from Jürgen Kuczynski's memoirs (1981), quoted in Merson (1986). Although Jürgen is referring to the illegal struggle rather than the secret but not life-threatening world of the London exiles, he writes of how the effect of such work is to make the comrades closer to each other, even though not always better people. Jürgen comments, as if he were describing Siegi when I knew him as my father, that such comrades become more distrustful in daily life but more confident about the world at large, with unlimited expectations for the world's future.

It was not just leaving the KPD that would have left Siegi increasingly adrift. By 1937, the Nazi regime, far from collapsing, had instead adopted increasingly systematic and brutal measures against the left and oppositionists. Siegi and Lotte would have followed events in the Spanish Civil War, closely aware of their political significance and of Brian's involvement. Siegi would have watched as the fascists pushed back the Republicans. By late 1936, the French Popular Front government under Blum had ceased providing the Spanish Republicans with arms. In early 1938, the nationalists bombed Barcelona; the earlier bombing of Guernica in April 1937 was immortalized by Picasso. By mid-1937, Bilbao had fallen. The USSR held tightly onto its purse strings and arms and turned its fire power against POUM. As if this was not all bad enough, in the UK, people on the left, whom Siegi might have looked to, were uncritical of the USSR's role in Spain. Kingsley Martin, editor of the *New Statesman*, supported the Comintern's tactics; Laski, a leading left theoretician, condemned those who criticized the USSR's tactics in Spain as being no better than the fascists. Orwell, outraged by such a slur on the POUM, wrote a rebuff in *Homage to Catalonia*, only to find his CP-leaning publisher, Gollancz, refusing the book. Siegi would have known Spain was a dress rehearsal and feared for the future.

What would also have increased Siegi and Lotte's sense of insecurity was the fear of Nazi agents working in the UK (and elsewhere). Although it was never proved, the deaths of Dora Fabian, a political activist and former member of the German Socialist Workers' Group, and Mathilde Wurm, an ex-SPD member of the Reichstag, were understood by most on the left as murder. Many leading left figures – some of whom have already crossed these pages and were known by Siegi, such as Ernst Toller, whom Fabian had worked for and knew well, Fenner Brockway and James Maxton – were involved in a campaign to establish the real cause of death. What they suspected and feared was that a German agent had murdered the women, especially as Fabian was actively involved in campaigning for SAP prisoners in Germany. They had grounds for their fears: there had already been evidence of Nazi activity, including abductions and murder, outside Germany; of particular relevance here is the case of Hans Wesemann who had been passing himself off as a socialist exile here but who had been unmasked as a Gestapo agent and who was suspected of having a hand in the women's deaths. However, the British state, though seriously concerned about Nazi agents in the UK, took the Communist threat more seriously. Siegi and Lotte would have known of the women's deaths/murders; indeed, Siegi probably knew Dora Fabian, and it would have made them even more anxious about participating in activity which could draw them to the attention of the Nazis, never mind the British state. (Anybody interested in this terrible but fascinating story should refer to Brinson and Dove (2014) on whose book most of this paragraph is based.)

Siegi must have felt alone and dispirited. He was living in a foreign land which threatened him with deportation if he was caught doing political work. He had no family here and would have become increasingly concerned about what might befall Hermann and Lotte's family far away in Germany. His Party had betrayed his ideals and, even if he did not think of it as counter-revolutionary, he no longer wanted anything to do with it or his erstwhile comrades. He had nobody here he felt he could trust or turn to. He had to think and speak in a second language. And his relationship with Lotte, deeply strained as a result of his emotionally exhausting flight from Germany, had not recovered, and never might.

1934–1938 Siegi's status as a refugee

Thanks to the MI5 files, partly confirmed by Siegi's correspondence, there is a limited record of Siegi's other activities during this period.MI5 kept records on all refugees entering the UK, through initial registration at the port of entry, as appears the case with Siegi, when they registered at Bow Street, by observing them in demonstrations (Edith Tudor-Hart, who will feature again, was picked up this way) or through the reports of MI5 agents (Brinson and Dove, 2014). Both Siegi and Lotte had reason to be anxious about being watched and the possibility of expulsion if they broke the known and less known rules.[162]

The Home Office was indeed playing a game of 'cat and mouse' with him (just as with Reimann). Siegi, who was not sponsored through the Jewish community but by the ILP MP, Maxton, had to apply for the right to remain in the UK every three months. According to his MI5 records, which we shall assume here are reliable, Siegi, who arrived here in the February, applied for permission to stay till 19 May 1935, then was granted permission to stay till 15 September; then he reapplied, for permission to stay till 31 December (only granted on 26 September 1935), and then he reapplied again. Each re-application had to be cleared by both the Home Office and MI5 on each occasion. That alone would make for a sense of insecurity (and we can also assume that he knew what had happened to people who had returned to Germany). Moreover, these extensions were far from automatic. Siegi and Lotte's letters to each other – for they were living apart regularly during this period – are full of angst.

Siegi became a part-time student of economics at the LSE between April 1934 and April 1935.[163] He worked his way from doing research work there for Gayer to being appointed as a Research Assistant, where he worked on trade cycles. In 1936, he got a job with the *New York Times*, a job he lost because of the refusal of the Ministry of Labour to renew his work permit (letter from L. Wohlfell, *NY Times*, 20 October 1936, in personal possession).

Siegi's job at the *New York Times* had to be revoked because of the problems he was having with work and residence permits. There is an open reference from the *NY Times* (20 October 1936), which states: 'The only reason we are dispensing with Mr Moos' services is because the British Labour Ministry has declined to issue a permit for his further employment with us... [as] he is a German national. We have found Mr Moos to be intelligent, loyal, honest and industrious.' Even his work as a Research Assistant at the LSE had to be cleared on a monthly basis by the Home Office (I have the letter relating to the period between 18 July and 18 August 1937).

Siegi writes to Albert Einstein on 21 October 1936, in the hope Einstein could help get him into the US. He writes: 'My uncle, Rudolph, recommended I address a request directly to you…Your wife, Mrs Einstein, knew my family and my father well.' Siegi then explains the circumstances of his leaving Germany and the failure of the British 'Ministry of Works' to extend his work permit so he could not continue with the *New York Times*. He continues: 'I have once more been forced to look around for another country and another life...I would be very grateful if you could invite me for a visit...I am in a hopeless situation.' Despite a double relationship to Siegi, through his wife and as a distant blood relative, Einstein does not appear to have replied. Siegi was not a person to beg and this last shot of a letter suggests a level of real desperation.

Siegi is clearly concerned. There is other fragmentary but convincing evidence of a variety of references/testimonials from the great and the good, including from his friend Ronald Wood in 1936, the American economist Gayer in 1937, and Bowen, the Director of the Oxford Institute of Statistics, in 1939 (all in personal possession), supporting Siegi's attempts to get into the US. Lord Hirst, a not-so-distant relative, who had earlier come out of Germany and had co-founded the General Electric Compagny (GEC), according to a 1937 letter from Hermann, recommended Siegi for a job at the New York branch of GEC.

Siegi's insecurity is reflected in a series of his letters to Lord Hirst, requesting his support for his applications to the Home Office. Hermann was closely related to Hirst: they came from the same (secular Jewish and highly bourgeois) family in Bavaria. Something could not have gone quite right. Hermann's letter of January 1934 to 'my darlings' (Lotte and Siegi) reads: 'Your reception at Hirst's showed me quite clearly how English this great gentleman has become, so different from when he was a truly Bavarian (sic) and family orientated youth.' Siegi however must have persisted. It seems he was very excited about the *New York Times* job, seeing it as a way into the USA and its relative safety. But as Siegi wrote to Hirst (dated 11 October 1936 and the last letter written in German), the Ministry of Labour 'in its correct policy of filling free posts with English staff...has refused me a work permit....There is the possibility of being allowed the work permit if an influential personality intervenes for me.' Otherwise, Siegi states, he will be penniless. We do not have the reply but as we already know, Siegi did not get his permit and lost the job – and, as it turned out, his chance to go to the USA.

In Siegi's next letter (22 October 1936) to Lord Hirst, he writes, in English: 'I have been asked by the Home Office to continue my studies if I want to stay in this country. I will now leave for the USA as soon as possible provided I get the visa which to obtain is extremely difficult for Germans.' Then we have Siegi's reply to Lord Hirst's reply, thanking him for agreeing to let his name be mentioned in his application to the Home Office. His permission to stay (though not to work) was granted. Christmas greetings were still being exchanged into the early 1940s between the comrade and the Lord!

The precariousness of Siegi's finances is highlighted by a further comment to Hirst in his letter of 11October 1936: his situation had been made critical because his uncle, Hermann, was now forbidden by German law to send him money. Hermann's financial support till then had clearly been crucial.

In May 1937, Siegi's German passport 'expired'. I now have a chilling set of SS, police and German Home Office papers, thanks to the help of Dr Weber, which show that in February 1937, Siegi went to the German Embassy in London to renew his passport. It seems unlikely he believed his passport would be renewed, but the Nazis' policy of removing citizenship from their undesirables was still new and Siegi must have thought it was worth the risk. However, the reality, according to these Nazi documents, is that Siegi (along with many other refugees, including Lotte) had their German citizenship revoked at the end of October 1937, following a lengthy bureaucratic process. The German State police provide an explanation: Siegi was a convinced and active member of the KPD and the Red Front. Moreover, when the police searched Siegi and Lotte's flat in Berlin, they found a considerable library of KPD literature (thus ended my fantasies about latterly finding this collection of opposition and Party literature under the floorboards). Although Siegi did not have a police record for criminal-political activities and there was no case for treason, nevertheless, because 'of his conduct... the Jew had lost his right to German citizenship.'[164] (Lotte also lost her citizenship, it was stated, simply because of her marriage to Siegi; there was nothing untoward in her conduct, according to the same records.) It is also of note that not all German Communist refugees lost their passports – this distinction may have been based on whom the German State saw as the activists on the ground and the more dangerous (rather than based on their prestige within the KPD or elsewhere), or it could instead be a consequence of German bureaucracy's irrationality.

MI5 note that Siegi no longer has a passport at the end of 1937, though they do not record any details. While it is impossible to know how important this was in Siegi's decisions, it would have made it almost impossible for him to travel abroad. This alone would have affected his decision not to go to Spain; it also limited his ability to travel to the US, as he, and Lotte, at points hoped.

What is also of interest is what does not appear in these (undoubtedly limited) MI5 records. Anti-fascist organizations continued to hold meetings and mobilize in London and elsewhere in the UK. By late 1936, there was an anti-fascist organization made up largely of liberals and radicals: the British anti-Nazi Boycott Group and the British anti-Nazi Council. In 1937, there was an attempt at a unity campaign, to include the ILP, the CP and the Socialist League (Pennybacker, 2009). But by 1937, I suspect, Siegi and Lotte were taking 'a rest' from politics.

Fortunately, in 1938, unlike so many of the refugees, Siegi finally got a 'proper' job, attached to Oxford University. Finally, in July 1939, both Siegi and Lotte received British certificates of identity to travel and were given the right to stay in the UK. The period of intense insecurity over the right to stay in the UK – and stay alive – was over.

Lotte, Brian, the USSR and Siegi

Lotte is evidently intertwined with Siegi's life, though this is not the place to go into the details of Lotte's trajectory during the period 1934–1939.[165] Lotte had been active on the revolutionary left in Germany. But she had met Siegi through an agitprop group, not through direct political activity and there is nothing to suggest she was concealing the truth when she told me that she had not been a member of the KPD in Germany. Whenever I asked, she always denied with great force that she had ever belonged to the Communist Party. Yet if we trust what she put in her CV when interned on the Isle of Man, from the transcript found in her MI5 files, it appears that she had been in the KPD from 1934 to 1936. But is this reliable? A question is raised by her absence from every list of members of the German KPD exiles in London. Not only is she not listed by name, she is not even referred to as Siegi's wife, as some other 'wives' were. Maybe, as she protests in her letters to Siegi, as she does not know whether she is being accused of spying for Germany or the USSR when she is in Holloway prison, connecting herself to the Communist Party seemed like a good idea at the time. (Lotte never had any difficulty concealing the truth, political or personal, if necessary.) Maybe she associated herself with the exile KPD group because of Siegi, without actually being a recognized member. Lotte certainly knew about the internal debates within the Communist movement in Germany, presenting a Brandlerite position about the USSR, which showed a detailed level of knowledge of the debates about the USSR's bureaucratic and class character.

But what is certainly the case is that Lotte maintained her identification with the left here, though less active than Siegi. She told me that she attended the Mosley rally in Olympia in 1934. She wished to give support to those disrupting it. She remembered how the ILP 'boys' had been chased by Mosley's thugs, some into the 'rafters' of Olympia. (Dozens were badly injured. The rally had the unintended consequence of showing up the British League of Fascists as thugs.) That took courage and political commitment – and a good dose of foolhardiness: she would have been deported if arrested. There is again an ILP link here. This fascist rally was not open to the 'public' but the ILP managed to obtain some tickets. So Lotte got her ticket from the ILP. We already know she had other ILP links.

When Siegi finally got to London, he initially moved in with Lotte. Later, he was to plead to the Home Office in Lotte's defence, that he was in no state to maintain any sort of relationship.

Lotte had become a part-time teacher of German at the Linguists Club in London in 1934. There she met Brian Goold Verschoyles. Maybe she fell for an attractive, lonely, young Irish Communist when she herself was suffering from a sense of displacement and isolation. It is not clear what the exact character of Brian and Lotte's relationship was, but Lotte was clearly willing to risk leaving the UK to travel across Europe without an extant passport to be with Brian in 1936. This was against strict Party instructions to Brian that she should not do so. Brian was being groomed to be some sort of low-level spy, probably not much more than a paper carrier, but significant for all that. Having a foreign woman unaccountably turning up drew an unwanted attention to Brian and almost from the time Lotte got there (itself an amazing and difficult feat), she and Brian got into serious trouble with their GPU (the Secret Police) handlers. Even people they thought they could trust turned out to be informers. Lotte and Brian behaved with irresponsible, naïve abandon, openly criticizing the Soviet system. This was 1936 and the show trials were just round the corner.

Based on Barry McCloughlin's evidence, I strongly suspect a deal was done. Brian allowed the GPU to send him to wherever they chose, in return for letting Lotte out of the USSR. One of the many intriguing aspects of this saga is that, throughout this time, Siegi was writing to Lotte, sending her money, at her request, and agitating for her release. Lotte was finally allowed to leave. 'More of an escape,' was how she put it to me, in those last months of her life when the existence of Brian had become official.[166]

Brian was sent to Spain, around Barcelona, by the Comintern, where he worked as a radio engineer, his official trade. (My guess is that both Brian's USSR minders and Brian himself would probably have had Spain in mind, where the USSR were in need of skilled staff in the burgeoning Civil War and Brian maybe believed he could disappear over the Pyrenees, if needs must.)

Safely back in London, Lotte continued to communicate with Brian, foolishly sending 'coded' messages, critical of the USSR, despite strict instructions to both of them that her departure was conditional on there being no further contact. This is corroborated in the NKVD (police force associated with secret police) transcript of Brian's lengthy interrogation and other of their notes (quoted in McCloughlin, 2007: 144, also other NKVD notes in private possession, thanks to McCloughlin).

That Lotte had sent Brian at least one card (in personal possession) and articles defending POUM would have, wrongly, fuelled the Russians' suspicions of Brian's 'true' political allegiances. In the hysterical political climate of 1936–1937, where Trotskyists were hiding under every bed, Lotte and Siegi were seen as 'active Trotskyists' (NKVD notes on Brian, quoted in McCloughlin, 2007).

In 1937, Brian was tricked onto a Soviet ship off Barcelona and taken back to a 'trial', in the USSR. Brian, when interrogated, was asked persistently about his relationship with Lotte and her circle of friends. He denied he knew any of her friends and assured them the only person who knew he and Lotte were cohabiting was Siegi. There is no way of avoiding the conclusion that Lotte's association with Brian helped send him to his death.

For the next 50-odd years, Brian and his fate disappear from view. But Brian continued to play in Lotte's memory till her death. When I cleared Siegi and Lotte's utterly chaotic home, there, under the sofa where Lotte lay all day (and often all night) was a small cardboard box containing carefully preserved, well organized mementos relating to Brian.

It is impossible to know how Siegi felt about his wife's disloyalty. We have a clue in the letter he sent her where he said she was all he had left to live for, a cry in which there is both personal and political despair. Did Lotte present her trip to Moscow as a political act, a desire to see how far the USSR was a 'socialist utopia'; or that she and Siegi might both need to flee again and the USSR would be one possibility? But I have my doubts – there was enough already known about the role of the Comintern and the nature of the USSR.

After all, Lotte had stopped living with Siegi fairly soon after he arrived in London. The relationship between Siegi and Lotte had already become rocky, prior to Brian's 'entry'. By August 1934, only a few months after getting to London, Siegi was living by himself in a property in Christ Church Road, London NW3, which belonged to a Mr Meyer (from the MI5 files; it is possible that this is the same Hermann Meyer from the KPD exile group, but it has not proved possible to establish this). When Lotte goes to meet Brian in the USSR, Siegi moves into her room in 9, Lawn Road, Hampstead, though still using Mr Meyer's phone.

Their relationship was not going well. In an amazing statement of support to the Home Office in 1940, to help argue Lotte's case and get Lotte out of prison, Siegi explained Lotte's behaviour by saying that he was in no emotional state to maintain a relationship. Such a terrible confession is unlikely, unless true. The previous few years have cost him dear psychologically. How does it feel to know that one could be caught, tortured or killed over a six months' period of an underground existence? When every little decision – whether to turn left or right at a fork in the path – can bring you up against the Gestapo? How does it feel to be hungry and fear hunger day after day? How does it feel to stop being able to trust anybody? Did Siegi also start to doubt that Lotte would wait for him? When Lotte went to London leaving him in Paris, did he doubt her commitment to him?

Siegi was emotionally drained out by the time he and Lotte met up again in London. He did not have enough emotional elasticity or resilience for his relationship with Lotte, who was not always especially sensitive to others' needs and was not enjoying living in a misty, alien country without family or friends. Lotte, the person whom he had, at least in part, left Germany (and then Paris) for, had now left him. The being he had loved and who had, in her own way, provided him with the rock of his existence, had deserted him.

I once asked my father, in a rare moment of intimacy, whether he had ever considered suicide. I did not know at the time that his brother, Aldolpho, had killed himself. My father's eyes took on a look as if he were seeing far-away sights invisible to anybody else and he said, 'Of course.' He added, 'Doesn't everybody?' I knew even then that he said that to reassure me. Can I second-guess how my father felt when Lotte left him to go to Brian in Moscow? He felt that he didn't want to live any more. He felt that his life had been in vain; that he had been defeated politically and now, he had been defeated personally. He had nobody to turn to, nobody who could comfort him. What was the point of being alive?

Lotte returned from Moscow with fearsome stories of shortages and, worse, of repression and fear. Soon afterwards, Brian's disappearance troubled her considerably. Siegi had already been encouraging and assisting Brian's mother, who also lived in Oxford, to put pressure on the Foreign Office to find Brian, though, correctly, Siegi had no expectation of success (personal conversation with Brian's nephew). Lotte, once back, also gave Brian's mother support, but my impression from personal interviews with Brian's nephew, is that it was Siegi, rather more than Lotte, who was principally involved in supporting Brian's mother. While this shows Siegi as behaving with extraordinary honour and comradeship, what he felt about the 'triangle' is another matter.

Even on her return, Lotte lived separately and headed off on a couple of occasions to France, sending cards back to Siegi from the area of the Pyrenees; she was almost certainly trying to find a trace of Brian among those fleeing Franco into France. By 1937, Siegi had moved to Nassington Road, and, as there is no alternative address for Lotte, one assumes they were, in some sense anyway, living together again after many years of separation. Indeed, they had not spent any sustained time together since the beginning of 1933.

Lotte was soon to head off to the US. In 1939, when in New York, Lotte tried to trace Brian by going to see Krivitsky, an exile Russian (a GPU defector with intimate contacts with MI5, unknown to her) who had had an article published showing knowledge of Brian's fate. She was desperate to find out what had happened to him. The official USSR line, which came down to her via the Foreign Office at some later point, was that Brian had been killed in a train transporting prisoners when it was hit by German bombs. In fact, McCloughlin recently established that Brian was in effect murdered in a far-flung Soviet prison in the Gulag.

Although the fate of Brian was not known, Siegi would have listened to his wife's stories of what had happened to her and the events taking place in the USSR. These would not just have been tales of bread queues and of her and Brian being spied on. The show trials had already started in August 1936 and somebody as acute as Lotte, who spoke and read Russian, would have sensed which way the wind was blowing. Individual victimization, apart from the treatment of Trotsky, had already taken place. In 1932,

Zinoviev and Kamenev, two of the triumvirate which took over after Lenin's death, were, falsely, claimed to be plotting to overthrow Stalin. Kirov, another old Bolshevik, had been assassinated in 1934. Zinoviev and Kamenev were then tried in 1935 for their involvement in Kirov's murder and in 1936, the case against them widening all the time, were sentenced to prison. Both agreed to confess on condition that they received a guarantee that their and their families' lives would be spared. The defendants were then sentenced to death and subsequently shot. The trial was taking place at the very time Lotte was in Moscow in August 1936. Moreover, Siegi, always an avid reader of all forms of revolutionary press, would probably have known about the 'Trotskyite' criticisms of the USSR that had already emerged, and have read about the trials. Lotte would have confirmed this 'news' for him. Siegi, probably more than Lotte, would also have understood Brian's likely fate within that context. It would have confirmed him in his resolve to leave the KPD.

It is not easy to understand the relationship between Siegi and Lotte at this time. They end up together and, from 1938 onwards, they were never again parted. Letters give us a glimpse into their lives. We owe it to Siegi that we have copies of Lotte's letters to him during the many periods when they were separated during the 1930s and early 1940s, including when she was travelling to the USSR. My father preserved the letters. Unfortunately, Lotte did not save Siegi's letters. I knew nothing of these letters till I found them when clearing their home. What right did I have to read their private correspondence? I have not found an answer to this. I cannot lay claim to bringing historical truths to light. In the end, curiosity overcame my qualms, but I find, having read the letters once, that I do not want to do so again.

Their letters, which at the beginning are written in German, are full of the minute details of living, inevitable when both of their circumstances are changing so very fast.[167]They both at points express, or refer to, deep love for each other, though Lotte, certainly around the time of her travels to the USSR, makes clear that she will always give support to, but, by implication, not necessarily love, Siegi. She professes eternal friendship, but she emphasizes that this is not the same as partnership. Lotte frequently asks for forgiveness. When she did not hear from Siegi, her letters express alarm and concern. But by 1937, she is again writing of her love for Siegi.

Siegi wrote a crucial letter to Lotte in August 1937, already referred to. Siegi writes (in English): 'I was glad to find your letter....Why do I love you? Because you are you and I have time and strength to discover you and because you are the only human being who makes life worth living...I very much doubt if I would live on without you as nothing is left of my belief from which I received my strength and my joy. And as my lost beliefs destroyed my energy, the only thing I have left is my relationship to you.' This is the most politically, and personally, explicit of all the letters. They were both too careful to write explicitly about politics. Lotte became all that Siegi had left to live for.

I cannot separate out my feelings as a daughter towards my parents. Although their move to London in 1966 seemed to finally bring them closer together, I do not feel that their prior relationship was easy. It was rather as if they were both stuck on a life-raft where they had to battle the elements together or they would drown. Brian, I was to realize, haunted my mother: it was his 'mementos' which lay hidden beneath the sofa where Lotte lay in the years after Siegi's death. My hunch is that Lotte's dalliance with Brian and his 'disappearance' ricocheted through Lotte and Siegi's relationship, doing unseen damage.

The period from 1933 to 1938 was one of continuous political and personal crisis for Siegi. Over a matter of five years, Siegi had risked his life in flight from the Nazis across the width of Germany, had risked being caught crossing from Saarland into France, had arrived in and left Paris, and, penniless, had finally reached London. Struggling to stay in the UK, forbidden from getting a job, rejected by, or rejecting, the KPD group in exile, never sure whether the police might come knocking to deport him back to Germany because of his forbidden political activities, his wife developing a relationship with another man, and without any source of income – Siegi must have felt adrift from all he had known and loved.

Endnotes

125. Hobsbawm (2002), describing his arrival in the UK in 1933, scathingly describes the strictness of British sexual mores, the overriding importance of its class rituals and traditions and how having the wrong sort of accent marked out the refugee as an outsider. Later, he describes how, nominated by the army for a cipher course, he was turned down because his mother was not British, which could cause divided loyalties. (Hobsbawm, born in 1917, was a vital thirteen years younger than Siegi, so was more eligible for conscription.)
126. Rudolph Olden, an anti-Nazi German writer and lawyer, arrived in England in November 1933 and campaigned and wrote, including in the *New Statesman* and *Manchester Guardian*, about the true nature of Hitler and Nazism (Brinson, Charmian and Malet, M. (1995) 'Rudolf Olden: Alerting the English', in *Between Two Languages: German Exiles in Great Britain 1933–1945*, 35–57). His non-alignment with the KPD/CP did not stop the British secret service finding him of great interest.
127. Otto Lehmann-Russbueldt, who arrived in October 1933, was a courageous and well-known peace activist (Furness, 1995) who had been arrested on 28 February 1933, the morning straight after the Reichstag fire (the night Siegi slipped into the underground), but, following a brief and vigorous international peace campaign, was released and

smuggled into Holland in March 1933. From there, he got to England where he campaigned steadfastly against political persecution in the Nazi regime and for the release of political prisoners; later he exposed Germany's secret re-armament.

128. Another writer and leading theatre critic, though one who had not been on the left in Germany, Alfred Kerr, was already in his 60s when he got out in February 1933 and finally arrived in England, where his prolific writings on the dangers of Nazism had some limited influence at an official level, including making contributions to the BBC (Vietor-Englānder, 1995).
129. Brinson and Dove: *A Matter of Intelligence: MI5 and the Surveillance of anti-Nazi Refugees*. MI5's history partly explains their obsession. MI5 had originally been established to tackle the threat of German espionage, but during the 1920s and subsequently, its concern had shifted to include tackling Communists, firstly in the UK, and then in relation to Soviet espionage here. Siegi (and Lotte) would have conformed to all their stereotypes.
130. In July 1938, the Evian Conference, organized by the US to deal with the issue of the Jewish immigration problem, reveals just how unwelcoming the British government were. The British delegate announced that Britain could not welcome more refugees, as Britain was already full, but he did suggest their going to the British colonies of East Africa which could take a small number of refugees.
131. An eastwards trajectory from Germany is illustrated by the case of Gerhard Hinze, an actor, and a member of the KPD from 1930, who, after being arrested in Germany in 1933 and released in 1934, went east to the USSR, as did a couple of thousands fleeing Germany. Hinze finally made it to the UK, after he was 'encouraged' to leave the USSR (based on a personal conversation with Hinze's son). Many of these

exiles, though the exact number is not known, seeking socialism in the USSR, did not survive.

132. In Margaret Dewar's autobiography, *The Quiet Revolutionary*, she talks of her friend, Vladimir one day 'disappearing' from Berlin in 1930. She discovered the Party had sent him to Paris. The idea of comrades accepting Party instructions as to where they should go is not as far-fetched as it might seem to us now.
133. The British-German Relief Committee for the Release of the Victims of Fascist Terror was established by a glittering group of people, drawn from a wide spectrum of the left, such as Havelock Ellis, Ethel Mannin, Harry Pollitt, Sylvia Pankhurst, Shapunurgi Saklatvala and Ellen Wilkinson. Its purpose was to raise opposition to fascism and to assist its victims. Isobel Brown acted as Secretary. Paul Robeson bestowed the proceeds of his performance in an O'Neil play. The ILP, for example, Maxton and Brockway, gave strong support (Pennybacker, 2009).
134. There is an intriguing overlap with Indian matters, as early committee statements bear the same names of the advocates of the Meerut defendants (Pennybacker, 2009).
135. Indeed, the Jewish establishment groups saw their role as to help to restrict the inflow of all refugees, Jewish and non-Jewish. Given crucial responsibility for vetting the refugees by the government, their recommendations were at points more restrictive than the government's.
136. Toller deserves more recognition in the UK. He had come to the UK after the Reichstag fire when he eluded the knock of the Gestapo because he was fortuitously in Switzerland. In fact, he had already visited here earlier when he had met with the ILP; in 1927, he had become involved in the setting up of the League against Colonial Oppression (with Münzenberg). Toller made the first of many reappearances between 1933 and 1938 in the UK, first testifying before the

Legal Commission of Enquiry into the Burning of the Reichstag (set up by Münzenberg) and subsequently campaigning against Nazism at a variety of writers' conferences, speeches which all received wide publicity, as well as speaking at the NCCL, WEA, various universities and the Anglo-Soviet Friendship League. But, unlike in his 1920s more Marxist self, Toller's denunciations focused on Nazism's attack on intellectual freedom and on innocent German writers, though this may be explained because he, too, had to avoid being seen as politically active (Dove and Lamb, 1995). He saw himself as a writer as having a moral responsibility to attack Nazism though, like Siegi's, his line was that literature should not offer 'neat resolutions or happy endings'. Again, like Siegi, he emphasized the importance of internationalism. (My father always had a soft spot for the UN.) In 1938, Toller anticipated Jewish pogroms, something Siegi got completely wrong. It seems highly likely that Siegi would have known him.

137. Just how difficult is illustrated by the failure of many of the SPD EC, a far more respectable bunch than the KPD, to gain admittance here, too often with deathly consequences (Jenny Taylor, talk on Social Democracy in *Exile*, IGRS 12 January 2012). Britain only accepted an estimated one in ten applications from Jews between 1933 and the outbreak of war (Pennybacker, 2009).

138. The ILP disaffiliated from the Labour Party in 1932, after having been one of the groups that set up the Labour Party initially. It is sometimes forgotten how much to the left of Labour the ILP was, Maxton in particular. Maxton had become leader of the ILP faction whilst still in the Labour Party on an anti-MacDonald, anti-gradualism, anti-class collaborationist platform, though there was also a strong pro-MacDonald, anti-disaffiliation minority in the ILP. Maxton was a key figure in pressing for disaffiliation from

the Labour Party after the dreadful 1929–1931 minority government and MacDonald's subsequent betrayal when he headed the National Government, composed largely of Tory MPs (Cohen, 2001). A sense of how left Maxton's politics were can be garnered from a meeting of the Second International in 1931, held in Vienna, when the 'social-democratic grouping', including Maxton the leader of the ILP delegation, urged the SPD to overthrow capitalism (Carr, 1982)! Maxton's sponsorship of Siegi was therefore not just the sponsorship of any left-leaning MP. However, Maxton was more wary of collaboration with the CP than the ILP as a whole, who were generally in favour of the organization collaborating with the CP around political prisoners and exiles, amongst other issues (Pennybacker, 2009). Maxton died in 1946, still a sitting MP. Unfortunately, a search of Maxton's accessible letters has not revealed any corroborating correspondence but this was one 'fact' about how he got into the UK that my father consistently insisted on.

139. I remember being astonished when I discovered that my parents' friend was the leader of the London County Council (LCC)!
140. My thanks for this point to Susan Pennybacker (in private correspondence).
141. Münzenberg at one point flirted politically with Strasser, the political leader of the SA, who claimed to represent the 'socialist' wing of Nazism and was purged by Hitler in 1934 (McMeekin, 2003), something I strongly suspect Siegi would have found very difficult to forgive. This further lessens the chance of the link being through Münzenberg to Maxton. Münzenberg was also one of the most strident and vocal Third Period anti-Social Democrat exponents, regularly calling the Social Democrats fascists (McMeekin, 2003), something else which would have kept him and Siegi

apart.

142. My thanks to Gidon Cohen for this idea (in private correspondence).
143. My mother once told me a story of regularly walking past a cake shop, and imagining choosing and eating one of the cakes. From memory, she was talking of her time in Paris but at least there she was earning.
144. Initially, Meyer appears as little more than a music critic, who may not have had much political gravitas, but he was almost certainly more important than that. He was born in 1905, one year younger than Siegi. The *Exil* analysis notes him as a bourgeois intellectual who joined the Party in 1930, in Berlin (like Siegi), where his close associates were Eisler, whom he had studied under, and Busch, both KPD musicians. He was active in various workers' music organizations (like Siegi) and a critic for *Rote Fahne*. He, like Siegi, had the role of putting his knowledge to use in the revolutionary struggle. He fled slightly later than Siegi came to London. Like Siegi, he was one of the very few political refugees who chose to come to London, arriving as early as July 1933, when he appears to have entered as a student of music (Brinson and Dove, 2014). MI5 were surprisingly uninterested in him. According to Brinson and Dove, he was not initially a member of the Party, though this is not what the different lists, referred to in the main text, reveal. He became a university and WEA lecturer on music. Unlike Siegi, he returned to East Berlin in 1948. In East Germany, Meyer became a famous and much feted musicologist and the darling of the East German/Soviet bureaucracy, close to the party apparatus, particularly Bush and Klempner. Although Eisler had also returned to East Germany, and wrote the East German national anthem, it appears there was later a serious falling out between the Eisler camp and Meyer. Meyer died a natural death in 1989 in East Germany.

Siegi must have known Meyer from Berlin onwards but my parents' failure to ever mention him, unlike Eisler, suggests deep political/ personal differences.

145. Such a source has to be interpreted in the light of Lotte trying to prove her innocence and MI5 trying to establish whether she was a spy for the USSR. Lotte claims she does not know what she is being accused of. For some time, I, too, wondered whether Lotte could have been a low-grade spy but the balance of evidence in McClouglin's *Left to the Wolves* (2007) persuaded me finally against this.
146. KV2/1012/24a.
147. MI5, despite keeping watch on Tudor-Hart, did not appreciate quite how important she was. They were far more concerned with Jürgen Kuczynski (see Brinson and Dove, 2014). Lawn Road's residents reveal a glowing array of leading Bauhaus exiles, as well as politicos. Gropius, the 'leader' of the Bauhaus movement, and Brener lived there in one of the few modernist buildings, and provided a social centre for the Bauhaus émigrés as well as modern British sculptors such as Henry Moore and Barbara Hepworth. None of them were in the exile group as none were Communists, so Siegi is unlikely to have known them, except as neighbours. Nonetheless, having German radicals as neighbours may have offered a limited comfort. Gropius, among others, left the UK after a couple of years for the more sympathetic culture of the USA.
148. One ironic parallel between Siegi and Lotte, and the Kuczynski clan was that many of them also moved to Oxford. Given that Siegi would have felt additionally vulnerable after leaving the KPD exiled group, the appearance of the Kuczynskis would, I guess, not have been welcome.
149. Jürgen served in the leadership group of the KPD until 1944, acting as political leader until 1939, and again from

June 1940 to July 1941, when he was replaced briefly by Heinz Schmidt, and then by his friend Siegbert Kahn (Matthew Stibb, 'Jürgen Kuczynski and the Search for a (Non-Existent) Western Spy Ring in the East German Communist Party in 1953', in *Contemporary European History*, 20, 1, Cambridge University Press, 2010). On the Kuczynski family as a whole, and in particular their roles in wartime London, see R. C. Williams, *Klaus Fuchs, Atom Spy* (Cambridge, MA: Harvard University Press, 1987); Anthony Glees, *The Secrets of the Service: British Intelligence and Communist Subversion, 1939–1951* (Jonathan Cape, London, 1987); also Anne McElvoy, *The Saddled Cow: East Germany's Life and Legacy* (Faber & Faber, London, 1992).

150. Much has been written by and about Jürgen, who returned to East Germany in 1945, in remarkable circumstances. (He was in the American Sector of the city, having returned courtesy of the US army.) He joined the SED and was appointed Professor at Humboldt University in 1946. He became a leading East German economist and published copiously on Marxist economics and theory. He served as the President of the Society for the Study of the Culture of the Soviet Union, 1947–1950, telling his members: 'He who hates and despises human progress as it is manifested in the Soviet Union is himself odious and contemptible,' though he was later purged because of Stalinist suspicions of those who had dallied in the west and, just as sinful, were Jews. (The leadership of the East German Communist Party were the people who had gone to, and subsequently returned from, Moscow, suspicious of those who had messed with the west!) Nevertheless, Jürgen prospered under Walter Ulbricht, and indeed became the adviser on external affairs to Honecker, Ulbricht's successor. He is still thought of highly by many 'ex' KPD members.

151. Hermann Duncker, originally in the SPD, joined the KPD

Zentrale at the very beginning; his role became the education of activists. Arrested in 1933, he managed to flee to Denmark in 1936, and finally got to the USA in 1941, presumably via the UK at some point from 1936. He returned to East Germany in 1947 and became an academic (Broué, 2005).

152. My thanks to Irene Fick for the loan of this letter.
153. One interesting statement in Ilse's letter is that Isabel Brown, a prestigious British CP member, had told Ilse that she had contacted Ellen Wilkinson, who had in her turn contacted Neville Chamberlain, who then, after the Munich agreement, had admitted 1,000 Communists, who had arrived here by plane from Czechoslovakia, to be greeted by Margaret Mynatt. But in the P.S. to her letter, Ilse makes clear that the number is disputed and might have been significantly less than this. I have not come across such a high figure elsewhere.
154. Margaret Mynatt's path to refugeedom was not dissimilar to Siegi's. She had lived in Berlin from 1929, where she had worked as a journalist, and joined the KPD and the circle around Brecht. She fled Berlin soon after the Reichstag fire and travelled via Prague and Paris to London, arriving, like Siegi, in 1934. It seems impossible she and Siegi did not know each other. Once in the UK, where she had rights of residence through her father, their paths diverged – Mynatt became and remained an activist, including, with her so useful British passport, ferrying money from the Comintern in the USSR to illegal Communist Parties in Europe (Brinson and Dove, 2014).
155. One need look no further than Trotsky's disappearance from the side of Lenin in the photos taken soon after the Russian Revolution. (See, for example, David King, 1997: *The Vanishing Commissar: the falsification of photographs and art*. UK: Canongate Books.)

156. The translation of Leske's work is thanks to Irene Fick.
157. Merker returned to East Germany and survived to become the main opposition to Ulbricht, who imprisoned him before he did anything, because he had been in the west and said something special had to be done for the Jews, and was therefore a Zionist imperialist agent.
158. Although it falls outside this paper, it is worth noting that Leske tells us that the KPD were able to maintain a 'German freedom broadcast', with the agreement of the Spanish government, from near Madrid, between January 1937 and March 1939, when Madrid fell to the fascists. Is it possible that the NKVD sent the Irish born, low-grade Russian spy, Brian Gould Verschoyle (who features in Lotte's story) as a radio engineer to Spain with this in mind?
159. The Gestapo had amassed the names of 60,000 Germans in exile, with a special responsibility for political oppositionists (J. and P. Barnes, 1993). I suspect my parents would have known about every suspicious death of left-wing German exiles – and there were a few in these early years – and trembled.
160. It is worth remembering that these arguments, which this is not the place to go into, are part of a much larger debate across the left at the time, and since, about the character of Communism in the USSR and when, or whether, it degenerated, or indeed was defeated. It took the suppression of East Berlin in 1953 and Hungarian uprisings in 1956 to open the cracks in the Stalinist monolith in 1956, almost twenty years after Siegi had walked away. Even in the 1950s and 60s, a regular – and, at the time, inexplicable – stream of publications used to arrive at our home in Durham relating to the USSR.
161. I did ask my parents why they had not gone to fight in the Spanish Civil War, and never received a clear answer. There are, I think, many reasons: they did not have the right to

return to the UK and so would have not left lightly. Siegi was already emotionally and physically exhausted. They supported neither the International Brigades nor, in Siegi's case, unambiguously the POUM. Nevertheless, my mother did, unusually, ask me on a couple of occasions: 'Do you think I should have gone?'

162. Karl Korsch had been Marxist and was forced to leave the UK in July 1935, when he was refused permission to extend his stay. However, the grounds for his exclusion were in part the suspicion that he had collaborated with Nazis (Brinson and Dove, 2014).
163. Lotte tried and failed to get into the LSE. Despite her Firsts in her first and second year studying economics at Humbolt University, Berlin, the LSE stated she would have to take the English matriculation before they would consider her. She then tried, but failed, to get an international scholarship for refugees to study there, and then gave up. She was understandably not willing to bow to the LSE's at best myopic nationalism. It was a turning point in her life, and not for the better.
164. A small irony: according to these Nazi (and indeed MI5) records, Moos left the Jewish religion on 5 March 1929. Did Siegi have 'Jew' on his birth certificate (although, as we have already seen, he was registered at secondary school as Protestant)? Whether he 'renounced' Judaism simply by failing to put 'Juden' into a census, or whether he actively renounced it at a synagogue, is not known.
165. Anyone interested should check MI5 files, Barry McCloughlin's *Left to the Wolves: Irish Victims of Stalinist Terror,* and David Perman's biography of Lotte: *Stranger in a Borrowed Land.*
166. *Left to the Wolves* by Barry McCloughlin (2007) includes both a substantial section on Brian and Lotte and a photo of Brian. I felt like a traitor when I confronted my mother, who

had never said a word to me of Brian, with his photo. I was crossing a deep emotional line – from respecting my parents' wish for silence to pursuing my wish for knowledge. Lotte's response was extraordinary, particularly as she was supposedly suffering from quite advanced dementia and her eyesight was poor. She held the book close up to her face, with Brian's photo on the frontispiece, and declared, 'I won't come well out of there.'

167. My thanks to Irene Fick for translating these.

Chapter 7

1938–1947 Life at Oxford: *'A whole world separates me from the line.'*

It is not possible to do more than surmise why Siegi's politics slowly shifted towards a more left social-democratic stance. Yet it is in this period, at the Institute of Statistics (IOS) at Oxford University, that we see the emergence of an 'academic' viewpoint which is more left-Keynesian, than 'conventional' Marxist. These years also were a time when the earlier personal upheavals in Siegi's life slowly calmed down.

It is remarkable how Siegi, a refugee and active member of the KPD, who only arrived in the UK in early 1934, had transformed himself into a reputable academic within four or five years. Here we will first examine Siegi's role at the Oxford Institute of Statistics (OIS), where he was appointed as a research assistant. In the early 1940s, he is doing work for the 'Free French'. Internment will form the next section. Siegi's (and Lotte's) involvement with *Die Zeitung* will then be evaluated. The final section of this chapter will look at other papers Siegi was writing at this time, where he attempted to develop an alternative basis to socialism and developed an economically-based critique of Nazism. The chapter begins with a brief overview of the situation of academic exiles in the UK in the mid 1930s, in particular at the OIS.

Siegi was one of over 100 German-speaking economists who fled Nazi Germany between 1933 and 1939 (Hagerman, 2006)[168] but he arrived too early to benefit from the measures which were rapidly introduced here. Many others were forced to leave after the Nazis had passed the 'Restoration of Civil Service Act' in April 1933, which encouraged the removal of 'undesirable people', including academic professors, who had civil service status. The Act also limited the number of Jewish students, to be followed by the 'Jewish' medical and legal professions. (My mother always told me she had been thrown out of Humbolt University, Berlin, because she was a woman, something I never doubted. In fact, it must have been under this Act.)

1,000 scholarships were created for exiled students at this time (Palmier, 2006), which my mother told me she applied for but failed to obtain, probably because she was already here. Universities and colleges took on 1,500 'exile' teachers (Palmier, 2006).

In addition, Beveridge, the Director of the London School of Economics, (and whom Siegi later worked for) set up the Professorial Council on 3 May 1933, which became the Academic Assistance Council and then the Society for the Protection of Science and Learning in 1936. The aim of the Professorial Council was to welcome these highly educated exiles and assist refugee scholars from Germany. It also established the Academic Assistance Fund. The Society mainly supported economists with an 'international reputation', often therefore middle aged. This did not include Siegi! Hagerman (2006) reminds us of what befell those scholars who did not get out of Germany, were caught in France and Holland, or never received permission to enter the UK: they died in the camps and prisons.

It is also worth reminding ourselves that anti-German feeling ran high even before the war, and increasingly so at points during the war. Prior to Kristallnacht, there had been only a limited number of people seeking refuge here. But by 1939, there was an exodus not only of Jews from Germany and Austria, but also of refugees from the Spanish Civil War; the invasion of Czechoslovakia and then Poland, and the increasing implementation of anti-Semitic laws in Italy caused tens of thousands to attempt to seek a life in the UK. Refugees fortunate enough to get admitted into the UK were increasingly seen as a destabilizing influence. Sympathy towards any group of refugees was uncommon, and rarely articulated in Parliament. Once war had started, German émigrés were explicitly condemned on occasions in the media as a German fifth column. Outside the remit of this paper, is also evidence for increasing incidents of anti-Semitism. Even in Oxford University, G. R. Driver, pressing for greater assistance to refugees, commented: 'There are in many quarters a disinclination to put such people on our governing bodies or ...our Common Rooms...with foreigners of whom we know personally very little' (Weindling, 1996,[169]; Kushner, 1989). Siegi and Lotte would have wanted to stay in the shadows.

Siegi joined the significant refugee academic community at the Institute in 1938. Marschak (1898–1977) had founded the Oxford Institute of Statistics in 1935. Marschak had been born in Kiel, but at Berlin University had fallen under Marxist influence, and been dismissed by the Nazis following the April Act of 1933. At the Institute, he gathered round himself other left-leaning economists he had known at Kiel, whose concern was also the business cycle, such as Fritz Burchardt and Jacob Marschak.[170] The Institute rapidly developed an international reputation for 'theory-guided empirical research' (Hagerman, 2006), and, against the back drop of the 1930s' depression, a concern with the business cycle and unemployment. It became the power house for Keynesian and post-Keynesian growth theory.

The need of Whitehall for economists, combined with the call up itself, quickly emptied the Institute of its former staff. (Siegi had also volunteered but been turned down because of his age.) From the late 1930s, émigré economists dominated the research work at the Institute: Marschak, Burchardt, Mandelbaum, Schumacher, the Hungarian born Balogh and the Pole, Kalecki, 'the towering intellectual figure' at the Institute between 1940 and 1944 (Hagerman, 2006) and often considered an equal to Keynes, but whose work was strongly influenced by Marx. Their excellence, as Hagerman states, was exemplified by the famous report, *The Economics of Full Employment*, collectively produced by this group of exile economists (plus G. D. N. Worswick) and edited by Burchardt (1902–1958). The main aim of the study was to 'give an outline of the strategic factors on a policy of permanent full employment in industrial countries'. Burchardt, another exile, who had already made a reputation as an economist in Germany and was a friend of Siegi's, attempted to combine Marx with the 'statuary circular flow'. Burchardt was delegated by the Institute to support Beveridge, whose reports *Social Insurance and Allied Services*, 1942, and the better known *Full Employment in a Free Society*, 1944, a tide-turning text, were closely associated with Keynesian principles. Burchardt had become the effective co-ordinator at the Institute in the later war years and after the war became its director. The Institute must remain an, if not the, outstanding example of academics in a position of influence attempting to produce policies based on a theoretical coalescing of Marx with Keynes.

Siegi at the Institute of Statistics

By the time Siegi got his job at the Institute in February 1938, he had managed to put together a credible CV. He had even, if briefly, had a job at the *New York Times* in 1936, which, as already mentioned, he had to give up because of the refusal of the Ministry of Labour to renew his labour permit. Gayer also recommended him on the basis of work Siegi had done for him on trade cycles at the LSE (letter 13 September 1937, in personal possession). Siegi had managed to obtain statistical research work at the LSE where he was subsequently appointed as a full-time Research Assistant from 19 May 1937 (letter of appointment from LSE, 13 May 1937, in personal possession). Here he worked for Beveridge on unemployment statistics (letter from Champernowne, 28 April 1937, in personal possession). These were not insignificant figures and provide a clue as to how he landed the job at the Institute.

Although the documentation does not seem to be available, Siegi must have acquired a permit to work at the Institute (and before that at the LSE). Presumably, by then, he had enough friends among the British establishment's 'movers and shakers', for example, men like Beveridge and Ronald Wood, for the Ministry of Labour to acquiesce.

It is easy to see that the concerns of the Institute would chime with Siegi's interests. Siegi used to insist that one should never talk of 'economics', only of 'political economy'. In other words, he rejected the possibility of understanding economics outside of its political context, in his case wanting to use political economy as a way of bringing greater justice to the downtrodden and to further (some sense of) socialism. Even his original interest in economics, when he studied at Munich as a very young man, was almost certainly because he believed that by studying the rules of capitalism, one would be able to better transform it.

How exactly Siegi got his job, initially doing computing work and assisting in research, according to Marschak's 1939 reference, in this prestigious setting is unknown. It is clear from references from Marschak (1939) (obtained from the New York library), Gayer (1937), and others, that Siegi's work was highly respected and that he was liked. Nevertheless, he had no degree and had not yet succeeded in getting his work published. Although the Institute clearly recruited many political exiles (some also Jewish), the suspicion has to be that Siegi was well acquainted with one or other of the people with influence at the Institute, most possibly Marschak whom he might well have known at Berlin University. There is an intriguing reference in a letter from Andrews (26 June 1966, in personal possession), another Oxford economist at Nuffield and a friend: 'Marschak could not believe that so good a poet [Siegi] could not be useful as a research assistant.' Maybe it was his contact with Beveridge, also confirmed in Andrews' letter.

Siegi called many of these men his friends and their names

cropped up regularly in conversations at meal times. Indeed Mr and Mrs Worswick became my guardians. I grew up being taught about Kalecki's theories of trade cycles, while other children hear stories about Red Riding Hood. Balogh, an exiled Hungarian who had come earlier than most to the UK and was formally attached to Balliol College but worked closely with the Institute, invited Siegi to stay in their 'little house in the Lake District' (letter, 29 September 1948, in personal possession). (Maybe it was Balogh who subsequently got him his job as one of Harold Wilson's advisers. Certainly they were still in touch in 1965 (letter, 24 March 1965).)

Siegi's initial area of research at the Institute was national investment in Great Britain (letter from Bowen, 2 April 1939) but this extended into research into the economic problem of mobilizing resources for war purposes and the distribution of scarce resources. The OIS was deeply involved in conducting surveys of various commodities, as part of their wartime contribution, work that was principally carried out by Worswick and Moos (W. Young and F.S. Lee, 1993). Siegi also wrote on, and had articles published by, the Institute on International Commodity Control (1941) and cotton exports (1942).

From the beginning of 1943, as the tides of war slowly turned, the Institute started to concern itself with post-war issues. In February 1943, the OIS published a special supplement to the normal bulletin containing three papers analysing the Beveridge Report on Social Security. In June 1943, the Institute lent Schumacher, one of their leading theoreticians, to Beveridge to help him with the economics of full employment (Young and Lee, 1993). My father told me he had worked for Beveridge at the Institute, though he was probably one among other research workers doing so, and it is now not clear exactly what his role was. He also contributed to one of the best known publications of the Institute: *The Economics of Full Employment*. Also in 1943, Siegi had his research into building policy and the prices and costs of building materials published (an issue Siegi spotted early as fundamental for the post-war period, especially for the working class, given the devastation of so many homes during the war), and subsequently into the light metal and aluminium industries (letter from Burchardt, 28 June 1950).

By 1945, he had been invited to teach several of the economics subjects on the prestigious Politics, Philosophy and Economics (PPE) course at the University (letter from Dean Jones, 9 October 1945, in personal possession) and had already started teaching his beloved Adult Education classes. I can only guess at what he thought of the rows of (largely) ex-public school boys (and very few girls) arrayed before him in his PPE lectures. Siegi's instincts were anti-elitist and I can imagine his not entirely positive surprise at the necessity to wear the uniform of the Oxford don when teaching.[171]

Siegi's precise attitude to the war is not known. He did not write explicitly about it, but I suspect that he supported the Allies without reservation. I doubt whether he held the more 'Trotskyist' position that one fought to persuade other soldiers that the fight was for world revolution, and he certainly did not take a pacifist position – otherwise he would not have volunteered. No longer a part of the Communist movement, and, I have no doubt, appalled by the Hitler-Stalin pact of 1939, he would have had a clear view of the Nazis as the greater enemy, and British democracy, however flawed, as preferable. The only injury he (or Lotte) incurred during the war was when, having volunteered as a fire fighter, which he did two nights every week, one of the other volunteers smashed his forehead open, swinging the nozzle of a hose. Siegi bore the scar for the rest of his life.

Siegi wrote extensively in this period, both work-based articles and other pieces, apparently unpublished, which were on a far more political and philosophical level of analysis of the world's events, considered in the next section. (Some of the articles listed below were published a few years after his leaving Oxford but can be assumed to be extensions of his work there.) In the late 1930s, he finished but never had published, a lengthy, well-researched economic analysis of Nazism, considered in the next section (which wrongly predicted that the Nazis needed the Jews). English publishers rarely took the risk of publishing the work of émigré authors (Palmier, 2006). But I imagine Siegi would have felt its non-publication a great loss.

Siegi's academic pieces included: contributions to *Studies in War Economics*, 1947, an Institute publication, a number of articles in the *Economic Journal*, at least some of which, according to a letter from Robinson (18 December 1944), he submitted directly to Keynes, including articles on the aluminium industry in 1945, and 'Laissez Faire, Planning and Ethics', 1945. Other articles were published in the prestigious *Manchester School Journal*, including one on aluminium, 1948 and another on coal, 1951. Siegi also had very many well-received articles published in the Institute's *Oxford Bulletin*, which, though primarily on the questions of raw material supply and prices, the building industry, manpower, and trade and distribution – for example, 'The Food Stamp Plan' and 'Incentives to the Development of Mineral Resources' – also included, 'Is Adam Smith out of date?', 1951. Although he was not one of the key movers and shakers at the Institute, this hot-house of Keynesianism can be seen as influencing the direction and perspective of his articles. He probably did not see himself as having turned his back on Marxism but rather bringing Marx up to date with Keynes. He is not the only one to have attempted this – and not the only one to have failed!

Siegi's move into the relative respectability of left academia has to be understood within the context of Nazi Germany's march through Europe, the subsequent outbreak of the second world war, and his disillusionment and despair at developments in the USSR. This is not the same as disillusionment with Marxism, but defence of democracy and preparations for peace became his professional priority.

It is worth mentioning here his work for the Free French Government,[172] which – given that the correspondence in 1942 (with an A. Morhange, with an address in SW1) from 'France Libre' was always addressed to S. Moos at the Institute – was, one assumes, negotiated through the Institute (in personal papers). Why it was Siegi who was approached can only be surmised. Maybe yet again it was the combination of his grasp of languages and economics, maybe some forever hidden political contact, perhaps from his time in Paris. However it happened, the Institute recognized his work for France Libre by awarding him a year's seniority from February 1943 (letter from Bowley, the Director who replaced Marschak at the Institute, 5 February 1943, in personal possession).

For the Free French, Siegi wrote extensive papers on French post-war requirements including the key issue of a future labour shortage, the tobacco industry, French agriculture, including sheep, British-French trade, and French foreign trade (all in personal possession). It was one of the few things about his past that Siegi proudly told me about – how he had helped the French against the Nazis, even suggesting he had met de Gaulle in an assignation in London. These papers reveal highly detailed statistics and almost econometric modelling. As with his research and published articles for the Institute, Siegi here is working hard to provide suitable and well-researched models for French rejuvenation under a democratic government, not to suggest any fundamental change in the balance of class forces.

Siegi was writing his articles in a second language, English. Never as eloquent as Lotte, he developed a fluency in 'academese'. Yet, as Lotte suggested in one of her poems, using a second language is never the same: it is as if you are borrowing somebody else's set of clothes and can never take it for granted that they are really yours. Yet, as we shall see, Siegi's work was considered sufficiently important towards winning the war (or defeating Nazism), to impress the Oxford University authorities.

Indeed, a transformation has occurred in Siegi's standing between his departure from the KPD exile group in 1937 and 1940, a mere three years. What becomes evident throughout this period is that Siegi is not seen as a suspicious 'Commie' or even a dangerous fellow traveller. Somehow, Siegi has succeeded in turning himself into a respectable and valued academic, on the left certainly but to be trusted to do his bit for the war effort.

Lotte and the USA

Lotte had not settled after her return from the USSR and the move to Oxford. From her letters, it appears that in 1938, she informed Siegi, rather than discussing with him, of her decision to go to the USA. She does not reveal her motives. (Of course, we do not have Siegi's side of the correspondence.) The tone of her letters (which, as she herself apologises for) is erratic and often bossy.

But there are enough clues to fairly reliably divine Lotte's reasons. She was bitterly disappointed that she had not been admitted to study economics at the LSE, despite her Firsts from Humbolt University. Her aim was to support herself while she finally achieved a degree in the US. She had made contacts and was going to get enough teaching to support herself. She also knew there were scholarships, which she did indeed apply for and won but was unable to take up. Her life in London was not what she wanted – she made bits of money by translation work but Lotte was a fiery and brilliant woman who wanted to be an economist.

Moreover, extrapolating from her letters, I suspect she did not trust the British ruling class to hold to an anti-Nazi position on Germany and wanted to get both her and Siegi far away from Europe. And she also wanted to get her parents out of Germany and hoped to put their names down on the long list of would-be immigrants. This is not a goal she emphasizes in her letters but then, until after the November pogrom (Kristallnacht), almost nobody anticipated the future extermination of 'Jews', including Siegi.

There is a final factor, which will re-appear in the section on internment. She was continuing to hunt for news of Brian, and may well have supposed, correctly, that she would find it in the US. She could not have known with what disastrous consequences.

In late 1938, Lotte finally succeeded in catching a steamer to the US. Thanks to her letters from 1939, which Siegi kept, we get the impression that she wanted Siegi to follow her. Written by now in fluent English, her letters are strident – Siegi appears not to be able to work out what to do and she gives him impatient instructions as to what is the best way to enter the US.

We do not have Siegi's side of the correspondence but the impression is that he was fearful that if he applied for entry as a student, this would not give him any future security. And he, unlike Lotte, by this point did have a good job. How far the option of going to the US was taken seriously by Siegi is not clear. I rather think that, by this point, it was Lotte who wanted Siegi to come over – she was finally studying for her degree and would not have wanted this to be again disrupted. (Sadly, she never finished, as she left to get back to England before the outbreak of war.)

That she did return marks, I suggest, her final acknowledgement that Siegi was the person she was going to settle down with, an acknowledgement however which, from the little she told me, was based as much on weariness as love. I did ask her why she came back, rather than finally completing her degree. (The US was still holding an essentially isolationist position so there was no reason for her, at her third attempt, not to finally finish her studies.) 'I couldn't start again,' she said. 'You do understand?'

One personal complication, which falls outside this story, was the arrival in the UK of Lotte's niece. R, who had come over from Berlin on the Kindertransport early in 1939, aged nine. It had been Siegi, as far as one can judge from the heart-breaking letters from Lotte's parents, R's grandparents (who were looking after R) who had negotiated for R to reach safety here. Siegi and Lotte accepted ultimate responsibility, but Siegi would not have realized, I suspect, that Lotte would not be around when R arrived. Fairly soon after Lotte returned, both she and Siegi were interned, Lotte, either imprisoned or interned, for close on a year. The young German girl was moved around from one place to another and when she finally became unhappy, it seems it was Siegi who finally succeeded in retrieving her. She lived with Siegi and Lotte for most of the last years of the war and until she went off to College in 1947.

The risk and reality of internment, 1940

Along with the experience of so many émigrés, Siegi's time at the Institute was not an entirely happy one. There was a real risk of internment and even of deportation. Altogether, during the course of the second world war, around 25,000 German-speaking men, that is, not just from Germany, and maybe 400 women, Jewish and/or anti-Nazis, were interned for varying periods in British prisons and internment camps (Brinson, 2003).[173] Kushner (1989) suggests that one factor behind internment was the growing anti-Semitism in the 1930s.[174] Anti-alien prejudice was incited by several newspapers, which had been pro-appeasement and soft on Fascism, and which were to the fore in suggesting that many refugees were really Gestapo agents (Calder, 1980).[175] The Joint Intelligence Committee supported by the British Minister at the Hague, Sir Neville Bland, was quick to proclaim its fears of a Fifth Column (Calder, 1980).

But Brinson and Dove (2014) present an alternative emphasis. Anti-Semitism, they argue, was commonplace in the 1930s; what motivated MI5 in particular, and the Home Office to a significantly lesser degree, in the policy of internment was their crusade against Communism and Communists, Jewish or otherwise. Kell (whom we have already encountered), then the head of MI5, even came up with the analysis that German and Soviet intelligence were collaborating, a position not supported by the Home Office (Brinson and Dove, 2014).

It had not been the original intention of the British government to introduce mass internment partly because so many of the refugees, certainly up till 1938, were different varieties of political opponents of Nazism and/or victims of anti-Semitism, not people likely to be rooting for the Nazis. But as the Nazi jack-boot subjugated most of Europe, the Home Office changed its mind (Brinson, 2003). Decisions on internment were taken at 120 Tribunals, which considered 73,800 cases, three-quarters refugees. Only a few hundred were put in Class A, to be interned immediately; 64,200 went into Class C, not seen as a security risk, although, as with Siegi, this could still lead to internment. Some Class B's were interned, others not. There appears to have been randomness in these decisions (Calder, 1980).[176]

In 1940, there were approximately 1,000 'aliens' in Oxford, of whom 477 were from enemy countries (Weindling, *The Times*, 25 May 1940).[177] Oxford University briefly demanded their blanket internment. The level of hysteria was acute. A reflection of the atmosphere at the time was that refugees were excluded from working in university hospitals, on the grounds they might have contact with military casualties; the Registrar was worried that 'aliens' in laboratories might blow the whole place up, and opined that 'enemy aliens' might commit sabotage and therefore should be excluded from all [university] departments (letter from Registrar to Vice Chancellor, 25 May 1940, from Weindling). He contacted the Home Office (21 May 1940), expressing his concern about sabotage and asking 'when the comb-out of aliens' was going to begin. At exactly the same time, Oxford's chief constable, afraid of German invasion in May 1940, was of the opinion that special security measures should be applied, a position supported in the same article in *The Times* (25 May 1940).

Weindling argues that the Home Office helped to diffuse the tensions after the Registrar, in July 1940, softened his line to argue that the Home Office could assist the harmless and academically useful. At this prompt, the Home Office suggested a series of alien gradings for academics at Oxford, which was later introduced by Oxford University's own Vice- Chancellor's committee in July 1940, ranging from 1 to 3, depending on usefulness and level of risk. The 'C' class was later applied to interned German and Austrian academics on 1August 1940.

Siegi's residence permit had been renewed on the basis of his job at the Institute. But, although the Oxford Refugees Tribunal found in late October 1939 that he and Lotte should be exempted from internment (McCloughlin, 2007), in 1940, after the fall of France, Siegi, along with Burchardt and many outstanding economists, was interned as an 'enemy alien'. A furious Keynes intervened on their behalf with the Home Secretary (Hagerman, 2006).

In fact, Siegi, along with only five other aliens out of the 40-odd Oxford 'alien' academics listed (Weindling, 1996) was categorized as Class 1, the most reliable and important group.[178] Class 1 referred to aliens 'engaged in work directly related to the war effort'. There was significant criticism from some Oxford dons of how few names were allowed into Class 1, and R.G. Collingwood protested at the irony of those fleeing to find freedom being interned (Weindling, 1996).

Siegi and his work achieved the highest rank! Yet, if one follows Weindling, Siegi would not appear an obvious choice for Class 1: the University committee was suspicious of younger men because of the instability of their allegiances, and, though Siegi was by now 36, this still was likely to be seen in academic circles as bordering on 'youth'. The committee also had a preference for men with good honours degrees in science and medicine which could be put to use – my father had no degree and knew no science. Nonetheless, of the six men in Class 1, three were statisticians. Siegi's work on the economic problem of mobilizing resources for war purposes and the distribution of scarce resources must have been seen as being of national importance. This categorization is testimony to his success in being seen as a safe pair of hands.

Siegi was interned on 22 July 1940, roughly at the time the University Committee put him into a Class 1 category. The effect, according to Weindling, of being a Class 1, was that the university would intercede most forcefully on your behalf to ensure speedier release. Apparently, release from internment was followed by an invitation to tea with the Registrar and an offer of further assistance. I wonder what my father's response was to that! The Institute independently also threw its weight behind Siegi's demand to be released (letter from Bowley, 22 August 1940, in personal possession).

In fact, Siegi did not have a 'bad' internment. According to him, he was sent to a camp in the Highlands (apparently via a stop-over in a disused mill in Derbyshire, according to a letter from Andrews, 26 June 1966).[179] Within days of his arrival, the High Command, my father told me, had realized their mistake (maybe because he was about to become an economic adviser to De Gaulle) and insisted Siegi join them at the High Table. 'I would much have preferred to be with the rest of the men on the floor,' he told me. 'I couldn't bear the High Table's airs and graces.' A few key émigrés, in particular Marschak, however, reacted more adversely to being interned and headed out to stay forever in the US. Siegi was let out, after only just over two months, on 3 October 1940, so was held for a slightly shorter time than the average three months, and a far shorter time than Lotte, presumably after the intervention of Oxford.

Siegi was put under further strain when Lotte's recent past

caught up with her. In March 1940, the Aliens Department of the Home Office declared Lotte to be a Soviet agent 'who should not remain at liberty.' Lotte was picked up instantly and taken to Holloway Prison. The speed and severity is more remarkable as far fewer women than men were suspected or interned. (This has mostly to do with gender stereotypes.) MI5 had been given the power to arrest all persons on its security list, though their concern was ostensibly more with potential Nazi sympathizers, than possible Soviet agents. Lotte insisted she did not know what she was being accused of. Indeed, she had good grounds for her 'confusion'– the first group of MI5 suspects 'included possibly as many anti-Nazis and Jews as it did genuine Nazis' (Brinson, 2003).

The reasons for Lotte's imprisonment in Holloway and then internment lie in her visit to Krivitsky in the US, whom she correctly suspected might know about Brian (McCloughlin, 2007). What she did not know was that Krivitsky had become an important agent for the British and suspected her – and other Communists, such as Kuczynski – of being a spy for the USSR and dangerous. It seems likely that Lotte never knew why she had been arrested, though her letters from prison (which she knew could well be read by the authorities) praised how she was being treated. Her imprisonment came only seven years since she had fled Germany and four years after she had escaped her 'confinement' in the USSR. She had had an eventful – and paranoia-inducing – few years.

Siegi was allowed to visit Lotte once a fortnight for 30 minutes, on receipt of a visiting order from her personally. This involved travelling to war-time London from Oxford, which would have required careful arranging. He again mounts a campaign to get her released from Holloway, revealed in their almost daily letters – which suggest they are now fully reconciled (in personal possession).

We have Lotte's many letters from this time. They are largely to do with the day-to-day trials of existence, first in prison, then in the Isle of Man, rather than with what Siegi is doing or any political issues. There is, however, evident concern that Siegi or she might be sent on to Canada or Australia, as were thousands who were interned (especially if Communists or suspected Communists, though there is no indication Lotte or Siegi knew that). The impression overall is that Siegi stuck faithfully and patiently to Lotte through a lot of thick and thin.

This time, Siegi's campaigning on Lotte's behalf was successful. Lotte was found not to be a high security risk, was sent on to Port St Mary on the Isle of Man in early June, and released in November (McCloughlin, 2007), having been forcibly kept away from home for eight months. It is arguably at this point, when Siegi and Lotte had both been released from internment and become central in the care of Lotte's niece, R, that they first started to feel that Britain was becoming their home.

Die Zeitung

Siegi became a contributor to *Die Zeitung* between 1941 and 1944. This was almost certainly as a result of Siegi knowing Johannes Uhlig, pseudonym of Peter Conrad, a left-wing German Social Democrat who had been the economics editor on the prestigious German daily, *Frankfurter Zeitung*, and who co-founded, and was a member of the editorial board of, *Die Zeitung*. Siegi will have known Uhlig as a fellow statistician at Oxford.

Die Zeitung was founded in January 1941, essentially supported by the British government, in the form of the Ministry of Information (Brinson, 1995).[180] Its political provenance, beyond appealing to anti-Nazi German speakers in the UK and consolidating pro-British feeling, was broad, and open to dispute. A German paper for German-speaking exiles had been mooted ever since 1938 when German refugees had started to arrive here in any numbers. There is some debate as to who set up *Die Zeitung*, and for exactly what purposes, but the support of the British government, both for its initial establishment and its – sometimes contested – continuation, was essential. It was presented as being essentially non-political, though resolutely anti-Nazi, a mechanism for giving German exiles in Britain some sort of united voice and, as the government saw it, helping to overcome the exiles' sense of grievance at having been turned into one sort or other of enemy alien. The paper's further purposes were supposedly for its distribution in the Reich, to influence neutral Germans to support the Allies, and for German POWs, but it is not clear how far any of these aims was achieved.

The government agreed on a run of 20,000, and that they would compensate the publisher in the likely event that subscriptions did not meet the cost of production (Abbey, 1995). Initially a four-page daily, it was to become a 12-page (probably more successful) weekly in early 1942 (Abbey, 1995). The government laid down as a condition of its support that it had its 'man' on the team, who, although he theoretically had the power to censor, seems to have operated more to curb excesses and even to try to resolve the very real acrimony with its German-speaking political opponents (Abbey, 1995). *Die Zeitung* ended with the end of the war.

Its small editorial team, including Uhlig, included many who had held positions of significance and responsibility in pre-Nazi Germany, with a tendency therefore amongst some towards conservatism. There was some ambiguity as to how far this team saw itself as providing some sort of mechanism for uniting all anti-Nazi forces and providing a form of alternative leadership in exile. There seem to have been some quite bitter disagreements on the editorial board about such a grand aim, and some of the Social Democrats withdrew. The Social Democrats may also have feared (wrongly) that *Die Zeitung* might become a vehicle for Communists, carrying on an old and deeply felt unwillingness to collaborate. The Communists, after the collapse of the Hitler-Stalin pact in 1940, did indeed want to write for *Die Zeitung*, but were firmly rebuffed.[181] The Foreign Office had stipulated that the paper should not become too revolutionary (Abbey, 1995) but it seems unlikely that the editorial team needed reminding of that!

Die Zeitung was criticized by its left opponents because Lothar and Haffner, two of the leading members of the editorial team, had left Germany 'late', that is, 1936 and 1938 respectively (Abbey, 1995) and were therefore not seen as proper anti-Nazis. Lothar defended himself in the *New Statesman*, a definitively left, though non-aligned, weekly (quoted by Abbey, 1995, from the *New Statesman* 3 May 1941): 'German Social Democratic Party...do not like us. Why? I do not know. Perhaps because some of us hold socialistic views without belonging to any 'party' or 'group'. Lothar's use of the *New Statesman*, confirms his willingness to be identified as on the left.

Many of the contributors to the paper were socialists (Palmier, 2006) and there was 'space' for a non-aligned left, such as Siegi (and Lotte). Uhlig worked alongside Hans Lothar, another of the moving spirits behind the establishment of *Die Zeitung*, and who became in effect its editor till his death (Abbey, 1995). Siegi was invited to write for the paper's economics page, presumably through Uhlig. (After the war, Uhlig made a new career for himself writing economics articles for German newspapers (Abbey, 1995).)

Siegi would have been careful about the company he was in and would not have wanted to write for either a CP-dominated journal or one controlled by the British government. Maybe Siegi's willingness to write for *Die Zeitung*, and their willingness to take his articles, was because of Lothar's unaligned but left-leaning politics, despite the paper being backed by the government, and with an essentially conservative editorial Board. Moreover, the editorial board's continuing refusal to allow CP writers would have reassured Siegi. As with his work for the Free French, it seems likely that Siegi saw his role on *Die*

Zeitung to do with carrying on, as best he could, given his limited opportunities, with the anti-Nazi struggle.

Lotte, released from the Isle of Man in late 1940, was writing for them by 1941. In effect, she was first imprisoned by the government and then wrote for them. In fact, the position of a leading MI5 member was that 'alien refugees [...are] likely to be useful for us for propaganda purposes in times of war' and that exemption for them from internment could be considered (Brinson and Dove, 2014).[182] While this can only be conjecture, I have often wondered whether some sort of 'deal' was done. Siegi and Lotte must have both taken the longer view and understood the paper's significance. Lotte, pen-name Maria Lehmann, wrote a series of short stories, some of which were much praised. Siegi, pen-name Alfred Lehmann, concentrated on a variety of economic issues, such as the importance of silver, allied shipping, South American economies and much else besides.

Siegi's many economic articles, written over about three years, are notable for being so politically unremarkable – this was the work of an economist wanting to do his bit for the war effort, not that of a revolutionary. Both he and Lotte stopped writing before the end of the war, as a result, I suspect, first of Lotte's, almost fatal, illness, and then, in 1944, my birth.

Siegi's writings 1938–1947

Hidden away in Siegi and Lotte's London home were the typed drafts of a number of political articles, none of which seem to ever have been published, written during the war about the future of the world and of socialism. Though not dated, their content strongly suggests they were written when the outcome of the war was still uncertain. Here Siegi is attempting to build up an alternative political philosophy to 'the God that failed'. He is still actively pursuing his commitment to socialism. The articles bear no resemblance to the neo-Keynesian economic work he is being paid for at the time. They suggest that Siegi did not consider an outright German victory likely but, with a profound awareness of the collaborationist tendencies in sections of the British ruling class, did not entirely rule out some sort of peace deal between the west and the Nazis. Some of his writings have the pessimistic tone associated with James Burnham and, later Orwell, in which Siegi feared the world might be divided between a number of quasi-authoritarian regimes.

Now outside the 'Communist' movement, Siegi raised a number of issues about a new basis for socialism. These are mainly based on questions rather than answers and try to combine a sort of ethical socialism with a rather economistic interpretation of Marxism, but end up simply putting the two next to each other without any real integration. Though striving for something 'new', his articles instead are woolly – Siegi has lost his political bearings. He is finding developing an alternative position to that of the KPD difficult.

Siegi refers to the ideas of 'Wintrinham and co.'. (The reference to 'Wintrinham and co.' is probably to the '1941 Committee', one of the predecessors of the CommonWealth Party).[183] Tom Wintrinham was a founder member of the British Communist Party, an officer in the International Brigade in Spain, who was then expelled from the Communist Party for marrying a 'Trotskyist spy' (Purcell, 2004, quoting from the head of the Comintern in Spain).[184] Like Siegi, Wintrinham never became a Trotskyist although he may have had some sympathies for the POUM, instead seeing himself, somewhat like Siegi, as a loyal Communist who had been forced out by a party that was going astray. Siegi's awareness of this figure shows how seriously he was still taking the debates on the left.

But Siegi shows no inclination to join him, despite some significant similarities in history and outlook. His disagreement with Wintrinham, who had become the most significant non-Trotskyite figure to the left of the CP, could have a variety of ostensible causes (see endnote 183) but the main one was probably Wintrinham's rejection of morality as a basis for politics; maybe, but less likely, Wintrinham's willingness to include the CP in a popular front. Nevertheless, Siegi's unwillingness to align himself with Wintrinham may have had just as much to do with Siegi's insecurity in Britain, both psychologically and legally (Siegi was not yet naturalized) as with Siegi's differences with him.

The most remarkable of the documents was Siegi's analysis: *Political Economy of the Nazis*. This appears in more than one version and it evidently kept on being rewritten between its inception in 1936–1937, when it was written almost entirely in German, and the final version in 1940–1941, written in English. (The absence of reference to the Hitler/Stalin pact of 1940 suggests that Siegi gave up before then, or perhaps gave up because of the pact.)

The lengthy document covers in extraordinary econometric detail – which must have required an amazing level of statistical research into wages, prices, production, etc in Germany – the changing situation of the many classes and class fractions in Nazi Germany, from the small farmer, through the artisan and shopkeeper, the worker and layers of the bourgeoisie, and how their class position was affected by Nazism. There is very little on the position of Jews, though Siegi does end by arguing that the Nazis will not exterminate them because of their economic usefulness. The document's emphasis is on the failure of the Nazis to fulfil the promises to their own voters, their links with big business and some suggestion towards the end that the regime remains unstable, an analysis, I suggest, as much a product of his Marxism as his statistics. But he did not appear optimistic that the Nazi regime would be replaced, suggesting at one point that some sort of right-wing coalition might be formed.

This unpublished book is unique – nothing of the sort, as far as one knows, was being produced in this sort of depth or detail at the time it was written, though other exiles and 'friends of anti-

Nazis' were doing some work and writing more 'journalistic' articles. It may also be the case, though this is conjecture, that Siegi's analysis of the economic situation in Germany could have contributed to an Allied war plan. Siegi's favourable internment rating indicates the importance of his research, which may well have included his economic analysis of Germany.

There is an intriguing letter from Orwell to Siegi, dated 16 November 1943, in Peter Davison's *The Complete Works of George Orwell*, which is a response to a letter from Siegi that is now lost. That Siegi should write to Orwell at all is itself of interest as it suggests Siegi's sense that Orwell was worth communicating with. Orwell starts by saying that what Siegi says is very interesting, but continues with criticisms, first, that Siegi underestimates the importance of communication in order to bring about change. Orwell writes: 'The greatest problem before intellectuals now is the conquest of power.' He continues: 'You speak of forming a new elite...', and states how problematic it is to do such a thing '*inside* [Orwell's italics] the powerful modern State which is controlled by people whose interest is to prevent any such thing.' Orwell's second criticism of Siegi's letter is that Siegi 'overestimates the danger of "Brave New World" – 'i.e. a completely materialist vulgar civilisation based on hedonism.' Instead Orwell posits the likelihood of the 'centralised slave state, ruled over by a small clique and in effect a new ruling class', whose dynamic would be 'rabid nationalism and hero worship kept going by literally continuous wars.' The suggestion here, even though implicit, is that Siegi was reaching the conclusion that change would occur through the creation of a new, apparently intellectual, elite, suggesting a profound pessimism on Siegi's part.

These political musings and analysis mark the end of the period of Siegi's life in which he was attempting to develop some alternative vision to that of the KPD. There is no evidence of any political writing after 1942–1943. Very likely, the near death of

Lotte, followed soon after by the birth of his child, would have provided distraction. But the break is more fundamental than that.

After the war, probably after 1944, Siegi seems to have stopped speculating, at least in writing, about the possibilities for, and possible nature of, socialism and disappeared completely into his economic work, though he did return to these ideas, finally, in the late 1960s. But Siegi has entered a period of life where his politics are expressed in less visible or active form

The Holocaust and its shadow

I want to finally focus in this section on the years immediately after the end of the second world war. Soon after the end of the war, Siegi and Lotte started the terrible process of trying to find out who was still alive. This occurred initially in Oxford, indeed even before the war had ended, but continued briefly after their move to Durham. This search was not known to me till I recently acquired my mother's and father's heart-breaking papers.

There I found that my mother believed she had found her father, whom she had been trying to trace since 1942, only to discover it was a different Samuel Jacoby, also from Charlottenburg, Berlin, with the same year of birth. Her father had not died of a heart attack, as she had informed me, but of his time at Theriesenstadt.

My father, I was to discover, had lost his beloved uncle, Hermann. Hermann had met a terrible death, which Siegi found out about within weeks of my birth (something I am now convinced must have affected his joy). Siegi's only cousin and family were captured in Yugoslavia and almost all murdered. Lotte's father, sister and, Lotte believed, mother, had all been murdered. Indeed, of the families Siegi and Lotte had left behind in Germany, almost none were still alive by the end of 1945.

In her last years, Lotte, as her inhibitions about speaking of the past became consumed by dementia, and she released the odd memory and word, would regularly repeat to me: 'I should have died too.' She had failed to save her family's skins while saving her own. She could not bear it. My father trod more lightly over the loss of so much, but he, like Lotte, also could not face that past and was therefore unable to speak of it.

There were other deaths, less personal but also pressing. Exile and the process of flight contributed to the suicides of literary and artistic figures, some of whom Siegi would have known or known of. Ernest Kirchner killed himself in 1938; Eric Toller, the playwright, whom my father may well have known, in 1939; Walter Benjamin and Stefan Zweig in 1940. And there were of course many others who were less illustrious. Exile 'de-roots' a person, turns them into an 'other', an 'outsider' who has lost country, language, comrades and friends. Siegi was not alone in sometimes wondering whether life was worth the candle.

As I grew up, I knew that both my parents wanted nothing to do with Germany, though now I suspect this was more Lotte's than Siegi's position. Somehow, aged only five or six, I knew that one of the hymns we sang at the services held for our Church of England primary school, which had the same musical refrain as 'Deutschland Über Alles', was *verboten*, and I, who was such a good little girl, would clamp my mouth tight shut and refuse to sing. Indeed, unlike almost all the 'Jewish' exiled community, including Lotte's living sister, Siegi and Lotte even had refused reparations because it was 'blood money'. As the British government files record, they were one of a mere handful to refuse. (They were later to accept their German pension which they saw as a right they had earned.[185])

The explanation Siegi gave for his job at the Institute ending in 1947 was that the policy was to give the jobs back to returning soldiers. Durham also had the advantage of offering him permanent tenure. Whatever the underlying cause, his contract at the Institute finished in October 1947 and, after spending three months 'commuting', he moved, in December 1947, into his first ever privately owned house in the 'bracing' and hilly university city of Durham, where he had finally, aged 43, got his first established university lecturing post in economics at St Cuthbert's College.

Among the letters my father kept (now in my possession) recounting who among the comrades had lived, and the many who had died, there is correspondence, in German, with somebody who survived. In a touching and illuminating letter from Harry Shulze-Wilde from Munich in 1947, who had founded the German journal *Echo der Woche*, based in Munich, Harry explains that he was doing OK, having survived nine concentration camps.

I thought I could not trace Harry till both an entry popped up on Wikipedia and I obtained some limited documentation from the *Bundesarchiv* just before I sent off this manuscript. Harry Schulze-Wilde's original name was Harry Paul Schulze, his other pseudonym being Harry Schulze-Hegner. In the 1920s, Harry had worked with Piscator and become a member of the KPD and, a left-wing journalist, left the KPD in 1932. He was arrested straight after the Reichstag fire and then, somehow escaping, got into Czechoslovakia, where, it appears that, although he was not apparently a member of the KPD, he coordinated with Johannes Becher and Willi Münzenberg, who were acting on behalf of the Comintern.[186]

It is not surprising that Siegi and Harry knew each other as their worlds evidently overlapped considerably. Originally a youth worker in the 1920s, Harry had been in Berlin from around 1928 when he was a member of the KPD, and, like Siegi, was a cultural activist and a journalist. As we know from Siegi's letter, they were involved in agitprop together in Berlin. Harry's departure from the KPD in 1932 suggests some level of dissidence from the KPD though his working for the Comintern a year or two after that – and after the Nazis have taken over – shows his willingness to work for the Comintern. Although Siegi was probably more 'on line' than Harry, Siegi may well have shared some of Harry's reservations. We also know from Siegi's letter that they met up again in Paris in late 1933/early 1934.

The following is drawn from Siegi's reply, dated 28 June 1947, to Harry's first letter. Siegi wrote:

> 'The fact that I write immediately is the best expression of my joy in being able to write to you [that is, that Harry was still alive]. We [Siegi and Lotte] often thought and talked of you. You had no small part in our meeting and we think back to our time in the theatre with unadulterated joy and there aren't many times I can say that about. How are you? When did you become Editor of "Echo der Woche"? I don't remember it from my Munich days.
>
> Politically we have completely withdrawn since 1937… We were worried you didn't get out of France in time. Paris was the last time we saw each other. We never heard from Ernst again. Otto was still alive in 1942 but we don't know after that. Berthe was involved in sabotage and "committed suicide".'

Harry had invited Siegi to the Second International Youth Congress in 1948 in Munich. It is still unclear what this Congress was or was supposed to be. It may have been a planned Congress of the World Federation of Democratic Youth. The Federation was founded in London in 1945 and was dominated by Communist-led groups. It had held its first International Youth and Student Festival in Prague in 1947 and was to hold its second in Budapest in 1949. Was the Munich gathering some sort of Congress planned for 1948 but cancelled under Cold War pressures? We know of one example of such a cancellation or maybe postponement: on 8 October and then again on 12 November 1947, any activities of the Cultural Union, suspected of being a Communist front, were forbidden by the US and

British military governments in their sectors. Germany, it has to be remembered, only finally 'divides' into West and East Germany in 1949. In 1947, it was still possible for the left in Germany to hope to build a united socialist Germany and cultural activities which embraced the revolutionary left.

We have a proposed schedule for a June Youth Congress (from correspondence between Farish and Graham Greene, who had also been invited to speak, in the Catherine Walstron archive in Georgetown University). According to Farish, 'the meeting will not have any political or propagandistic tendency. Its only stated purpose ... is to further the spirit of understanding between Germany and the world.' But there does not appear to be any other record of this Congress, which strongly suggests it never took place.

Siegi was enthusiastic about the invitation. He might, he wrote, give a lecture on economic/social questions, or the relationship between ethics and economics, or the problems of planning. Siegi appears to have been trying to build an alternative ethical socialism to the Stalinist model. Although it is impossible to know how to interpret Siegi's proposed involvement, one of the attractions of Harry's invitation may well have been that Harry came out of a Christian revolutionary tradition, for whom, therefore, ethics would have had greater priority than for the average comrade.[187]

In response to Harry's suggestion that they may have gone separate ways politically, Siegi writes: 'A whole world separates me from the line. When I hear the line, then I realize a whole world separates me.' 'The line', one assumes, refers to the position of the KPD/CP.

The letter is full of the contradictions of a past that could never be undone. Siegi warns Harry that he would need to sort out passport difficulties (although by then he is naturalized). He writes: 'I have lost more than an essential part of my past but there is nothing to be done about it.' Siegi shows an enthusiasm for returning to Munich as the place of his birth. The people who had bound him to Munich had been murdered but it seems that returning to some sort of political profile in Germany could outweigh this. Siegi was willing or even keen to return to Germany given the right circumstances.

But, for whatever reasons, nothing came of the plan. The Cold War was already looming, in 1948, in the 'Russian domain', there had been a 'Communist coup' in Czechoslovakia, and the removal of non-Communist elements across 'coalition' governments in Eastern Europe. The Berlin blockade had started in mid-1948. In the 'West' the expulsion of Communists from Italian and French coalition governments was already taking place. Harry's initiative may have been timed out – what was possible in 1947 was no longer feasible in 1948. One element in Siegi's decision was likely to have been the descent of the Iron Curtain.

Intriguingly, there is no further correspondence between Harry and Siegi, although both lived on for at least thirty years (or at least none that Siegi preserved). Although we do not know whether the Congress ever occurred or Siegi decided not to attend (or both), I suggest this moment marked a key break for Siegi from his former comrades (who were still alive), and a break with his aim, since he had left the exile group and the KPD, of developing some sort of alternative basis for socialism. Siegi has for now been defeated. He has not just lost 'more than an essential part of my past', he has lost the intention and probably desire to rethink the basis of socialism. It also symbolizes Siegi and Lotte's decision that they would never return to their former 'homeland' and were now facing a future in the UK.

Endnotes

168. My thanks to Professor Herald Hagerman for kindly sending me a copy of *German speaking economists in British exile 1933–45* (2007).
169. My thanks to Paul Weindling for sending me his article:

'The Impact of German medical scientists on British medicine: A Case-study of Oxford 1933–45', in *Forced Migration and Scientific change*, eds. M. Ash and A. Sollneer, German Historical Institute, 1996, CUP.

170. Marschak failed to 'get' Lowe. Lowe, whose economics was also influenced by Marxism, a Jew and an architect of the Weimar Republic, also had to flee Germany in 1933, but escaped to Manchester, not the Institute, and, after internment, left for the USA.
171. I remember how, when I got into Oxford University, my father proudly gave me his long flowing Oxford university gown. But I had no use for it: the undergraduate gown was of course of a different, and shorter, cut to that of the don. Siegi kept the gown till his dying day and I sadly threw it out when I cleared my parents' home; it had become the living quarters for a million moths.
172. De Gaulle, who was recognized as leader of the Free French on 28 June 1940, is often now seen as the accepted leader of the 'legitimate' French resistance but this was far from the case at the time. Churchill and, even more so, Roosevelt were not enamoured of him and tried to build up a couple of figures with more Petainist tendencies, but they failed. Siegi's work for the Free French was more politically partisan and less illustrious than it might seem now.
173. Brinson (2003): *In the Exile of Internment or Von Versuchen, aus einer Not eine Tugent zu machen; German-speaking women interned by the British during the Second World War. Politics and culture in twentieth-century Germany*, eds. Niven, Jordan, Rochester, N.Y., Camden House, pp 63–87.
174. Kushner (1989): *The persistence of prejudice: anti-Semitism in British society during the Second World War.*
175. Calder: *The Myth of 1940.*
176. Internment experiences were highly mixed. The Isle of Man, where many were detained, had its compensations; with so

many distinguished intellectuals present, a rich cultural life emerged: musicians had time to practise; artists improvized paintings and sculptures (Calder, 1980). The Dadaist, Kurt Schwitters, after years of neglect, relished his captive audience: 'His pièces de résistance, …were made out of the remnants of porridge,… collected from breakfast tables but the mice soon got them' (Calder, 1980). Sir Claus Moser, a Jewish German refugee, who was to become a leading British economist, was only one among many able exiles who was interned but 'forgave the implicit insult to their integrity, and went on to make distinguished contributions to British life' (Calder, 1980). According to my mother, being interned on the Isle of Man was a cross between being at university and a holiday camp. Without wanting to detract from others' experiences, she seems to have enjoyed herself – but then she had just come out of Holloway Prison.

177. Weindling: *The Impact of German medical scientists on British medicine: A Case-study of Oxford 1933–45,* in *Forced Migration and Scientific change,* eds. M. Ash and A. Sollneer, German Historical Institute, 1996, UK: CUP.

178. The others were Burchardt, also from the Institute of Statistics, Kosterlitz: psychotherapy, Oldern: history, Steiner: medicine and Siegi's good friend Uhlig: 'medicine statistics'. (Weindling: Society for the Protection of Science and Learning: 129/1 UA CQ/11/17). Uhlig, for reasons unknown, was interned for six months, having his first attempt to be freed turned down. Siegi and Uhlig (my father always referred to him as Uhlig, not by his first name) stayed in contact even after Uhlig's return to Germany.

179. Jacobsthal, another German émigré from Oxford, is recorded as first being held at a disused cotton mill, Warth Mill in Bury, Lancashire, probably but not definitely a different place.

180. Brinson, Charmian and Malet, M. (1995) 'Die Zeitung', in

Between Two Languages: German Exiles in Great Britain 1933–1945, Vol. 59, 215–244.

181. Hobsbawm was also an (unlikely) contributor to *Die Zeitung*, as he was a Party man and they did not take Communist contributors. He wrote to the literary editor, Wolfgang von Einsiedel, a relative of Bismarck, who accepted Hobsbawm's literary contributions. Presumably, Lotte also dealt with von Einsiedel. Both my parents totally refused to ever go to hear Hobsbawm speak. I'd always assumed this was because of his Party allegiance but maybe their paths had also crossed.
182. Brinson, Charmian and Dove, Richard (2014) *A Matter of Intelligence: MI5 and the Surveillance of anti-Nazi refugees 1933–1950.*
183. Although he had been a senior member of the Communist Party, who had narrowly escaped death in the Spanish Civil War, Wintrinham was given the choice of his Party or his wife. 1937, the year of mass trials in the USSR, was also when significant CPGB notables in the UK were disciplined for 'Trotskyist tendencies'. Even Pollitt, the General Secretary of the CPGB, was accused of being a spy for British intelligence. Wintrinham believed his expulsion was as much to do with his belief in the Popular Front, rather than seeing the Popular Front as merely one tactic. Wintrinham, who, like Siegi, had dedicated his previous life to the Party, always remained (again, similar to Siegi) a Marxist.

    Early in the War, Wintrinham and some other International Brigadiers were involved in plans to set up partisan-type units in the event of a German invasion. His approach was regarded with suspicion by the authorities and his group was dumped and replaced by the far less activist Home Guard. He was described by Orwell as 'a notable voice stemming the tide of defeatism' (Purcell, 2004, from Orwell's letter to *Partisan Review*: 3 January 1941) and briefly became a much loved figure, though not by the government. Wintrinham was very critical of the CPGB's position at this point not to fight, though he believed the government's prosecution of the war was as much to do with defeating socialism (USSR) as fascism. He wrote that the war should be a fight for freedom, including by the colonies. (Amazingly, in 1942, Cripps asked Wintrinham to go to India to report on the possibilities of guerrilla fighting, and Wintrinham subsequently retained an active interest in this area, another overlap with Siegi.)

Wintrinham was later a founder of a grass-roots, revolutionary movement, the Common Wealth. His slogan was, 'Turn the imperialist war into an antifascist war.' But he insisted he did not want to attack the CPGB and wanted them as part of a popular front, to bring about 'Victory through Democracy'. His position was to support Churchill in his war against the Nazis, but to campaign for its own policies. One of the groups Wintrinham spotted to be part of his alliance was the '1941 Committee', referred to by Siegi (see main text) as 'and co'. It was largely a group of respectable, even if generally radical, well-informed and often influential journalists or publishers, with whom Purcell suggests, Wintrinham felt comfortable. I can imagine Siegi's hackles rising at this class allegiance. Common Wealth then contested (and won) by-elections on a leftist basis during the war when the main parties had agreed a pact. Acland, a practising Christian, had become deeply involved and there was a disagreement between him and Wintrinham, a committed atheist, over the importance of 'morality in politics' which Wintrinham deplored, a disagreement which came to dominate and weaken Common Wealth, which was closed down after the General Election in July 1945.

184. Purcell, *Last English Revolutionary: Tom Wintringham*

1898–1949.

185. This is, however, only part of what happened. Siegi had to contact an uncle who had left pre-Nazi Germany for the US, to provide a testimonial for the German government that Siegi had worked for the *liquer fabrik.* When I visited Los Angeles in the early 1970s, I was introduced to said uncle, now an elderly man, as Siegi's daughter. He told me that he had stood on the roof of his factory in 1919 in Munich shooting at the revolutionaries!

186. http://de.wikipedia.org/wiki/Harry_Wilde#cite_ref-becher 1989_7-0, accessed 25th March 2014. Harry had a fascinating career. He survived the war, moving repeatedly from one country to the next. He knew Plievier well, another person of working-class background, who combined writing with revolutionary activities, a feature of the wide-ranging character of Germany's revolutionary left at the time. After fleeing to the USSR, Plievier returned to East Germany after the war, but then moved to West Germany where he became a leading cultural figure. Harry moved in with the Plievier family.

    After the war, Harry wrote copiously, including on Rathenau (a distant relative of Lotte's), and in the 1960s on the Black Power movement, and put together a book of photos of, and extracts on, Trotsky. He was also involved with a documentary on Trotsky's murder. He seems to have developed an interest in Trotskyist ideas rather than any identification with Trotskyism. Maybe this also contributed to the distancing between Harry and Siegi, as Siegi, in so far as he held a coherent position on the USSR, though fundamentally critical of the USSR, seems to have retained a belief in the possibility it could still be changed from below.

    Although it is impossible to know, another possible cause of friction was Harry's sexual 'identity'; Siegi was a puritan on such issues. Harry appears to have had a close relationship (or probably rather more) with a fascinating figure, Jef Last, a Dutch 'anarcho-Communist'.

187. Among my father's books in his office, was the autobiography, *Angry Young Man* by Leslie Paul. Paul was the founder of the Woodcraft Folk (a sort of left-wing, co-ed alternative to the Boy Scouts) who became its leader from the 1920s into the 1930s. Paul had come out of a Christian tradition, joining the CP during its Third Period, and then returning to Christian Socialism, in fact becoming a priest. Here is a parallel with both Wilde and Pleviers, both of whom had come out of the tradition of Christian socialism. There is a shared concern with ethical socialism which had become Siegi's preoccupation in his search for a new form of socialism after leaving the KPD.

Chapter 8

1947–1966 The Durham years. Drowning ghosts

Siegi and Lotte moved to Durham in the winter of 1947, finally leaving again in 1966. Although not an exact fit, these were also the years when the Cold War was at its height. In fact, Siegi may have been lucky – another year or so, and the tentacles of the Cold War might have precluded his getting a new university job. Although Siegi continued his political activities by virtue of being a branch officer for the Durham branch of the University Union (AUT) (as I was delighted to discover) and teaching Workers' Educational Association (WEA) classes of miners and shipbuilders (which he loved), he does not appear to have been involved in the (very limited) debates about socialism or in any direct 'socialist' activity during this period. His move to Durham and into academia represented a loss in his earlier self's sense of agency.

It is too easy, observing Siegi's trajectory, to take it for granted that he and Lotte stayed in the UK. Taking the job in Durham represented for Siegi and Lotte finally closing the door on any idea of returning to Germany, though this might not have been a conscious decision. We already know that Siegi had deep reservations about accepting Harry's offer and, in 1948, he also failed to respond positively to an invitation from Brecht to work with him at the Berliner Ensemble in East Berlin. The failure to accept such an offer reveals that, by around 1948, for Siegi, there is no going back.

On 9 September 1947, Siegi became naturalized (Certificate A231511, National Archives). Without naturalization, there was no certainty that he, and other refugees, would be allowed to stay in the UK. Again, we forget that naturalization was not something the refugees could be certain of; indeed, many refugees were most concerned they would be returned to their countries of origin after the end of the war. The wartime British government, unlike the American, refused to grant British citizenship to the refugees, even if they were serving in the forces. Almost all initial rights to enter the UK had been given on a temporary basis, though, with the outbreak of war, the government ceased to pursue issues of possible deportation. Neither Siegi nor Lotte could have taken for granted that they would get citizenship.

Aliens could theoretically apply for naturalization after five years of residence in the UK, but the influx of refugees in the 1930s had increased the existing backlog in the Home Office. More seriously, Morrison, a Labour member of the National Government and later a Labour Home Secretary, opposed naturalization, voicing the opinion that too many refugees/Jews would risk an explosion of anti-Semitism (London, 2003). Similarly, R. G. Somervell, the Labour interim Home Secretary in 1945, stated that it was unwise to offer refugees settlement. The government should not accept liability for the refugees who had been admitted on transit visas. Repatriation should be considered, although without the use of force (London, 2003). Chuter Ede, the subsequent Labour Home Secretary, refined this position: aliens of good character should not be arbitrarily expelled but he planned to enforce deportation orders against 'undesirables', a position endorsed by Clement Attlee, the Labour Prime Minister (London, 2003). Churchill, ironically, stood out against deportation. Ede employed delaying tactics in the processing of applications, but the Labour government never carried out their threat of deportation.

However, there was an extra threat against people who were seen as Communists. Although we know that Siegi had come to be seen as contributing to the war effort, as the Iron Curtain slowly came down following the end of the war and snapped shut in around 1948, the climate towards Communists in the UK grew more frosty. A secret Home Office letter from the Home Secretary, in reply to Mr Roland Robinson MP, asked about the difficulties arising out of divided allegiance as disclosed by the Fuchs' case. Fuchs had been found to be 'spying' for the USSR.[188] I quote from the last section of the letter:

> 'I therefore intend for the present to refuse applications for naturalisation from (a) known members of the British Communist Party or of any foreign Communist Party
>
> (b) persons who, though not avowed or known members of a Communisst [sic] Party are associated with Communist activities in such a way as to cast doubt on their loyalty
>
> (c) persons who in the past have been members of a Communist! P a r ty [sic] or have been closely associated with Communist activities' (National Archives, CAB/129/38).

Although the Fuchs' affair spills open after Siegi became naturalized, the memo reveals clearly that an especially close eye was kept on Communists or people associated with Communism.[189]

Naturalization must have come as a relief to Siegi (and Lotte). He was now settled in the UK and could finally stop worrying about the possibility of being deported. It also allowed him to bring up his young daughter as British. He could turn his back on the horrors of the past. How far he succeeded in this is another matter.

But Siegi, as a political refugee who had remained on the left, was unusual in preferring to remain in the UK. Many Communist refugees and exile organizations did plan a return to Germany. Towards the end of the war, the *Freie Deutsche Bewegung*, a covertly Communist organization, among others, made extensive preparations for the return home and the deployment of activists in key areas in post-war Germany, going as far as matching names to places (Brinson, 2011). In a separate piece of research I conducted, I established that two of the four KPD parents exiled in the UK, whose 'children' I interviewed, returned to Germany, in one case to the East (or rather the area under Soviet control), the other to the West. The third person's father was in the KPD for only a couple of years as a young man and had then drifted rightwards. In the fourth case, the father had fled to the USSR, then to the UK, and had eventually become 'apolitical'.[190] Unlike the refugees who came here as a result of anti-Semitism, and who tended to see the UK as their future home, the political refugees hoped and prepared to return to their countries where they had been political activists and where they planned to try to build socialism after the ravages of Nazism. I suspect that the 'comrades' who were most likely to stay in the UK were those who had fallen out with the KPD.[191]

But there were many reasons why Siegi and Lotte would never have gone back. They did not want to return to a country which had just murdered many of their family and comrades. In terms of returning to Western Germany, Siegi knew that the system of government had not been de-Nazified. Nor could he return to East Germany because he and, even more so, Lotte were paranoid – though with good reason – that the Stasi were out to get them. Moreover, I suspect Siegi had the sense to realize that returning to German soil was never going to return him to the political scene he had once been active in. Indeed, according to Palmier (2006) the 'comrades' and literary figures who did return apparently did not have a good time: though they were initially feted, there soon developed a suspicion between those who had left and those who had stayed. Life had moved on and there was no way back.

Siegi and Lotte moved into a terraced house, built in the 1860s, on a hill so steep, there was a handrail to help! Durham city was built on seven hills, it was said, like Rome! The house's renovations over the intervening 80 years were restricted to a built-on tiny galley kitchen (where my mother erratically produced amazing Germanic three-course meals) and a freezing microscopic bathroom. Siegi had borrowed the money to buy the house from Lotte's anglicized relatives who, as I gather from the correspondence, did rather well out of the deal, which left Siegi very cross.

Durham was their first real 'home' since Berlin and they had no furniture or anything else to put in their house. There was linoleum on the floors; most of the furniture my father picked up at auctions, which were sources of an assortment of rather wonderful, at the time unpopular, heavy Victorian furniture, odd bits of already worn carpets and some once fashionable sets of very old beautiful plates, bowls, cups, etc. Somehow or other, our 'silver' had come out of Germany and we ate with exquisite gold- and silver-plated cutlery.

I certainly remember us as having little money. The house was hardly heated, except for one room with its ever-hungry anthracite stove. I was so cold at night, I could not sleep. I never received pocket money. But what my parents did spend money on was a biennial foreign holiday. I think this was one of the few times they were content. Yet I remember once, in Paris, probably around 1949. It was 14 July and the streets were full of the noise of celebration. Suddenly my parents pulled me violently into the nearest church. Terrified, I asked what was wrong. 'The policemen were carrying guns,' my father told me in a voice which said: Are you an idiot that you didn't notice? Then I was told how the Nazis fired from the 'balconies' at De Gaulle as he marched down the main aisle of Notre-Dame to celebrate the liberation of France in August, 1944. For my parents, that was yesterday.

Where they refused to go was Germany, except on an occasion, probably in 1948, when, I now realize, they needed to be in situ to try to sort out some unresolved financial matters. The trip was a disaster. I was at the time a little girl with a halo of fair curls. A man approached us and picked me up declaring, 'Ein arisches Mädchen'. My parents turned grey and fled. Then there was a second incident. In a rare break in their normal silence, they actually told me that one man whom we had encountered had been castrated. My inexpressive parents were overwhelmed with distress.

I have no nostalgic feelings for Durham, though this was where I spent my childhood and grew up. But there were good moments. My father regularly used to take me for walks with the dog, though not with my mother (who usually said she was too busy). We could walk straight into the countryside from the back of our house and we used to go for long strolls with the dog, past well-cultivated, large allotments and small farms with their assorted livestock. The older I got, the more difficult my father found me (and I him) but for the first ten or so years of my life, my father would make a point of taking breaks from his work to spend time with me and, as I now realize, behaved towards me as if my being a girl made no difference at all to what he expected of me.

Siegi settled into Durham university life. Hobsbawm (2011), a life-long Communist, casts light on how Siegi may well have felt. Writing about the impact of the Korean conflict on him, Hobsbawm says: 'To me, a young fellow, the conventions and courtesies of college life could barely conceal that many, perhaps most, of those I dined with at high table regarded me as a potential or actual traitor.' He continued that the possibility of internment again seemed real. Hobsbawm also reminds us of the execution of the Rosenbergs at this time in the US for being 'atomic spies', and how sensitive the British authorities were to American pressure about spies and 'Commies'. The Cold War did not just make enemies of 'Communists', it created an ideological climate in which left-wing ideas became dangerous.

Even if Siegi's university colleagues did not know the details of his past, his left-wing tendencies would have been evident because of his trade-union activities. The heating up of the Cold War would have made Siegi's time at St Cuthbert's College more difficult and would have reinforced his and Lotte's (understandable) tendency to paranoia.

But Siegi was a hard working lecturer, much liked by his students. He used to invite them home, I remember, for afternoon tea, an approach he may have copied from his Oxford days, but which surely marked him out in the conservative corridors of Durham. Harold Evans had been Siegi's student back in the 1960s and kindly gave me his impressions of Siegi (private conversation, 2012). He described him as whimsical, and 'slightly savvy': sufficiently interested in scholarship to make other, more mundane, matters of less concern to him. He marked students' work with generosity and was very popular with the undergraduates. Evans told me that Siegi stood in a Keynesian tradition; his teaching of economics emphasized the humanitarian, and focused on the impact of government economic policy on the life of the ordinary man and woman, particularly appropriate in the Durham area, with its history of unemployment and deprivation. What was endearing was his enthusiasm for his subject and how relevant he made his teaching. Siegi, Evans said, was very different from many of the other members of the faculty whose heads were buried in Ancient Greece and in Latin, but, regrettably, the students, with their own preoccupations, never really found out what made this unusual lecturer tick.

In 2011, Roger Till, who had been on the staff along with Siegi, wrote to me:

> 'I have pleasant memories of Siegi when he taught at a course in Durham for Trade Unionists [probably in The General and Municipal Workers' Union in the early/mid-1950s, R.T.] which was organized by Peter Kaim-Caudle ...in the University Extra-Mural Department... I could tell how fond of Siegi his students were, not only because they said so but because it

> soon became obvious how successful he had been. With his friendly appearance and sense of humour he had the gift of making his subject really interesting and relevant to the lives of the industrial workers he was teaching' (in personal correspondence).

Siegi also continued writing and getting published regular articles during his time in Durham: 'Price formation and price maintenance in the aluminium market', 1948 (and therefore probably started at Oxford); 'Is Adam Smith out of date?', 1950; 'The scope of automation', 1957, and 'The effect of automation on industrial relations', 1959. This theme crops up repeatedly. 1959–1960 was the year Siegi attended the fourth World Congress of Sociology in Milan as a delegate and read a paper on automation (something I remember his being very proud about). In 1963–1964, he read a paper to the 'Northern Economists' on 'Problems of Mixed Economies', and gave a paper on automation to the National Economic Development office. Apparently 'Mr Moos' got a sabbatical in the first term of 1965–1966 to continue his work on automation, which he hoped would be published (sadly, it never was), but which there was no trace of amongst his voluminous papers. Siegi also read a paper on 'Problems of automation' to the London Conference of the Industrial Welfare Society as well as 'taking part in Extra-Mural activities'. I do not have a copy of this paper, but find its title significant.

My memory of him was that he had an abiding interest in automation, which he saw as having the potential to free labour-time, and as having the potential to end scarcity – therefore as helping to bring about socialism (not that this is ever what he actually said). He was, though this is only a suspicion, disappointed by the relative lack of interest in his progressive take on automation. For him to see automation as problematic suggests a growing awareness that the social relations of production were, as ever, going to thwart this new technique's potential.

We get a brief glimpse of other aspects of his university life from 'The Durham Colleges in the University of Durham [annual] Report by the warden'. The first available report is from 1953–1954, where it is mentioned that Moos, among others, published 'A Survey of Newspaper Reading by University Students'. In 1956, the university rewarded him by conferring on him a Master of Arts. I suspect this was his first ever degree! He seems generally to have maintained a higher profile in relation to the students, than I imagine was customary in the 1950s! There is a reference in the 1957–1958 report (and, less specifically, in following reports) to Mr Moos and two others having read papers to 'very successful' staff-student seminars (also referred to in Siegi's own papers). He seems to have been an active participant in the university's staff-student academic seminars, addressing them in Michaelmas Term 1965 on Britain's economic predicament. He was one of only three staff members who participated in this staff-student cooperation in the late 1950s.

These reports also reveal his abiding interest in extra-mural work, that is, the teaching of non-university students. This is often now seen as good practice but was then seen generally as less prestigious; not by Siegi, who actually wanted to teach the trade unions' students and courses. From 1955 to 1959, 'Moos', again among others in Social Studies, shared the teaching of a course on management problems and other unspecified courses at different times at Sunderland Technical College, Lambton Castle and Durham. In 1958–1959, 'Mr Moos and Mr Odber undertook other extra-mural teaching'. Mr Till's reference to extra-mural teaching provides us with the detail that this was probably to GMWU (General and Municipal Workers' Union) members. Indeed, from 1960 to 1961, the report shows Mr Moos's apparently increasingly radical activities (It is of course possible that these pursuits had previously not been recorded). Mr Moos 'addressed the Trades Councils', a remarkable inclusion in these august and dry reports. The report states that, in 1962–1963, 'He participated in managerial and trade-union courses at Stockton and Conset', (presumably to steel-workers).

Though it does not appear in these reports, I know that throughout his time in Durham, he taught at the WEA classes for miners and ship builders. Maybe these were organized under a separate non-university contract. He would come home from the university, and go out again soon after, to far-flung pit villages and then, even further, to the docks. If he loved anything during his time in Durham, it was this. Not even sickness (for his chest suffered from the climate) would stop him. Here, I suspect, he was able to 'let go', to tell the truths of how the capitalist system really worked, to people who wanted to learn and were open to understanding. Indeed, I wonder whether one attraction of taking the Durham job was not the reputation of the WEA's Newcastle 'pitmen painters', reawakening a belief that he could, after all, still be an 'organic intellectual' in the class struggle. I suspect that, as he watched the Cold War slowly loosen its grip (though Cuba was yet to come), Siegi was gradually feeling safe enough to involve himself in activities, while only on the margins of the class struggle, at least remotely attached to it.

But he was also busy on other fronts, according to the university reports. With Mr Odber, he attended the annual Conference of the Association of University lecturers in Economics, and, alone, attended a Conference of the University Industrial Relations Association in Oxford. In 1958–1959, he gave lectures at Sunderland Technical College to the Prudential Assurance Company and to chartered accountants. In the late 1950s, 'Mr Moos' attended a conference in London on Pay Structure (but no more detail given). In 1960–1961 and the following years, he addressed the Bernard Gilpin Society, as well as giving two talks to the British Association for the Advancement of Science, the Rotary Club (!), the National Coal Board and the Socratic Society. In 1962–1963, 'Mr Moos' lectured at the Commonwealth Institute Conference. Though no details are known, my guess is this would have been a task he prized because of its internationalism. In 1962–1963, Siegi also attended the International Congress of Collective Economy in Rome, where he met for the first time, at least in a very long while, his cousin, Lorre, who had escaped from Germany, while still a teenager, to Italy. [192]

But the reports also highlight by omission what Siegi was not involved in. Professor Morris-Jones was a visiting professor of Commonwealth History in India; Dr Bromhead was a visiting professor of Social Sciences in Florida; Professor Morris-Jones conducted a round-table Conference on Civil-Military relations (!) among many other roles; Mr Allen was a member of the research committee of the North East Industrial Development Association. Not to ignore Dr Blair, who gave a course of extra-mural lectures on law. (In subsequent years, it is stated, 'Dr Blair made frequent appearances on Tyne Tees Television' and lectured to police cadets. And, yes, it is the father of the warmonger, a leading Conservative: the Chair of the University Conservative Association and a figure whose legalistic idiocies I remember my mild-mannered father getting heated about over our meals.) My father appears to have largely stuck to his teaching, I suspect in part, because this was his preference, and because his politics did not encourage his being put forward for more 'prestigious' roles.

This was the 1950s and first half of the 1960s, a period still under the thrall of the Cold War. Outside a very small group of revolutionaries, mostly Trotskyists, and the CP, which Siegi would not have touched, there were few places in which to be politically active, especially in Durham, far distant from the early political rumblings of dissent in London. Siegi's main forum was his AUT branch, where he had many arguments with the right faction in the union, in particular with Leo Blair.

Clearing my parents' mountains of papers, I unfortunately threw away most of the union stuff, but a couple of items slipped through. There is Siegi's letter against the appointment of Chairs of Department in favour of their election, a really radical demand for that time (and still for this), and another letter against the University Grants Committee's unachievable intention of measuring student effort as a basis for monies to be bestowed (how topical that is today!).

Siegi's final year in Durham was 1965–1966. The general election of 1966, which confirmed Labour's hold on power, took place in March and Siegi left Durham soon after for his job at the Board of Trade. The university report is more fulsome in its praise than was often the case. It states: 'Pleasure is tinged with regret on the retirement of Mr Moos [who was 62 in 1966]...Mr Moos has been teaching Economics at Durham since 1947...The Department and the various waves of students who have been taught Statistics and Economic Organization by Mr Moos owe him a great debt for his patience, insight and generous bestowal of his time.'

Outside the umbrella of the University, though noted in their Yearbook, was that 'He took a leading part in local activities in connection with the Freedom from Hunger campaign.' Later on, and not included in these reports, was his activity in 'War on Want' (unfortunately, I threw away this documentation also). I recall that he was their local treasurer, and seemed to put a lot of time into their activities, frequently departing for their evening meetings. This is hardly a display of his earlier active politics but does show his continuing commitment to justice and equality. Whether it was through his involvement in Freedom from Hunger or War on Want, placards and paintings to be sold to raise funds sometimes appeared in our house, not that, in its chaos, one would really have noticed.

Siegi continued to campaign, even if it was mainly through letters and articles. It seems from a letter to the *Observer* in 1962 that Siegi was campaigning against Britain joining the Common Market (17 October 1962). I have a copy of a letter he sent to *The Times* on 23 March 1965. Clearly aware far earlier than many about the growing war and American atrocities in Vietnam, he condemns *The Times'* leader for assuring their readers that the gas used in Vietnam was less serious than in the first world war. 'Why,' he writes, 'did you not add not as bad as Hitler's gas chambers? Then we would have felt thoroughly comfortable.' It was not published.

He wrote frequently for the *Northern Echo*, a prestigious local paper, then under the editorship of Harold Evans (before he rose to higher things), who was, as already discussed, once a student of Siegi's. Harold Evans explained to me that he thought of Siegi as a practical thinker and was glad to get him into the *Northern Echo*, indeed was touched that Siegi was willing to help him out. For example, in April 1962, Siegi wrote the key analysis of the Budget (3 April 1962, letter from Evans) for which Siegi was thanked profusely (12 April 1962, letter from Evans, both in personal possession). There is another intriguing letter to Siegi, from 1965, from McAlpine, representing a Scottish company, which was some sort of cooperative made up of trade union representatives, community centres and churches, which wanted to produce ethical products. There is no way of knowing how this all developed, but it is interesting that, of all the people possible, it was Siegi whom they approached.

I used to find my parents' paranoia when we were in Durham not only oppressive but also unintelligible. Why on earth would they think our house was watched? Did they have to cover the phone with cushions to stop their conversations being overheard? But they might have had cause. The CIA requested Lotte's file from MI5 as late as the first years of the 1950s. Moreover, recently opened MI5 files have divulged that they were still keeping a close eye on Peter Pears in 1951 on the grounds that he was the Vice-President of the Musicians Union for Peace and a member of the League for Democracy, both described by MI5 as 'Communist Front organizations'. Two years later, in 1953, MI5 were concerned with Pears' partner, Britten, as a well-known pacifist. MI5's file on Priestley started in 1933 and effectively continued till 1960. What alerted them appears to be that he was a member of the early National Council for Civil Liberties in the 1930s. The files reveal they were opening his letters, keeping a collection of articles by and about him in the press, and as late as 1956, had a report, presumably from a 'spy', of a meeting which Priestley attended about police powers! He was, they said, associated with left-wing causes, but the appreciation that 'none [were] Communist inspired' did not stop the surveillance (KV21/3774/5).[193] My parents' 'paranoia' may have been well founded, after all.

Life in Durham was not a happy time for my family. My mother, unlike Siegi, had no public role to play beyond that of mother and housewife, and, though this may have fitted in with the 1950s' image of what the married woman was all about, it certainly did not suit her. She loathed Durham's provincialism and conservatism. Unknown to me, she spent much of her time writing, hidden away in my parents' bedroom. She succeeded in having a play put on in the West End in 1962: *Come Back with Diamonds*, which was a dramatization of her time in Moscow and did not present the Stalinist regime in a positive light. It was booed off the stage by, my mother stated, a Stalinist mob who sat in the front seats – this event is even recorded in the reviews. So much must have been riding on this final success after so much loss that for the play to be withdrawn would have been devastating. I imagine how much she would have wanted to turn her back on Durham and the evidence suggests she did not start writing again till after their move to London.

Durham was also where I grew up and when Siegi, generally working, and Lotte, generally out of reach in her bedroom, had to bring up their daughter. Looking back, I am aware, as I was not at the time, of how deeply isolated our little family unit was, without any extended family to speak of. My parents never talked about their families and I was aware from an early age that this was a forbidden zone, about which one must never ask. Moreover, we lived in a small conservative ecclesiastic city where my parents had few friends. (Gary Sargent, the artist, was an exception, but they only got to know him and his wife, Val, in their last years in Durham.)

While I loved my father, he expected his child to conform to rules which even in the 1950s would have seemed archaic in many households. He had a room in the house which was his study (my mother had to use their bedroom for her copious writing) which I was not allowed to enter and I expected to get shouted at if I did dare to knock at the door. I had to find a way to amuse myself as a child which is how books became my best friends. Till about the age of 15, when I finally rebelled, I was banished to my tiny bedroom at 7pm and would sit in bed reading and miserable. I guess the ghosts of the past were allowed out after I was sent off to bed and Siegi and Lotte could talk to each other out of earshot about what they never wanted me to hear.

My father took occasional breaks from his work to go for walks with me and the dog. I suspect to make up for the absence of a family network, he found dogs to befriend me, which indeed they did. My mother did not sympathize with this initiative and never had anything to do with either of our two dogs. The second dog, Biscuit (after the brandy), was a lurcher which my father obtained from a farm, a mix of a collie and a greyhound and absurdly fast. Talking to Ken Worpole, it appears my father told him after Biscuit's death how much he liked lurchers because they were the dog preferred by the Durham miners.

The older I got, the worse things became. As I reached adolescence, my father increasingly frightened me. There was a dress code that I would not have dared to break, of wearing loose demure clothes. As my mother told me, 'Your father does not want to see your breasts.' (!) I stopped wanting to be anywhere near him. Even in the sixth-form, I was rarely allowed out and my friends were not welcomed. The appearance of a 'boyfriend' was an emotional disaster and effectively caused me to end my relationship with my father till I became pregnant decades later. It is difficult to square my father with Siegi, the man who lived in bohemian Berlin in the late 1920s and dedicated himself to revolutionary struggle. My guess is that both he and my mother were walking on such emotionally thin ice, that they could not cope with any sort of 'disturbances' in their lives.

My parents adopted a consciously assimilationist perspective to my schooling. I was first sent to a Church of England primary school and then to the local grammar school. My parents had rejected the route most middle-class Durham parents took of sending their daughters to the private school, or of sending me to the more prestigious and predominantly middle-class grammar school in Newcastle. Durham Girls' Grammar School's pupils were, most unusually, largely from families where the father was working at or down the pits. While I had few friends at grammar school, I learnt from the parents of those I had, rather than from my 'socialist' parents, about the working class, the importance of trade unions and class solidarity. This affected me in a way that my parents may not have anticipated and did not always accept. My father actively discouraged me from any political interest, banning me, for example, from joining CND. I assume he thought he was keeping me safe. Far from my following in my parents' political footsteps, as most people assume, it was my act of rebelling against their politics which took me into the revolutionary left. I escaped from them to university at Oxford in 1962.

Once, already at Oxford, I enquired of my mother whether I was Jewish. I remember clearly that I assumed, correctly, that the answer would be 'no'. Like many émigrés who had had to leave Germany because of their left-wing politics, my parents rejected any label of 'Judaism'. My father defined himself in terms of a much broader political struggle, in which Judaism played no part. (Indeed, my mother, in her controversial way, always insisted that the German Jews had not fought back against the Nazis, so were no use to anybody.) In their desire to bring me up to be safe and integrated, they had left behind their pasts. It was left to me, already in late middle-age, to try to find, and wonder how to remember, our two families' murdered dead.

Siegi and Lotte moved to London in 1966. This was made possible by the election, for the second time, of a Labour Government, under Harold Wilson. My father was invited to become a special adviser at the Board of Trade, a post he took up in 1966 and which lasted till Labour's defeat in 1970. He had known Balogh at the Institute of Statistics in Oxford and stayed in contact with him ever since. (The last letter to Balogh, in his records, is from October 1962, commenting on how the *Observer* had chosen Balogh's article over his (probably anti-) Common Market submission.) Moreover, he also knew Harold Wilson from the Institute. My father never boasted but once told me in his matter-of-fact way that he and Wilson (and a third person whose name I cannot remember) had worked together on a project for Beveridge. It seems likely that this combination of contacts put him in a good position to get the job at the Board of Trade and finally got him and Lotte their ticket out of Durham.

Endnotes

188. Emil Klaus Fuchs joined the German Communist Party in the 1930s but was forced to flee to Britain in 1933 when the Nazis came to power. In 1939, when the second world war broke out, he was detained on the Isle of Man and, as happened more frequently with Communist refugees, was sent to Canada. He was allowed to return (to Edinburgh) in 1941. His scientific expertise led to his being recruited to join the nuclear weapons programme and, in 1946, he was offered a post at the UK Atomic Energy Research Establishment. In late 1941, Fuchs contacted the German

Communist, Jürgen Kuczynski (referred to earlier in this study, and who was a Soviet spy – although Special Branch appeared unaware of this). Fuchs offered the Russians information and subsequently passed on secret atomic research. Fuchs continued spying until he was finally exposed in 1949. Fuchs later stated that he had been motivated by a belief that the Soviets had a right to know about the atomic bomb project, not out of a desire for private gain. He was sentenced to fourteen years' imprisonment and stripped of his British citizenship. Granted an amnesty after nine years, he spent the rest of his life in East Germany.

189. It was not just Communists the government were suspicious of. In 1950, MI5 recommended that 'members of the Revolutionary Communist Party, a group to the left of the Communist Party, "should not in general be permitted to acquire the citizenship".... The Home Office seems to have agreed the slightly more nuanced position that "applications from existing members of these parties or groups [RCP (Revolutionary Communist Party), Jehovah's Witnesses etc.!] and from persons whose present or past associations with these parties or groups were such as to cast doubt on their loyalty, should be refused".' (From I. Birchall, *Tony Cliff: A Marxist for his Time* (Bookmarks, London, 2011).) Indeed, Tony Cliff, who arrived in the UK from Palestine, was consistently refused naturalization, despite the support of Michael Foot the MP, and, for Cliff's later application, the Deputy Leader of the Labour Party, because of Cliff's revolutionary beliefs.(My thanks to Ian Birchall for this point and source material.)

190. Gerhard Hinze was under constant surveillance by MI5 as a suspected Communist and indeed had only been allowed to disembark at Harwich in 1938 after the intervention of the MP, Ellen Wilkinson, who agreed at the last moment to act

as his guarantor. Hinze was one of the Communist refugees who were deported to Canada from their internment on the Isle of Man. Soon after, he was allowed to return to the UK. Appearing before an Aliens Tribunal, he denied being a member of the Communist Party. Disillusioned with the Communist Party, he was one of the very few 'Communists' who did not consider returning to Germany. He took his British acting career increasingly seriously and, by 1950, MI5 opined he had become an anti-Communist (Brinson and Dove, 2014, and personal conversations with Hinze's son).

191. In my extensive wanderings around the 'second generation' in the UK, that is, people who were the children of the refugees from Nazism, I have not come across anybody else whose parents had, like mine, fled Nazism for the UK as committed political/Communist refugees, had stayed on the left and chosen to stay in the UK. The one person with some similarities is Hinze's son, but his mother was British; his parents first fled to the USSR, and then, when they did 'return' to the UK, the father moved completely away from the left. Siegi and Lotte's isolation must have been intense.
192. Lorre was not Jewish which may have helped her survive under fascism, although her husband, a diplomat, was a resistance fighter in the mountains in the North of Italy.
193. As late as 1959, MI5 were still concerned with some of the leading members of the British 'literati': Priestley, Pears, Britten, Dame Peggy Ashcroft, Stanley Spender and Michael Redgrave amongst others. (KV2/3215, 3822; *Guardian*: 'MI5 targeted JB Priestley, Peter Pears and Michael Redgrave, released papers show', 28 February 2014.)

Chapter 9

1966–1988 London. Beaten but not defeated

The Board of Trade and Harold Wilson

Through the good works of a very distant relative, my parents succeeded in renting a beautiful Crown estate maisonette, opposite Victoria Park in Hackney; Siegi was eligible as an official of the Crown. Siegi had an 'office' in the lower ground floor and here he stored all his old manuscripts and economics books (and a lot else besides, which I was only to discover when I finally emptied their home). He decorated his desk with shells and bits of driftwood which the sea and sand had sculpted. He hung a picture of Mandelstam, a Russian poet sent to the camps under Stalin who consequently died, right by the door where it was impossible to miss.

I imagine that their home on the edges of the East End suited them, reminding them of the bohemian/working-class areas where Siegi had lived in Berlin, even if where they lived, next to Victoria Park, was a middle-class enclave. But they would not have wanted to live in a bourgeois area such as Hampstead had become. They did believe, though, that their area would 'come up', that any moment now local shops selling their favourite coffee beans would appear – and they were right, but this did not happen till after their deaths. Being away from the conservative claustrophobia of Durham and back in an environment where ideas were important and debated suited them both well.

Till the fall of the Labour government, Siegi continued to work at the Board of Trade, as an adviser to the Labour government. The Board of Trade remained as a product of a 'social-democratic' perspective on the role of the state in the economy. Although this is not the place to go into the arguments about the beginning of the 'social democratic decline' or the growing importance of the 'world' economy, the Wilson government had a commitment to trying to bring up the less developed regions and to limit the control of the multinationals. Wilson's concerns were the importance of the 'white heat of technology', and that British economic innovation and production were being increasingly overtaken. Wilson committed the government from 1964 to putting state resources into Research and Development (R and D), something Siegi was also strongly in favour of. Siegi wrote for a variety of Board of Trade anti-monopolization papers, something which allowed him to combine his criticisms of capitalism and his belief that the role of the state included intervention to prevent industrial injustice and monopolization. When the Conservatives were elected in 1970, Siegi, then 66, finally did retire, though I doubt if he had a choice.

The growth in the left, particularly in the UK but also elsewhere, maybe the denunciation of Stalin (even if in limited terms) by Khrushchev in 1956, the convulsions of Europe in 1968, including the (thwarted) uprising in Czechoslovakia, left Siegi and Lotte feeling more able to go back onto the streets in support of the many demonstrations, in the late 1960s and early 1970s, against the Vietnam war. Even so, they would march on the pavement, alongside the demonstration. 'Come on, join us,' I chided them, if we met. But their fear ran too deep. Later on, after 1979, both of my parents hated Thatcher, understanding her as a class warrior and both wrote excoriating poetry about her. After my father's death, I remember my mother coming out in support of the miners. By then, she marched with us and I was proud of her.

My father, somewhat to my surprise, did accept the copies of *Labour Worker* I arrived with, though my mother was probably the keener reader. I would discover, well concealed of course, copies he must have bought in public places, a sign that, by the early 1970s, he was no longer as terrified of the shadows in his past. I guess the founding of International Socialism (IS) in the early 1960s, with its politics of 'neither Washington nor Moscow', would have felt like the lifting of a very dark cloud. I can imagine he was very aware of International Socialists /Socialist Workers Party increasingly becoming a rival to the influence, ideologically if not numerically, of the CP. Not that he ever agreed with the position of state capitalism or a more Trotskyist position more generally. Though his reasons were opaque, I suspect, he maintained an abiding hope that the USSR would turn out all right in the end. My suspicion is that, despite his awareness of the 'disappearance' of Brian, he continued to believe that the USSR still had the potential to become a socialist society if there were enough pressure and organization from below.[194]

When I came to sort his piles and piles of old papers, I found hidden away copies of old *Solidarity* papers and a variety of shop stewards' movement literature from the 1970s. He had, in other words, maintained his interest in left debates. Despite his very real fears that political engagement could lead to his removal from the UK till his naturalization in 1948, despite his severe disillusionment with Stalinism, despite the political amnesia imposed by the Cold War, he never left behind his youthful commitment to socialism or lost his interest in the debates amongst the revolutionary left, even if he could no longer place himself within them.

Some time during the late 1960s, he did finally return to some of his ideas from the period after he had left the KPD. Probably inspired by the New Left and the student revolts and mass strikes of the period, he wrote a major manuscript aimed at laying a new basis for Socialism, which was rejected by publishers – we know because in this case he kept the rejection slips. Siegi's political writings represented a noble but failed attempt to make socialism relevant to the present day, not helped by his position on the USSR, a defining issue by the end of the 1960s, which remained opaque, and his ambiguity about the possibility of left reformism, which detract from the usefulness of this work.

Around the same time, Siegi also had a brief political dalliance with Ralph Miliband,[195] who was looking around for comrades to help build a new socialist organization, albeit one which Miliband increasingly saw as much as a pressure group on the Labour Party, as acting outside it. Although I believe letters were exchanged, this project came to nothing at the time.[196] Although initially excited by the prospect of working for a non-Communist/anti-Stalinist and non-Trotskyist/non-'ultra-left' organization committed to non-parliamentary as well as parliamentary activity to bring about change, Siegi may well have been deterred by Miliband's failure to emphasize class as the fulcrum of change and his orientation towards working within the Labour Party. For all that, the fact that Siegi was willing to think about re-entering the socialist fray, bears testimony to how far he was revisiting old political pastures.

Despite working as an adviser to the Labour government, Siegi was never tempted by membership of the Labour Party. There is an apparent inconsistency here. But working within the state to limit capitalism's excesses is a classically left-reformist position. Siegi's refusal to align himself with the Labour Party is more significant given that the British Labour Party had never had the opportunity to betray the British working class as had the SPD, so Siegi's non-involvement should not simply be taken for granted. After all, Siegi and Lotte's first good friends in the UK, the Woods, were to become key Labour stalwarts. Their best friends in Oxford, the Worswicks, were also strongly committed to the Labour Party.[197]

But Siegi had seen the Social Democrats at work in Germany and would have remembered their betrayals in 1918–1919, the murder of Liebknecht and Luxemburg by troops under a Social Democratic government and, later, their refusal to collaborate in an anti-Nazi alliance. According to Sylvia Worswick (in private conversation), Siegi broke off all contact with David Worswick, his oldest living friend, who had run the then prestigious National Institute of Economic and Social Research for seventeen years, when Worswick accepted a CBE in 1981. Siegi did not believe in accepting honours from the state, particularly when it was the Conservatives, the class enemies, in government. Though David lived till 2001, twenty years after their political falling-out, Siegi refused even to send David Christmas cards after that. My father's revolutionary instincts ran deep. Siegi had seen too much of the deadly effects of reformism to ever countenance joining the Labour Party.

The betrayal of the 1919 German revolution

Clearing his papers, I found an article, I presume written to commemorate the 50th anniversary of the defeat of the German uprising. It is illuminating in terms of how constant Siegi's political concerns still were in the late 1960s, as well as being a comment (albeit limited) on the event itself.(Like so much of his political writings, these papers have no title, author or date, and virtually no referencing.)

The article's purpose is to demonstrate a clear connection between 1919 and the coming to power of the Nazis. This seminal event in German, and indeed European, history followed the abdication of Kaiser Wilhelm, as a result of Germany's defeat in the first world war and the declaration of the Weimar Republic. Its defeat dented Lenin's and the Bolsheviks' hopes of the USSR not remaining isolated. It also ended with the murder of Luxemburg and Liebknecht and sowed many seeds of fundamental hostility towards the SPD by the KPD.

Siegi's emphasis is on the betrayal by the Social Democratic leadership. He writes of what was happening in the 'Councils':

'They were victorious, the "moderate left". They had routed

> the left "extremists". Proudly they formed a coalition government...with the premiership and the chief ministries in control of the army, police...Less than fifteen years later, a national socialist [government] formed a "Government of National Concentration" [on] January 30 1933. This is how the moderates' victory over the extremists ended.'

The article continues by describing the start of the German revolution. The 'flag of revolution' was first raised in Kiel on 5 November 1918. The first meeting of the Council of Workers and Soldiers was attended by some 3,000 delegates, containing equal numbers of representatives from the majority Social Democrats and the USP. The 'inner cabinet' was similarly to be made up of three from each constituency. But, Siegi laments, the nominations for this Committee did not come from the deputies. Instead, the 'Chairman of the Deputies meetings' simply appointed them.[198]

The adviser to the 'Council of Soldiers' Deputies', was Noske[199], the article reminds us, who was soon to become the 'butcher of the radical left'. Always sympathetic towards the military, Noske was to actively encourage the Freikorps in its murder of the left. The Freikorps was effectively the old German Army, banned by the victorious western allies, but now operating as mercenaries under the command of rightist generals. Noske's first pronouncement, in the name of the Soldiers' Councils, was that 'unauthorised persons' (that is, except the military and police) must immediately surrender their arms. Karl Liebknecht, the 'leader' of the extreme left, proposed that all executive, legislative and judicial power should be handed over to the Workers' and Soldiers Councils, a proposal rapidly scotched by the Social-Democrat majority on the Council.

Siegi's analysis is detailed, revealing the process whereby the revolution was lost. Only three weeks after they had been established, many Councils had been attacked and dissolved, including by the army. There was then a crucial showdown. The

Chairman of Congress put forward the following demands: 'immediate arrest of the generals, disarming of the officers, formation of a Red Guard...to disarm the counter-revolution'. Congress accepted the 'seven Hamburg points', including that the Councils of Soldiers' Deputies were to be responsible for maintaining discipline and electing their own officers.

However, Ebert, who professed himself to be a socialist,[200] argued that these positions were only advisory – final orders should be determined by the Cabinet of Six (point 8). Although initially this position was defeated, Ebert, after talks with General Groaner, who promised him the loyalty of the Reichswehr if he stopped this nonsense, informed Congress that it was army control that had to be maintained. Only two of the USP deputies strongly objected: Congress would become a mere talking shop. Ebert argued successfully that 'the decisions of Congress were not to be carried out until the administrative orders for transacting them had been issued.' The Councils were thus deprived of power. The revolution... had been broken.

The moderate left, [particularly as represented by Ebert], felt justified in their pseudo-democratic actions by what they interpreted as the needs of the hour – to protect the new order, to save the economic life of the country, to prevent anarchy and the new [Weimar] Government being overthrown by right-wing forces' and to stop civil war. Ebert was moreover committed to stopping the 'militant left...which wanted a *"genuine grass-root- democratic society"*' (my italics).

The catastrophic consequences of the defeat were soon seen, for not just the 'extreme left' but the moderate left as well. The German army, the *Reichwehr*, was formally established, some of whose units supported and fought for the ultra-right Kapp Putsch in 1921, only two years later, wearing the swastika on their helmets (at that time the symbol of the new Kapp government). Siegi understood the centrality of class action. He wrote: 'Workers' resistance led to the collapse of the putsch', but, he reminds us, only one of its leaders was ever punished.

But the Social Democratic fudge with the military did not keep them in power. By mid-1920, the moderate socialists themselves had lost the key positions in government. In addition, 'between January 1919 and June 1922, the right committed 354 political murders.'[201] The *Reichwehr* were to become Hitler's willing executioners, marching through and subjugating Europe and murdering or forcing into exile *all* opponents, including many of Ebert's own supporters. All over Europe, the strong democracy that Ebert had promised proved strong against the radical left and weak against the radical right. This carnage [following Hitler's take over] was nothing less than the direct outcome of events in the early years of the Weimar Republic. They were victorious then, the 'moderate' left. They had routed their 'extremists'.

The article reveals how strongly Siegi had held onto his convictions. There is no doubting from this analysis that the Social Democrats are seen (correctly) as responsible for the crushing of the revolution and that they thereby laid the foundations for Hitler. Siegi's politics from the early 1930s shine through in this article, almost as if nothing had happened in between. Yet there is fudge – when he writes of 'democratic rank and file' action, one can hear his attempts to distance himself from the autocratic pattern of the KPD, but what this phrase actually meant is obscure. Siegi was also, I suggest, positioning his – and so many others' – exile as a long-term consequence of the betrayal by the moderate left in 1919.

The last years

One of my most touching memories of my father was when he turned out to support a demonstration in favour of the Kilburn Four in 1983. I and three others were being threatened with expulsion from our union, NATFHE, for supporting a black colleague, John Fernandes, who had gone to the media with accusations about the racism of the police cadets he was teaching. The management of the College of North-West London initially supported the police and were going to sack John, but after a vigorous campaign, kept him on. The union leadership and some of the CP however took a dim view of our campaign. The hearing to consider whether to expel us (which we won) was in the Imperial Hotel (given the nature of this dispute, this name seemed remarkably appropriate!). Unannounced, my father arrived and stood with the small crowd of people shouting slogans in our support. I was hardly on speaking terms with him at this point and I still do not know how he knew about the demonstration. I will always remember him for supporting me that day. Indeed, carefully filed away amongst his papers, is a letter to the *New Statesman* written in our support by another member of NATFHE (T. Butler).

Although my father's appearance at the Kilburn Four case encouraged me to see him and Lotte, I still had little to do with them till I became pregnant in 1986, only two years before his death. But, from his letters, I gather that he had kept involved in the local political scene: he wrote letters and went to meetings to defend the wonderful Victoria Park, which lay a stone's throw from their front door, and was also active in the local Pensioners Campaign, penning letters to MPs and councillors demanding more money for pensioners. He told me that he sometimes used to go the local magistrates and Crown Court and even on occasions to the Old Bailey and, dressed in his smartest clothes, would sit bang opposite the magistrate or judge, who, not knowing who this well dressed gentleman could be, would feel more cautious about handing out unnecessarily punitive sentences to the local working-class miscreants. I am sure Siegi saw this as a form of political activity which he could keep doing sitting down!

After retirement, Siegi also started to go to painting and framing classes and an amazing stream of expressionist pictures, undoubtedly influenced by the expressionist styles prevalent in Berlin in the 1920s and 1930s, started to appear all over the house; stacks of his work made his office almost impassable. He won second prize one year in the Hackney local artists' competition. Here were miners crouching in the Durham earth deep underground, 'No ballgames' notices fixed on the walls of council estates, a woman lying in her blood– called 'To the Unknown Soldier'. But there were also pictures of my mother, hat on head, looking out to some past future, and a picture I have on my bedroom wall to this day of the Paratroopers in the 1974 Portuguese revolution, who had gone over to the side of the left, standing guard on a roof top. Look, his picture says, there is always ground for hope.

He and Lotte became active members of a local community cultural centre in Hackney, and, later, in other local writing groups, in particular the Approach Tavern group, and my father happily returned to writing poetry, much polemical, railing against injustice, a collection of which were published posthumously, called *Mind the Gap*. He had already started to select poems for a volume, I think to be published by Centerprise, while still alive, but Lotte, with the help of Ken Worpole and others, completed the task.

Ken Worpole ran the Hackney Writers' Workshop which met at Centerprise in Dalston from the early 1970s to the mid-1980s, and became Siegi and Lotte's friend. He kindly gave me his impressions of them. He was first introduced to them via Celia Stubbs some time in the mid-1970s. Celia Stubbs, who was then a local Hackney community worker, had met Siegi and Lotte and, discovering their literary interests, introduced them to Ken. From then till his death, Siegi eagerly attended the fortnightly evening meetings with Lotte, and, even in his 80s, come rain or shine, had caught a bus from Mare Street to Dalston and back again, a journey which required a change of buses and a solid walk to the bus stop. It was a very mixed group; the average age was in the late 20s – Siegi and Lotte were far older than anybody else. But the others appreciated and warmed to Siegi and Lotte, as Siegi and Lotte appreciated them. Lotte was the more dominant in the relationship, Ken told me, something which impressed the group, unaccustomed to such feisty older women (and this was after all 'only' the mid- to late 1970s). They were constructive about others' work – Lotte was the more discerning and astute, Siegi more benign. 'They enjoyed the Writers' Group, as we enjoyed them.'

Siegi and Lotte were both more prolific than anybody else. Their poetry was well received. But there was a difference in their styles. Siegi's poetry used rhyme and was often written in ballad form, of a Brechtian type, which could have been declaimed in a theatrical setting. Lotte on occasions brought wonderful short stories, inspired in part by Greek mythology which she introduced some of the group to. Siegi and Lotte's writing carried a strong political commitment; they eschewed writing which focused more on the confessional or the more personal, though most of the group were in fact political. They started to attend public events and read their work. Some of these took place with Hackney and Islington Music Workshop, a fruitful mix. Lotte became relatively well known and started to be invited to a variety of gatherings in her own right, including by feminist circles.

But Ken Worpole said that, nevertheless, although they were both very sociable and very charming, they remained something of a closed book. 'Together, they were an impregnable force.' Neither ever attended without the other and they were 'loyal and defensive' of each other. Ken knew they came from Durham and almost nothing else. He had been invited to their home for tea two or three times, and they to his, a few times for supper. They kept themselves to themselves, Ken stated. They came across as a couple who had known difficult times. People guessed that they had had a troubled earlier life and kept a respectful distance. Yet, for all this relative absence of intimacy, it was Ken whom Lotte turned to on the death of Siegi – suggestive of the absence of really close friends.

I have chosen three short poems from the posthumously published collection *Mind the Gap* and selected from a fourth. The first is, I presume, essentially autobiographical; the second polemical; the third, four-liner, a bitter sweet comment on how Nazism and repression had not bowed Siegi, and the fourth, written I suspect in his very last years, reveals how far Siegi may have been beaten but had never been defeated.

HOW

How to sow
When no longer
The seed harbours life

How to harvest
When the fruit
Has not ripened

How to work
When the hours drag
Drained of joy

How to rest
When so much
Needs doing

How to celebrate
When the soul
Feels numb

BACKLASH

The Tolpuddle martyrs
Entered the fray
There happened a 'backlash'
They were sent away
Now children learn the lesson
Avoid all strife
And live forever
A Good Dog's life

TO HELL

I know the type of face
I know the type of phrase
And I say 'No'
For socialism's sake.

RESURRECTION

Where can I find you
Dreams of my youth?...

I dreamt
That all did share
Their labour's fruit
Their joy and pain
That all did care
For all…

I went and searched…
[And] found a tombstone

Weathered
With the inscription
'Born in innocence
Murdered
By enemies of hope…'

Dream
Dream…
Under tomorrow's sun
All equal
None outcast.

Siegi's return to writing and reading his poems to a radical audience of semi-working class and professional people, for the first time since 1933, must have helped him feel that it was good to be alive. Many of the people he and Lotte rubbed shoulders with were to become famous for their radical and working class orientated writing – Ken Worpole, Roger Mills and others – and I can imagine my father enjoying their, then, youthful comradeship and interest in what he represented and had experienced.

But friendship was another matter. There is a fascinating letter, dated 9 November 1979, from Ron Barnes, a London artist well known at the time for his 'naif' portrayal of working-class life, lamenting the loss of the friendship of Lotte and Siegi. Although the exact cause is not clear (and maybe never was), it appears that what Lotte and Siegi held against him was his lack of punctuality. Ron laments in the letter that he had to work and therefore laboured under that tyranny. No wonder my parents had so few friends given this level of exactitude. (I do remember when my mother was asked by a psychiatrist during a case conference, one time she was in hospital, to tell me one good thing about me. 'She is punctual,' is all she said.)

Lotte and Siegi were getting on well; indeed, I suspect that it was in these twilight years, that their relationship blossomed. But activity was getting more strenuous for Siegi. He was still going out and doing the shopping, carrying back two heavy shopping bags, his lips turning slightly blue.

The birth of his grandson, Josh, was a source of unbelievable delight to him. He, and not my mother, visited me in hospital almost every day (I'd ended up with a caesarean and was in for almost two weeks). His pleasure was palpable. I did not appreciate at the time quite how significant the birth of a grandchild was to him. Indeed, it was many years till I worked out that Josh was almost certainly the only direct descendant of any of his family going back to his eight great-grandparents. Although I'd given Josh the surname of 'Moos' because of an embedded feminism and in no way to please him, I think that knowing his family name lived on, and just maybe even more so because it was the surname of a boy, must have made him very happy.

My pregnancy also had the profoundly important effect of bringing us back to speaking again. He was so uncensorious when I explained my situation to him, that I realized, after avoiding him for the previous 20-odd years, that I wanted to see him again. It was in the nick of time. He had just over a year to live. I and Josh saw him and Lotte as often as possible, though he found the demands of an energetic baby (who walked at eight months) increasingly difficult to cope with.

After a fall in the house, he was taken to Homerton Hospital. They showed little interest in this old man and after a few terrible days he died. But as he lay there, tubes coming out of everywhere, an oxygen mask essential for him to breathe, he pointed to the wall at the non-existent television screen. 'Rubbish!' he announced. 'Football. Another opium of the masses.' As he lay dying, unable any more to speak or make a sound, he wiggled his toes to the beat as I sang him the Internationale.

Epilogue

My father, despite the terrible losses which would have felled a lesser man, kept an insistence on hope. When I was a teenager, he banned me from reading *1984* and *Brave New World*, a prohibition which only encouraged me to read them. The realization came far later that, despite the defeat of the Communist principles he had fought for, despite the evident horrors of the USSR, despite the bloody defeat of the left in Germany and the destruction of his and Lotte's families, he did not want me to suck in the message of despair that these two books impart.

I remember him soon after Gorbachev came to power, about a year before he died, astonishing me when he said, 'Marx never said the revolution could not come from above.' (Both my parents excelled at logical niceties in argument.) I argued, but, looking back, I realize that my father wanted to grasp at any straw of hope. Not for him the slide into hopelessness, not for him a belief in the inevitability of oligarchy and the impotence of the left, not even for him the parliamentary road.

Yet, as we watch this revolutionary from the early 1930s, we cannot but observe a slide towards left-Keynesianism, a commitment to reforming the role of the state, maybe because this was the only way he could earn a living, maybe because in the absence of any real revolutionary movement in the UK, left-Keynesian was as radical as it got.

After he left Durham, for all his, very real, commitment to his students and his research, I never sensed any feeling of loss. I suspect that the last 20 years of his life, when he was back in London, back in the thick of debates about writing and its role in the struggle; when my partner brought the debates into his home about the nature of the USSR and argued volubly for state capitalism; when Siegi returned to participating in the occasional demonstration against the Vietnam war; when he went back to writing his powerful poetry against injustice – that is when he was able to remember and retrieve the person he felt he truly was.

At Siegi's funeral, my mother read, so appropriately, from William Morris's, *A dream of John Ball* : 'I pondered all these things, and how men fight and lose the battle, and the thing that they fought for comes about in spite of their defeat, and when it comes, turns out not to be what they meant, and other men have to fight for what they meant under another name.'[202]

Endnotes

194. This is a position akin to Deutscher's. See, for example, Isaac Deutscher *Ideological Trends in the USSR* (1967), 8 April 1967, at a conference on 'The Soviet Union, 1917–1967' at the State University of New York. Binghampton. http://www.marxists.org/archive/deutscher/1967/ideological_trends_USSR.htm, accessed 12 January 2014.
195. Ralph Miliband is not just famous as the father of Ed and David, but as the author of a couple of brilliant books critical of the parliamentary route: *Parliamentary Socialism* (1961), his best work, and *The State in Capitalist Society* (1969). Miliband had been thinking about the possibility of building an independent socialist organization since the days of the first New Left in the late 1950s, but it was not until the publication of *Moving On* in 1976 that he explicitly delineated the crippling effects of a belief in working within the Labour Party and argued for the formation of a separate party (Blackledge, 2011).
196. In the late 1970s and early1980s, there was a more sustained attempt to establish a Socialist Society, in which many leading names who were to the left of Labour were initially involved – for example, Raymond Williams, Stuart Hall, Robin Blackburn, Perry Anderson, Tariq Ali, Hilary Wainwright, Mike Rustin and others. From the very

beginning, there was an absence of consensus as to whether its purpose was to pressure the Labour Party or be an alternative to it, and it quickly evaporated (Newman, 2002). But Miliband was already thinking about such an organization at least ten years earlier, when he would probably not have been so caught up by the Benn mystique.

197. The softness of at least some of Labour towards the USSR in the late 1930s will also have kept Siegi distant. He would not have missed the implications of the disappearing question mark, after, the Fabian, Webb's tome, *Soviet Communism: A new Civilisation?*, published in 1935, lost its '?' in the second edition of 1944.
198. The committee membership was: from the Social Democratic majority, Ebert, Scheideman, Landsberg; from the USP, Haase, Dittmann and Barth.
199. A butcher by trade, he had become a SPD MP in 1906.
200. Ebert had been one of the leading Social Democrats to support involvement in the First World War. In 1918, he become the first Chancellor of the new Republic and was responsible for sending in the Freikorps against the Sparticist uprising.
201. Siegi wrote that these included not just 'the left, like Liebknecht, Luxemburg, Leviné, and Jogisches but also a former Deputy Prime Minister [and] Minister of Finance, the Christian Democrat Erzberger, and the Foreign Secretary, Democrat Walther Rathenau, the pacifist Hans Paasche, and the Independent Socialist Kurt Eisner.' Leviné was sufficiently important to Siegi and Lotte for Lotte, many years after Siegi had died to attend a lecture by Eugene Leviné, Leviné's son, at the Ethical Society on 27 June 1993 (something she would have done for Siegi, not for herself). Its analysis chimes almost completely with Siegi's, although it ends with the horror of his father's being shot.
202. Morris, William, *A Dream of John Ball* (serialised 1886–1887,

book version1888, from John Ball's sermon on Blackheath in 1381), kindly lent me by Ken Montague.

Appendix 1

Five articles by Siegi Moos on the role of revolutionary theatre, first published in 1930–1931 in *Arbeiterbühne und Film,* edited by Weber. Translated by Ian Birchall.

AGITPROP

Siegfried Moos

These lines are intended to encourage discussion. The ATBD [German Workers' Theatre Federation] has made a major step forward. It has recognized by a massive majority that today there can only be one form of workers' theatre: the theatre of struggle. To raise this theatre of struggle to its highest possible level, to rid it of all harmful dross, must be our next task.

The first target is the 'happy ending' of every play. Just as bourgeois art usually ends with a kiss, so we end with the class enemies being thrown out by the powerful fists of the workers. The difference is that the bourgeoisie wants to have a pacifying effect, whereas we want to have a rousing effect. If we use our happy endings very sparingly over the course of time, we can have a rousing effect. But if the happy ending of chasing off and defeating becomes a habit, it will eventually lose its effectiveness, until it turns into its opposite, and has a pacifying effect on workers. They see their desire to defeat the capitalists accomplished on stage too often. But in the real world they feel too often that these capitalists are still exercising their rule. The events on the stage, which should be a piece of reality, become an empty game. It is better for our acting to leave the spectator with a feeling of dissatisfaction than one of complacency. How effective is the conclusion of the play by Die Nieter [The Riveters – a Hamburg agitprop troupe] *God-Given Dependence,* in which the capitalist lords it over the proletarian, calling out: 'Look, he is already nearly asleep!' Here the spectator realizes what a lot of work there is to be done by the workers who are already awakened.

Our acting serves the class struggle. What the class struggle demands from the working class at the present moment, we must put on stage and shape it so that the worker recognizes what he has to do today in order to achieve his final goal, the overthrow of the capitalist social order and the establishment of the proletarian dictatorship. If we move into an acutely revolutionary situation, i.e. if armed struggle for the conquest of power is impending, then we shall show in our plays only and exclusively the victorious working class on the attack. And in this acutely revolutionary situation we shall not merely provoke applause, but assist in provoking struggle, assist in bringing about the moment when we can exchange the stage for a different arena of struggle. We don't want applause, we want to be the dynamos of class struggle. So we have to ask ourselves: what are the tasks that the revolutionary worker has to fulfil today? We have to mobilize the working class against the raging of class justice, against witch-hunting of the Soviet Union, against the already existing and imminent bans on revolutionary organizations, against cultural reaction, against preparations for war, against the Young Plan, against wage cuts and sackings, against the existing order of society. We must win, by discussion, apathetic Social Democratic and Christian workers for class struggle and revolutionary organization. We must fight the scum of the bourgeois press and promote the revolutionary press. We must defend ourselves against fascist murderers. We must ensure that positions of responsibility in the working class – works councils, shop stewards, trade-union officials – are filled by trustworthy revolutionaries. We must win the woman worker for active class struggle. Out of these tasks our happy ending is also produced: a Christian worker who is convinced by the facts that his ideology is distorted and his leaders are corrupt, tears up his old party membership card and joins up with the revolutionary workers. – A worker, who is signing up subscribers to the revolutionary press, the visibly increasing circulation of this press and the decline of its opponents. – A victorious defence against a surprise attack by the fascists through workers' fists. (Caution! The law for the defence of the Republic!) – How a revolutionary represents the interests of the employees to the management. – How mass action prevents wage cuts and sackings. – How a working woman becomes class conscious: These are examples of real happy endings.

You know what I mean. The working man and woman who attended must not go home and say: 'That was wonderful! What a splendid theatre group!' They have to become active fighters in our ranks. They have to carry on agitating for the things we have agitated for on stage. They have to advance through us in their class consciousness. We don't want the sort of audience which takes pleasure in our acting as it would take pleasure in a good gymnast or a bad singer. The pleasure, applause, recognition that we arouse must only be by-products of our primary goal: agitation. Our agitation shall and must be lively, a fresh breeze must blow from our boards, but our impact must derive as much as possible from agitational content and as little as possible from theatrical stunts. Agitating must not be pushed out or stifled by entertainment. If we have an audience of workers, who have already recognized the role of the press, the church and Social Democracy, and we put on stage the representatives of the church, press and Social Democracy as if they were imbeciles, lackeys of capitalism, clowns and whores, then we have produced popular entertainment and not agitation. If our audience consisted of a hundred per cent revolutionaries, we could afford to do that. But it consists mostly of people who are just on the way to us, who are beginning to doubt their previous way of looking at things. We have to win these people. We shall not win them, we shall not convince them with clowning; mostly we shall repel them.[1] A good play about the press would have to show, in caricatural form, what the bourgeois press does and what it doesn't do, in order to expose its tendency to stupefy. It would have to investigate the causes of the wide circulation of the bourgeois press, such as tradition, the placing of advertisements, novels, sensations, refer to its antagonism to the working class and to the Soviet Union; and then prove that only the revolutionary press represents the interests of the workers. – We must show in our plays how and why the leaders and upper layers of the [Catholic] Centre Party, of the SPD and of the Nazis have interests that are different from those of the mass of the workers. We must put on stage the facts about their hostility to workers in workplaces and in parliament. But we have a superfluity of such facts. So it is the task of the revolutionary to tear through the tissue of lies produced by capitalism, and to bring the truth about things to the masses.

How easy we make for ourselves, for example, plays against religion. How many crimes the church has committed over the years! But Marx and Lenin have taught us that the origin of religion is of an economic nature. Lenin said: 'We are unconditionally opposed to the slightest offence to the religious conviction of workers who have still retained their belief in God.' But in our plays the priest is a semi-idiotic clown, who may well be able to offend religious feelings, but is not able to recognize how strong and dangerous the church is, to recognize that it is one of the most harmful enemies of the working class. The church and war, the church and exploitation (see for example Bebel's speeches, published by the Neuer Deutscher Verlag), the church and the Soviet Union, the church and justice. What a lot of material there is there! It is only about two years ago, that a fascist arms depot was discovered in the St Michael's church in

1 Satire and clowning are different things. Satire is biting and aggressive; clowning is merely amusing.

Munich. In Germany there is a man of the Centre Party, Brüning, who is a relentless enemy of the working class, etc.

What I want to say is that our opponents are not clowns but enemies. Enemies! And against enemies we need sharp weapons, not toys. Workers' theatre is theatre of struggle. Our troupes must be troupes of struggle, our words must be arrows and the laughter of our audience must be bitter as gall. That is agitprop.

Arbeiterbühne und Film, No 6, June 1930.

MARCH – THE POLITICAL CONTEXT AND THE SITUATION IN THE ATBD [German Workers' Theatre Federation]

Siegfried Moos

> *A crowd of rioters raised mutinous and impudent demands .... Since their furious advance led to fears that they had evil intentions, the square had to be cleared by mounted police riding in step with sheathed weapons; two infantry rifles went off accidentally. A rabble of miscreants, mainly consisting of foreigners, filled the inflamed minds with thoughts of revenge, and thus became the fearsome instigators of bloodshed. The troops first used their weapons when obliged to do so by several shots.*

A familiar text! 'Rioters', 'mutinous demands', 'rabble', 'foreigners', 'instigators of bloodshed'. Come on! This text is a bit dusty. A proclamation by His Majesty, King Friedrich Wilhelm of Prussia 'to my dear inhabitants of Berlin' on 18 March 1848, when two shots 'which went off accidentally' and injured nobody led to 200 barricades springing up from the pavements. The March Days.

Friedrich Wilhelm has been rotting for quite a long time. Kings and emperors came and went. One century died and another was born. The monarchy passed away and the republic came into existence, but the 'rioters, mutineers and instigators of bloodshed' remained. Herr Grzesinski, Herr Severing! You can be proud! Your wise ideas have blue blood in their veins!

> *The King's speech pleasantly surprised us. Praise for the Constitution and peaceful progress is a statesmanlike thought of the first order.... We have long stood on the principle indicated by the King and we continue to resist all endeavours that are unconstitutional and against the state.... All those who conspire against the foundations of the state must be put into confinement.*

Now this is not another text from 1848, but is taken from the central organ of the Bulgarian Social Democracy, *Narod*, of December 1930, where the leader of the Social Democracy, Pastuchow, is celebrating Tsar Boris of Bulgaria, the ruler over the land of white terror.

Herr Grzesinski, Herr Severing, your comrades! You can also learn more from your comrade MacDonald, an English gentleman and British Prime Minister. You should be aware that the revolution of the Indian people against its British oppressors has been drowned in blood by the bombs, tanks and machine guns of the British 'Labour' government, that 'mutineers' were thrown into jail, strangled and tortured. Isn't that so? Perhaps it might interest you that the government of your comrade MacDonald has issued annually the appropriate 'Honours Lists' on the birthday of His Majesty the King and Emperor and at New Year. Comrade MacDonald understands the need for honours. The police chief of Bombay, the police chief of Punjab, who have hundreds of human lives on their consciences, were elevated into the hereditary nobility. Altogether 82 members of the police forces were honoured for their heroic deeds. But that was not enough men deserving honours. 60,000 political prisoners are languishing in Indian jails. Comrade MacDonald did not forget them. Comrade MacDonald understands the need for honours. The prison governors of Sylhet and Visapur, prison officials in Bombay, Bihar and Orissa were singled out for honours. The chief judge in Bombay was elevated to the nobility. And so that God also should distribute his blessings, archbishops and missionaries received the Kaisar-i-Hind medal for 'public service'. Herr Grzesinski, Herr Severing, you're out of luck. If you had lived in the British Empire, you would already have been elevated to the hereditary nobility. You're out of luck. But perhaps you can take things even further in Germany. Five million unemployed, three million unemployed, 2.6 million impoverished agricultural workers, that's ten and a half million with their families condemned to hunger and death by starvation, so there's plenty of work for rubber truncheons and tougher weapons.

Every day in Germany 18,000 workers lose their jobs, 3,000 become ineligible for unemployment relief, 45 people are killed by rationalisation, 20 people are driven to suicide.

Every day Herr Krupp earns 43 thousand marks. The People's Republic.

In the year 1930, 69 workers were murdered by the police and fascists, 5,200 injured, 1,400 imprisoned. In January 1931, in one month, 19 workers were murdered by the police and by fascists. The road to socialism. The ordinary mortal is taxed on every last cup of coffee. In one year, through flight of capital, capital robbed the revenue of twelve to fourteen thousand million marks. National sentiment. In the last two years national insurance was cut by two-and-a-half thousand million, in the last year workers' income was reduced by between six and seven-and-a-half thousand million. But Siemens is distributing fourteen per cent dividends just like before. And again wages are reduced and social expenditure is cut and again new taxes are raised for the masses. But not an iota is removed from the thousands of millions spent on armaments, not an iota from the hundreds of millions for the police. – That more is spent on the maintenance of a police dog than for an unemployed person merely testifies to the statesmanlike intelligence of our rulers. – Not an iota is cut from the hundreds of millions for the church. The church has earned it. Pius XI joins in with the loudest voice to incite against Soviet Russia, 'for the persecuted Christians'. Pius XI, pope by divine providence, has already issued an encyclical about Christian marriage. Against the economic, political and sexual liberation of women. 'He shall be your master.' Birth control and abortion are forbidden and shall be punished. Marriage shall be indissoluble. 'It is the foundation of a healthy state.' Thus speaks the Holy Father. Everything clean and proper as in Hitler's programme. With particular pleasure the Pope reports the 'solemn and fortunate agreement in the spirit of Christ between the Holy See and the Kingdom of Italy.' In the spirit of Christ, when in Mussolini's Italy out of five to six million rural workers 80 to 90 per cent have not found any work for months, when out of four-and-a-half million workers in industry, trade and commerce, one million are unemployed and two million on short time, when the wages and salaries of workers and employees are continually reduced, when the average hourly wage of an Italian worker does not even come to 1.50 lira ((0.30 marks), when during fascism's eight-year rule real wages have fallen by 45 per cent. 'Happily the Italian people have not yet got used to eating more than once a day.' (Mussolini on 13.12.30) Such are the blessings of fascism in the spirit of Christ.

And these people dare to incite against Soviet Russia. Reports are coming out of the Soviet Union which are already beginning to be unimaginable for us. Demand for two million new workers. In the capitalist world there is unemployment of around fifty million, in America alone ten million, and here is a country with the problem: where shall we find two million extra workers? Or else: the Five Year Plan in three years. The Five Year Plan, which was regarded as ridiculous chimera and fantasy because of its gigantic figures, has already been fulfilled to such an extent that even the target of 'the Five Year Plan in four years' has become too small. What an inconceivable development of strength in the land of the proletarian dictatorship, in the land of 'Bolshevism which destroys everything'. Capitalism is fully aware of the danger which threatens it through the triumph of the socialist system in the Soviet Union. Hence its feverish war preparations, hence the suppression of the revolutionary proletariat with the methods of fascism.

Our task is to arouse mass struggle against fascism. Ahead there are big strikes – in March the wage agreements for over six million workers expire. – Ahead are the elections for the works councils, and Youth Day. In the coming war youth is one of the most decisive factors. We have to win them over, we have to fight for every single young person, just as we fight for every Social Democratic worker. The works council elections will give us a new opportunity to measure the strength of the revolution against our opponents. In wide circles of the SPD is appearing an honest opposition to the politics of the SPD, a strong need for a united front of struggle against fascism. Never was the situation so favourable as today for forging such a front. It is up to us to use this situation with all our strength. It is not yet too late. All the Marches are not yet past.

II

Is the workers' theatre armed for the coming tasks, are our weapons sharpened? Our art seeks to shape in concentrated form the connections, which are decisive for the class struggle, between our class and the world around it, and to activate it for the daily struggle, in which it will turn not only to intellect but also consciously to emotion. Would we for example have achieved this with a happy ending in which the workers drive off the capitalists? No. In such driving we have formed in concentrated manner the emotional relations of the workers to the class enemy and aimed at a corresponding effect. But the situation in which we acted was not yet ripe for driving off the capitalists, but rather the tasks ahead of us were the organization of the masses, promotion of our press, propaganda for strikes, etc. Only when our plays are burningly topical in their impact do they carry out our tasks.

They will continue to carry them out only if they are thoroughly grounded. The fatter the belly, the bigger the cigar of the capitalist or the party boss, the easier it is to obtain an effect, but also the less substantial is the political value. Our task is to show the *rôle* of capitalism, the *rôle* of the bureaucracy in the class struggle, independently of the fatness of their bellies or the size of their cigars. The possibility of artistic effect is not reduced by the correctness and depth of the political content, but is only created through it.

If it's possible to find many examples where the raising of the stage effect is achieved at the expense of political depth, we can find just as many where the political effect of a good political content is lost because of the defective quality of the stage methods.

In a spoken chorus words and movements must be as precise as possible, the tone, stress and tempo of the chorus must be well polished. If we want to give form to a political content, we have to seek the form that corresponds to the given relationships, the content and the purpose. *Form* and *content* are in contradiction if we sing about the 33 dead of May Day 1929 in the form of an Alpine folk song, or if we tell the story of the German workers' movement since 1914 in a short sketch. *Content* and *means* are in contradiction, if we imitate the terror of war with children's trumpets, if an important sentence is spoken by a bad speaker (too quiet, too lofty, too theatrical), if an important part is badly cast. *Form* and *purpose* are in contradiction if the purpose of our agitation is to win over Social Democratic workers and the form is the ridiculing and mockery of their leaders without investigating the basis for their betrayal of the workers and the overwhelming factual material against them, and indeed making this central.

> *The Social Democratic worker is bound to the treacherous leaders of his party by the trust which he has put in them, and he defends them, in order to justify this trust, and we can only win him over by taking this fact into account.*

Furthermore the economic structure and the immediate political situation are essential for the form. Rising unemployment reduces the income of performances and troupes, and thereby the possibility of improving resources. Increasing long-term unemployment weakens the will to fight of many comrades both physically and mentally. Increased exploitation through the new wage system drains the last remaining energy out of those who are working. With the deterioration of our economic situation, the conditions of our work deteriorate too. On the other hand the political situation is getting ever more serious. The class struggle is getting sharper. The masses are looking for a way out. Increasingly those who have previously been apathetic or who have disagreed with us are coming to us to get an answer to the question: What is to be done? And we have to discuss with them honestly, and show them the way: the cause of their impoverishment, the connection between their everyday needs and the capitalist economy based on profit, between wage cuts, fascism and war, public opinion – press, radio, cinema – the trade-union bureaucracy, fascism of all shades. (The scope of fascism is broader than the storm troops of the Nazis. To the forces of fascism belong the millions who sympathize with fascism, whom we must win over to our side, all fascist and fascistic parties and associations, and fascist methods of government such as paragraph 48, emergency decrees, sequestrations and the stripping of immunity.) And finally we have to show the way: Soviet Russia.

In order to win over those who disagree, we have to enter

their conceptual world. That means: 'the strong man', 'the German people', 'colonies', 'Jews', 'the big and the small', the 'career' of white-collar workers, the 'existence' of small business people, the fear of 'expropriation' by the middle class which has already been expropriated, the 'tradition' of bourgeois newspaper readers, the hatred of the 'city' among peasants, 'intellectual weapons' and 'freedom of conscience' for the intellectuals, hope of putting his party back on the right road and confused ideas about the unity of the proletariat for the Social Democrat, 'Moscow gold', which is the standard argument of all counterrevolutionaries. We have to demonstrate the unviability of these ideas, so that they no longer find a home in any brain.

Our conditions of work are getting worse, but our tasks are growing. We have to be topical and we have to be fundamental. The more superficially we treat a problem, *either* politically *or* artistically, the more superficial is the effect *both* politically *and* artistically. Better two more rehearsals. Better to launch the play later, but well. Moreover, a good orator is better and a bad agitprop troupe damages the reputation of all the others and hence harms their ability to make an impact.

Our job? Work! Work! Work!

Arbeiterbühne und Film, No 3, March 1931.

THE NATIONAL CONFERENCE: EASTER 1931 IN BERLIN

Siegfried Moos

It was a working conference. All the delegates – 88 delegates representing 13 districts and 126 local groups – were inspired by one single wish: learn, learn, learn. And there can hardly have been a single delegate who did not return to their local group with new stimuli.

The conference heard greetings from the Central Committee of the Communist Party, from the national leadership of the IFA [Community for Workers' Culture], from the actors' RGO,

[Revolutionary Trade-Union Opposition], from the editorial board of *Die Rote Fahne*, and the Struggle Community for Red Sports Unity. Two representatives of the Russian workers' theatre were refused entry to the country. Written greetings were received: from the national committee of the RGO, from the presidium of the IATB [International Workers' Theatre Federation], from the workers' theatres in Czechoslovakia and Ukraine. The Polish workers' theatre published greetings to the conference in German in its newspaper.

The essential feature of the conference and of the discussion was an enormous difference in level. On the one hand there were theatre groups who were still performing old-style dramatic works lasting an entire evening, on the other there were agitprop troupes of enormous political seriousness, bubbling with vitality, activity and initiative. In between there were agitprop troupes that were in process of development, whose scripts and acting style were still superficial and politically defective. This difference of levels was revealed in the discussion, and also in the practical performances of three agitprop groups which were placed in the middle of the conference and turned out to be especially useful. The most advanced agitprop troupes are no longer satisfied with acting and recruiting; but when they discover organizational weaknesses, they intervene helpfully, in order to get things going. Thus a troupe is due to play to the assembly of a factory which has taken over its management. The previous time it performed before an almost empty hall. This time it organizes things for itself. It takes care of the production of leaflets, organizes and helps with distributing them, helps with the factory newspaper. The hall is full for the performance. The troupe recruits new comrades from among the employees in order to do the revolutionary work required in the factory. The older comrades acquire a new enthusiasm. Another troupe goes into the countryside. No success. They organize agitation for the next performance. They come back, recruit thirty members and found the local group of a revolutionary organization.

The national conference showed the correctness of the line of the ATBD [German Workers' Theatre Federation]: *training, helping the weaker to keep up, links with big factories*.

The troupes that had the best political training were also the most effective agitationally and the most advanced in their political work. For the further development of the troupes, and especially also of theatre companies, which are lagging behind, helping them keep up is (see No 4 of *Arbeiterbühne*) urgently required. Since this work can be carried out fruitfully only on the district level, our next task is *the rigorous and thorough organization of individual districts*. Links with large factories are still extremely inadequate. We can see that it is difficult to establish contact. In order to overcome a certain degree of estrangement between the comrades in the factory and the agitprop troupe, it is necessary for the agitprop troupe to make itself available for donkey work in the factory, helping with the production and distribution of leaflets, and with the factory newspaper. Such assistance must always remain only a means to the preparation and utilisation of our theatrical agitation. *This*, now as always, remains the centre of our work.

Questions took up a lot of time: methods of work and the crisis of the programme. The report 'Methods of Work', on a high theoretical level, showed the situation at the present moment and the perspective for the workers' movement. Discussions and the use of performances by the troupes were also fruitful. The essence of the workers' theatre is the unity between actors and audience. Increasingly the boundary between the stage and the audience is breaking down. Our aim is that the audience should be pulled into the play by questions, interjections and discussions. The auditorium becomes the stage and the spectators become actors. The actors are lost among the spectators. The actors and spectators become a unity. The raised stage loses its significance. This development, of which the first signs are already present, will lead to further progress. One speaker giving a report states that the bourgeoisie, of course unintentionally, is correcting our methods of working. Something we've been fighting against for a long time, the crude ridiculing of representatives of the church and the government, is now being punished by imprisonment as a result of the emergency decree. The emergency decree has raised the possibilities of our effectiveness to an extent that we could not have dared to dream of. We can no longer put the pope, members of the national and regional governments, police chiefs and other important 'public figures' on the stage, as we otherwise could have dealt with them, so that ..... we can no longer express, but we can *suggest*. And it is an old rule of effectiveness, that a much greater effect can be achieved through suggestion than by direct statement. (Though this must never happen at the expense of ideological clarity.)The audience understands, and has the pleasure of having thought through what was suggested.

In Berlin now performances are only permitted on the condition that agitprop troupes do not appear. At Easter alongside the national conference of the ATBD was held the national troupe conference of the Communist Party and of the KJVD [German Communist Youth League]. The *Berliner Börsenzeitung* [Stock Exchange Newspaper] devoted its front page to this conference and openly urged the public prosecutor to 'intervene immediately'. We have to say that this fear of agitprop troupes does us almost too much honour. But now we must publicly attack every harassment. The bourgeoisie wants to block our work. Now they can ban our troupes' songs, strip our troupes of their costumes, confiscate our properties. But they can't forbid us to *show the facts with our means and with new methods, to show the concrete things of everyday life as every reporter does. Our programme and our methods of work must be adapted to the new conditions.* The main thing is to connect to the way the masses think about the concrete facts of everyday life, to show how things are connected and their backgrounds! The connection between collective reporting and theatrical representation (for which of course we shall also use satire), working with the most primitive properties, the greatest possible topicality and flexibility of our plays, the most rigorous discipline of the troupe collective, that is the necessary form of our future work.

Resolution unanimously agreed at the National Conference:
Since the last federal conference in Dortmund in 1930 the contradictions between capital and labour have become very much sharper. The progressive intensification of the industrial and agrarian crisis on a national scale is forcing the bourgeoisie to take ever more brutal measures against all working people.

Because Germany lost the war the crisis is particularly acute here. The German bourgeoisie is making desperate efforts to overcome the crisis at the expense of the working masses.

As a result, it finds itself obliged to completely abandon the ground of the pseudo-democracy which has existed hitherto, and to entrust the Brüning government with the establishment of fascist dictatorship. It is actively supported in the carrying through of these measures by the stance of the SPD, whose leaders are publicly mobilized for the fascist course of Brüning, and by the Nazis, who are increasingly exposed as agents of the terrorist suppression of the working class.

The fighting working class is faced with the enormous task of organising a popular revolution against fascism.

In relation to this overall strategic solution the ATBD must make more concrete the tasks it set itself at the Dortmund conference. The local groups of the ATBD must increasingly prove themselves capable of developing themselves as cadres and specialists in their special field of agitation and propaganda, i.e. as struggle units with a responsible function.

In order to enable the national organization and each local group to accomplish these tasks, the national conference of the

ATBD resolves to carry out the following plan of work:

1. **Politicisation of the members** by systematic training within the troupes as well as on a district level. – Deeper study of the daily press and periodicals; the hostile press must also be included.
2. **Activising of the troupes** by links with a large industrial or agricultural enterprise. Practical participation in the work of the RGO and ideological support with the aim of taking over **responsible** agitprop work in the RGO apparatus. – Close cooperation with other proletarian mass organizations, especially with cultural organizations allied in the IFA, with the aim of involving them in the work of the RGO. – Becoming more competent and polished in our methods in relation to the rural population and the petty-bourgeois intermediate strata. – Activity towards hostile organizations with the aim of reducing their influence on the masses and winning over their members.

In face of the sharpening persecution of the revolutionary workers' organizations, which has already made itself felt also in the ATBD, we have a duty to make up for time lost in the past as rapidly as possible and to work with the greatest energy for the carrying out of this plan.

On the offensive against fascist reaction is our response.

Mobilisation and Counteroffensive!

Arbeiterbühne und Film, No 5, May 1931.

REVOLUTIONARY THEATRE

Siegfried Moos

Some very confused ideas about revolutionary theatre are still around. Some people regard left-wing partisan contemporary theatre, which critically confronts immediate situations, as revolutionary theatre. Others consider revolutionary theatre merely as frivolity, while yet others see it as one-sided party theatre.

I

A play is not necessarily revolutionary theatre because it shows the misery of the proletariat and criticizes the present-day organization of society, and when one of the characters says correct things from a revolutionary standpoint on the stage. It only becomes revolutionary theatre when it shows how circumstances are conditioned by class and presents a revolutionary alternative, when the proletariat appears on stage as the decisive revolutionary element, as a class, as an oppressed, struggling, rising class, which will overthrow the existing social order and will be the bearer of the new social order. It is only revolutionary art when the people on the stage (or in the film) are genuine representatives of their class. For example to put public prosecutors, doctors, judges, factory managers with humane feelings on the stage is only legitimate if it is also shown that they are hypocrites or insignificant exceptions. Exceptions, who are much more dangerous than their fellow class members. For they cover up the laws of class; those characters with 'humane feelings' conceal them with the veil of their 'humanity'. Even to show a doctor, judge etc. with revolutionary inclinations only makes sense if we want to demonstrate to intellectuals how their interests are linked to those of the entire proletariat. In other cases for us the appropriate representative of the proletariat is not a doctor, a judge, etc., but the worker, the working woman, the young worker. Theatre is only revolutionary when its effect is unequivocal, so unequivocal that it clearly expresses the statement: For us there is only one way out, only one way, that of revolutionary class struggle.

And then the spectator. Our spectator is primarily the proletariat. Only where the spectator and audience form a united totality, only there can something healthy and united come into existence: revolutionary theatre. In the framework of bourgeois commercial theatre all these fundamental conditions for revolutionary theatre cannot be fulfilled.

Revolutionary theatre is and remains the task of the workers' theatre.

II

Revolutionary theatre as frivolity. In the history of bourgeois theatre there are a series of examples of how theatre can have a revolutionising impact. The impact of *The Marriage of Figaro* in the revolutionary days of 1789. *The Dumb Girl of Portici* in the days of August 1830. The impact was so strong that the audience, in the spirit of the performance, demonstrated through the streets, destroyed a hostile print shop, and burned down the houses of the Minister of Justice, the Chief of Police and hated journalists. In these pages already enough has been written about the importance of the workers' theatre and worker actors for the class struggle. The free time of the worker actor is filled up with rehearsals, acting, meetings, political education. He is a true agent of the working class. For workers' theatre is not frivolity, but the most vital, effective agitation for the class struggle.

III

Revolutionary theatre as party theatre. – In our ranks there is a place for everyone who stands on the ground of class struggle. We want to put forward the teachings of Marx, Engels and Bebel on the stage, applying them to today's conditions. For instance, when Bebel says: 'If I, as a Social Democrat, enter into an alliance with the bourgeois parties, then I will wager a thousand to one that not the Social Democrats but the bourgeois parties will be the winners, and we shall be the losers.... Party comrades must take care that the party leaders do not do any harm to the party.' Or 'Either monarchy or bourgeois republic, both are class states, both are a form of state for the preservation of the class rule of the bourgeoisie'; or when Engels says: 'So a unitary republic, but not in the sense of today's French republic, which is nothing but the Empire without the Emperor'; or when Marx says: 'Between capitalist and Communist society there is the period of the transformation of the one into the other. Corresponding to this there is also a political transition period, whose state can be nothing but the revolutionary dictatorship of the proletariat.' And in the *Communist Manifesto*: 'Let the ruling classes tremble at a Communistic revolution. The proletarians have nothing to lose but their chains.' So it follows that we have the duty, in the shaping of our plays, to apply these teachings. What Marx and Engels, and in the continuation of their thinking Lenin, have said, must be the foundation of our plays.

Workers' theatre is not frivolity, nor is it party theatre. We want revolutionary theatre. Revolutionary theatre, which can only be achieved, which must be achieved, through the workers' theatre.

Arbeiterbühne und Film, No 7, July 1930.

RECRUITMENT

Siegfried Moos

'Here!! The fiiirst new member!!!! Here!! The seeecond new member!!! The thiiird, the fourth new member! Hello! Hello! Where is the tenth new member??!! The tenth new member?!!! Hello! The tenth new member! Where is the tenth new member? Here!! The tenth new member!!!' It's fun. While the recruiter shouts himself hoarse, you can hear below in the audience: 'Fresh salty bread', 'Membership forms for the….', 'Acid drops'. That's right, membership forms are being pushed just like acid drops. The man with the membership forms has it easier than the acid drop seller, only because he is still backed up by the recruiter. But it's amusing. Isn't it?

Where is the tenth new member? 'Come on, give it here!' says someone from the audience to the man with the membership forms. He doesn't ask anything else; for example what duties he's taking on thereby. He fills the form out. He has filled out the tenth membership form. He. Yes, he. Yes. Isn't that splendid? Hello! Here's the tenth membership form. Yes, perhaps you think that I'm writing about the fairground. Far from it. You'll see. So: Three weeks later they ring at the door of the man who was recruited. 'Listen, comrade, how about the money? Admission fee and subs?' 'Look, I've already told you that I don't have any money.' 'This is the third time I've come here. You signed up.' 'Yes, well .... back then I didn't know what it meant.' And six months later none of the ten new members is left.

Not one. Because we recruited the wrong way. Every troupe is proud, when it can say: 'We've made so many new members. Aren't we splendid?' But we don't want completed membership forms, we want people who are convinced of the necessity to be organized, we want fighters. With market-trader methods we may dazzle people for a moment, But we don't win their strength for our movement. So let's get rid of our complacency about the quantity of new members. Our first aim is quality. It isn't a rejection of quantity, but rather a precondition.

'So how should we set about it?' you will ask. There is, I think, only one possible way to recruit successfully, and that is individual, personal recruitment. We can and should as far as possible support this from the stage. We can announce a recruitment target.

This recruitment target should not be fixed too high. A target that has been exceeded is more inspiring than one which has not been reached. We can make a big diagram (on linen or cardboard) with big figures that go from the bottom to the top, with a big pointer, a red flag or some other symbol of the revolutionary working class, which moves upwards according to the current increase in new members. Perhaps its silent impact will be greater than the effect of marketplace methods. One comrade has suggested that we should put on stage a recruitment scene, in which one comrade is recruiting and other comrades are being recruited. The comrades who are acting as 'unorganized' will make the usual objections, which will be answered by the recruiting comrades. We can develop this suggestion, by having the comrades who are recruiting in the hall repeating aloud to the audience and the stage the objections that are made to them, providing that they are not of a particularly private nature. The reply then comes from the audience, or, alternatively, the objection is repeated by one of the 'unorganized' comrades on the stage, and is refuted by the comrade who is recruiting. Recruitment thus becomes alive, effective and enlightening. We must draw into the individual recruitment and into the public replies of the audience the numbers of organized comrades who are present at almost every performance.

Personal recruitment goes best when we go up to a comrade and discuss with him so loudly that the people around him listen and if possible help with the recruitment. The troupe must have factual material at its disposal, in order to be able to give information about work that has been done already and about tasks lying ahead for the organization in question, and above all about how money collected in subscriptions is used. The members of the troupe must exchange their experiences of recruitment and be prepared for objections. For example: 'No money? But in fact we are the organization of the impoverished masses. A few cigarettes, a glass or tankard of beer less, and the subs can be paid. The fewer sacrifices we make for our organization, the more sacrifices we shall have to make for the capitalists', etc. In addition the comrades must make connections with topical events, in order to base the necessity for the organization or newspaper in question on the current situation. So get a move on and write to us about your methods and experiences of recruitment, so that other troupes can learn from you.

In short: Individual recruitment backed up with good, not

fairground-style, ideas from the stage. Not only quantitative but above all qualitative recruitment. And no more of: 'Where is the tenth new member??!' and 'Membership forms for the....' but 'Comrade, are you already in the .... organization? Won't you help us with our work?'

Arbeiterbühne und Film, No 12, December 1930.

Appendix 2

Researching the KPD 1929–37. Conversations with three members of the KPD in the 1930s

I had started to look for people who either might have known, or at least known of, my father, because of writing his biography, but I had left it too late. I concentrated instead on trying to understand the lived experience of being in the KPD in Germany between about 1929 and 1933. Very little has been done on the lived experience of KPDers as opposed to the KPD 'line'.

I was very lucky to find and be allowed to interview three centenarians who had been in the KPD in the early 30s and who are now living in Berlin

There has been little attention or research into this area or indeed these people, particularly in East Germany. Who became celebrated, who not? After all, the East Germans, unlike the West Germans, celebrated their heroes. But which heroes? I suggest that it is those who in one way or another, always with unbelievable bravery, fought and resisted fascism during the war who have received the accolades, rather than the far less visible – though always courageous – underground fighters of the period leading up to and soon after Hitler's ascendancy who, after all, 'failed' to stop the Nazis.

I will first introduce the three Berliners. As luck would have it, the three people represented a cross section of society: in the early 1930s, Elfreida had been a writer, Hans a white-collar/skilled worker (later on, he became a senior police officer in East Germany) and Rudi had been semi-unemployed. All had been active members of the KPD, though in different areas. My principal concern was with the three areas of my father's political activism – agitprop, the Red Front and the Proletarian Free Thinkers – but I was also interested in the Berlin 3's total political experiences in the early 1930s. My focus was not on their lives in a fuller sense or in what had become of them after 1945.

Another limitation was that I speak little German. I was and am therefore dependent on the good will of others and, in this case, I have to thank Irene Fick for translating for me so generously. But this cannot be the same as being able to follow up for oneself the issues of interest in the interview.

Another problem which was in itself fascinating was how difficult it was to persuade the three to separate out their experiences before and after January/February 1933, which makes interpreting what they said more difficult. I had grown up in a family where the Reichstag fire of 28 February 1933 had marked the beginning of exile, an assumption reinforced by most academic literature on this period, which presents the January/February events as a division, between supposedly democratic Weimar Germany and the start of Nazism.

What quickly became apparent was how active the SA were before 1933. Rudi's testimony highlighted how active they were among the unemployed. Hans also reported their activities amongst white-collar workers: the employers, for example in metal, tobacco and coal, would give SA men jobs, pay for their uniforms and different sorts of handouts. Elfrieda talked of the nightly battles between the SA and the Red Front in Prenzlauerberg in Berlin.

Rudi lived in a hut on his allotment in Wedding, the red centre of Berlin. Every day involved a battle with the SA. There were daily attacks, blood flowed, and many people murdered before 1933. He described their lives as if it were a military operation. They had people on bikes and 'courting couples' as look outs. He wrote, printed and then distributed the illegal leaflets by putting the leaflets under the baby in the pram which his wife pushed. You could never trust anybody, nobody at all. He talked about how careful they had to be because people talked, friends of friends could not be trusted. You always had to have an exit strategy. He and his wife distributed leaflets without anybody else knowing.

Of course, as Rudi stated, there were differences according to region and place, but certainly in Berlin and Leipzig, Hans' home at the time, the battles between the SA and Red Front were daily. The SA were organized into groups (and, as many of their members were unemployed youth, they had the time to roam) and would attempt to attack most left meetings and demonstrations and indeed any informal group of lefties who made the mistake of walking the streets as a group. That all three, from their different class fractions, attested to this, increases its reliability as a source.

Rudi was arrested near Roder before 1933 during an illegal demonstration, and had experienced and witnessed many beatings up, prior to 1933, by the police in Berlin under a Social Democratic authority. 'One must remember never to remember names.'

The Red Front was part of the daily lived experience of these young KPDers. The Red Front was an anti-fascist organization set up by the KPD which had been made illegal in 1929 following the 1 May demonstration and consequent repression (see main text). Yet the Red Front is not an organization that most historians spend time on. However, talking to these three old comrades, I suddenly realized it was not merely one of many of the KPD front organizations, but was the key organization for protecting not only the comrades, but also local left meetings, streets and left taverns.

What also emerged, especially from Rudi, was that the Red Front recruited from a wide range of political backgrounds. What mattered was where one lived, so young people who sided with the Social Democrats would join the Red Front if they lived in an area where it was organized and where the SA were a threat. (To that degree, the Third Period line of working with rank and file Social Democrats was working in practice.) Rudi was the leader of his small group of seven or eight young Red Fronters; their aim, he said, was to be defensive until attacked. But Rudi also attested to how some members were out for trouble and he had to calm them down. Rudi walked a tightrope, or so it seemed to me, between cooling down his hotheads and defending his comrades by whatever means necessary. Rudi appears to have experienced the growth of the Nazis, the SA at street level, and while his resistance to them was a consequence of his Communist politics, he seems to have understood far more clearly than most of the KPD leadership the importance of consistently opposing the SA.

My impression was that this had little to do with the line of the KPD and far more to do with the reality of the situation and expediency. Though it is hardly necessary to remind the reader, it was unusual, at an official level, both within the KPD and the Comintern, to prioritize the fight against Nazism till almost 1933, yet for Rudi and the two others, there was a daily need to defend yourself against the SA. Though, like Rudi, the cadres of the Red Front were generally KPD, the Red Front can clearly not be reduced to the KPD, although conventionally it has been presented as no more than its military adjunct.

How far was Rudi, with his amazing illegal printer and leaflets, seizing an opportunity, rather than being a part of some organized KPD underground? Really we have very little evidence about how far an underground existed. Indeed Elfrieda's story indicates how unaware the KPD were of the importance of secrecy. After January 1933, Elfrieda's home was used for the KPD leadership's secret meetings. The CC met there for the whole of 1933, and, predictably, were finally picked up and arrested there.

But there are wider questions. Given the essentially random nature of the sample, how can it be explained that the KPD leadership was so out of touch with their members' everyday experiences on the street? Secondly, how far did these comrades' experiences really change with January/February 1933? Rudi certainly did not remember the Reichstag fire, not even roughly the year it took place, but did say that, in 1933, he went to hide with his parents-in-law for a few weeks till everything calmed down. So he did not conceptually distinguish the two periods, but did remember the need to hide. The KPD CC itself did not at first recognize that the January election and Hitler's becoming Chancellor marked a fundamental shift. So is it so surprising if some of the members did not either, especially as many were 'loose' members of the KPD?

Another issue deserving more research is how far there were attempts by the KPD to draw members of the SA over to them. SA spokespersons were invited to speak at KPD meetings, even in the early 1930s. Both Elfrieda and Rudi talked about this. Elfreida's writers' group had a member, Felix, who was a member of the SA, indeed, arrived in his uniform and ultimately betrayed them after 1933. Felix becoming a member was agreed to, even encouraged, by the KPD 'boss'. I got the sense that it was thought more important to draw from the SA, than from the SPD.

But Rudi provided an eloquent explanation for this policy: the people who joined the SA were workers too, he said. They belonged to the same families, had gone to the same schools, lived in the same streets and were often good friends. Families were divided between the SA and KPD, and this could make things very difficult. This semi-official attempt to draw over workers may have helped legitimate what happened next. Rudi talked of counter-recruitment but noted that most of the traffic was one way, especially after 1933 (his dating) because some Communists were so harassed by the SA and so afraid, that they joined the SA and then they stayed. Rudi knew that, as the going got ever tougher, especially after 1933, it was KPD members who joined the SA, not the other way round, though he was not clear about how far this was expediency, how far ideological.

As Ian Birchall has highlighted, the initiative for debate in the 1920s did not come from the KPD. Nationalists were attending KPD meetings, not in order to disrupt them, but to try and engage Communists in discussion. And, as Victor Serge reported, the debate was already taking place on the streets, where the unemployed congregated until late at night, while Communists, Social Democrats and Nazis argued their rival solutions.

Hans was the only one of the three to be employed in the relevant period. He was a skilled worker. Hans joined the Social Democratic union in Leipzig, not the Red Union, which was the KPD line (for the most part). The union was his main area of activity. I tried to find out in the interview whether there was a Red Union at his place of work, but failed. Hans also referred to working with individual members of the SPD prior to February 1933. Of course, Hans lived in Leipzig where the SPD, most unusually, were in the leadership of the struggle, so Hans' experience may not be typical. Hans' emphasis was on how difficult it was to be politically active before 1933. If it was known one had said something left-wing, even outside the workplace, one lost the job. He was beaten up, maybe more than once, by members of the SPD. He said his trade union officially never discussed working with the KPD.

On the issue of the Freethinkers, only one person, Hans, had been involved, but he was not clear whether or how the Proletarian Freethinkers differed from the Freethinkers, whom he saw as under Social Democratic control in Leipzig. (The right to abortion, something the Catholic Church stood against, was apparently not a demand.) Again, there is the question of the specificity of the Saxon experience. Hans changed sports club because the one he had been attending was SPD dominated and he was not comfortable there and went over to a Red Sports Club, run by the KPD! Here the Third Period line held! But it still is not clear how far a separate Proletarian Freethinkers was a feature of Leipzig. Although the conversation became a bit confused at this point, Hans connected the Proletarian Freethinkers with the *Fichte*, which he said were a Berlin phenomenon, aligned with the KPD. Until around 1928, it had been a united organization, but then it split into SPD and KPD. Hans seemed to suggest that the Red Sports organizations were banned as early as 1931.

What emerged from Rudi and Hans in particular was how far their politics was still influenced by Third Period politics. Hans, although decrying the use of the term 'social fascist', went on to blame the SPD for the defeat of the left. Rudi, the person most active on the front line against the SA through the Red Front, had already been subjected to much violence and persecution before the Nazi takeover, and did not recognize that the Nazis' gaining power and the Reichstag fire were a turning point. In none of the interviews did I get the impression that these comrades saw their task as to draw those sympathetic to the SPD over to them, though Rudi did refer to some SPD youth joining the Red Front. Indeed, the absence of reference to Social Democrats reinforces the impression that they were not seen as particularly relevant.

Yet I suggest that, although the 'social fascist' line was a historical disaster, seeing January/February as a fundamental turning point was not most comrades' lived experience. They had been doing battle with the Nazis long before 1933, and had already had serious confrontations with the police, who were under SPD control. Their leadership, moreover, did not suggest there had been any sort of qualitative break which would have provided a framework for them to reassess what was happening. My suspicion is that their voices are not untypical of this layer of KPDers who experienced the 1930s at street level and survived to live in East Germany.

What was also interesting was that none of the three considered flight or were not able to do so. As Rudi suggested, to flee, one needed money.

The person most aware of the significance of Hitler becoming Chancellor (followed by the Reichstag fire), was Elfrieda. The

Nazis had immediately banned their Bund of Revolutionary Writers in January 1933. When they went to their usual meeting place in February, the SA were there waiting for them and they had to instantly scatter. During the burning of the books, they all individually turned up and were able to conduct discreet conversations as their books burned. They subsequently formed into small groups of five or six.

Elfrieda was arrested in October 1935, after Felix's betrayal. She was tried before a Nazi judge and held in isolation in prison. She was released in 1936 but had to check in with the Gestapo three times every week. She ended up marrying a man who was not an active anti-Nazi but who provided her with a safe home and a child. She left him as soon as the war was over.

Hans was also arrested on 21 March 1933 after an illegal meeting, appeared before a proper judge (it was still the old system, he said) and was in prison for one year. Initially he said he was arrested twice, once for activity with the Freethinkers, once for the KPD, but he never returned to that, despite encouragement.

But we must not let the tragic mistakes of this period cloud our awareness of the bravery of these people. I will end this section with a comment by Rudi: By 1945, none of his old comrades from the early 1930s were still around. They were, he said, dead, exiled or in prison, but his emphasis was on being dead.

Appendix 3

Hermann Binnswanger

Hermann, as seen throughout this biography, was a key figure in Siegi's life, and probably crucial in providing Siegi with funds. My guess is that Siegi had sufficient confidence that he could survive, first on the road and then jobless and penniless in a foreign land, because he expected (or anyway anticipated) that Hermann would provide for him. (From what I can gather, the amounts were small but sufficient to keep him alive.) Hermann's affection for Siegi shines through the letters he sent Siegi and Lotte from 1933 till it became impossible to do so. Rather than break the thread of Siegi's story in the biography itself, this appendix allows more space and attention to consider Hermann's letters and Hermann himself.

Although the letters from Siegi's uncle are not overtly political (indeed how could they be, given the conditions in Nazi Germany between 1933 and Hermann's 'death' in 1944), they do illuminate Siegi's life. I did not even know of Hermann until a few years ago when, clearing my parents' house, I came across a brown and battered packet, buried deep beneath my father's copies of *Economic Journal*. In the envelope, were hundreds of sheets of paper, many written in archaic German handwriting, which proved very difficult to translate. I had no idea who they were from. Very slowly, the truth unfolded from these dusty and fragile sheets and I discovered that the 'home' my father had described had been with delightful Uncle Hermann and not with his mother or father, as I had presumed (and been led to assume). (See end of this appendix for extracts from these letters.) As already outlined, the exact scope of this relationship is not known but, if we judge from his letters, Hermann cared a great deal for his nephew. We have no copies of Siegi's replies to his uncle – which is curious, as Siegi kept copies of so much he wrote to others. Happily, Siegi preserved Hermann's letters.

The letters are written with amazing frequency till Hermann was removed from his home. But much is written in heavy code, so any interpretation is open to question. It took me some time to realize, for instance, that the frequent references to somebody called 'Fritz' actually referred to Siegi!

Hermann, Siegi's only real family, is clearly doing everything he can to support his beloved nephew and his wife, Lotte. Hermann had no children and, as was more the way then than now, he and his wife, Rosa, took over the care of Rosa's brother's child. (Siegi's father, Rosa's brother, died when Siegi was little and his mother (supposedly) when Siegi was still young.)

From 1933 till about 1936, Hermann reassures Siegi that he will do whatever is possible legally to support Siegi, although transferring money gets more and more complex and potentially dangerous. (The issue of legality appears to have mattered to Hermann morally, as well as because he wanted to stay out of trouble.) In December 1933, probably before he knew that Siegi has arrived in Paris, Hermann writes to Lotte: 'Every hour my thoughts and my heart are with you, dear Lotte... I would love to make my contribution with all the strength still at my disposal. I do insist on it.' However, he urges her to respond to his letters, as her failure to do so (something she was never good at!) 'irritates my nerves.' In a later letter from December 1933, he assures her that the next instalment is on its way. Hermann regularly reminds Siegi (for example, in a letter from March 1934) that Siegi (and another person he refers to as 'August') will inherit a large amount each. (This was never to be, but that is part of another story!) In March 1934, he writes that he has opened a new account for them.

But it is getting increasingly difficult to transfer money abroad and, by April 1936, Hermann is finding it difficult to send his monthly transfer. He tells them: 'I can only watch with my heart bleeding...Should you ever get into dire financial circumstances, show these lines to Lord Hirst.' We know Siegi was in contact with Hirst so he may well have done so. By 1937, draconian financial restrictions were being enforced to deprive Jews of their property. Hermann is creative in finding ways of supporting Siegi and Lotte. He appears to get money to Siegi via business contacts in the UK and through the USA, and even suggests – and probably does – sending stamps. By March 1938, although he offers to send them his old furniture (which is legal), Hermann laments he cannot help them financially with their move from London to Oxford. In a sombre letter from April 1939, he writes about how many people now need his financial support. Was Siegi's ability to flee Germany in part predicated on the knowledge that, if it came to it, his rich uncle would help him out? Certainly, he has no evident source of income till he starts his part-time job at the LSE in 1936.

Back in 1933, Hermann wrote a letter to Lotte giving her a variety of possible contacts in Paris, which she had reached before Siegi, and where she knew nobody. These contacts included reference to members of the Dreyfus family (relatives of Alfred Dreyfus of the French Dreyfus Affair in the early twentieth century) – related through Rosa's mother; also to cousins of Albert Einstein, also blood relatives of Siegi's, as well as the exact address of another branch of the family that had apparently lived in Paris ever since the early nineteenth century! These illustrious connections indicate that my father's family, at least on his father's and uncle's sides, had deep roots in the radical wing of the nineteenth-century European bourgeoisie. Whether Lotte made use of these contacts is unknown, but their existence surely must have been comforting.

The tensions and insecurities of Siegi and Lotte's relationship after they had both separately fled Berlin also show up in Hermann's remarkably non-judgemental letters, though sometimes obliquely. Some of the passages, even written as early as 1933, require detective work to decipher. Hermann writes: 'I can agree that the London traffic in question could play a part. If husband and wife can be together... the traffic should not play a big part, at least not for the next few years and then you can see which way the wind blows.'

Certainly, Hermann shows continuing concern for their relationship – as we know, not without cause. He expresses great anxiety ('I am in a state of total groundlessness.') in a 1936 letter about Lotte's planned departure (though it is never stated, it was to the USSR) but wants to know if he can provide her with anything for her trip, as long as it is lawful to do so. In the same letter, he assures Siegi that he has the addresses of relatives in the USA and offers to pay for a ticket to the USA directly to the shipping company, confirmation that Siegi is seriously considering leaving for the US and, again, suggesting deep problems in his relationship with Lotte. (Hermann's repeated attempts to purchase tickets were frustrated.) Hermann expresses much hope when Lotte returns: 'You are still young enough that the difficulties of the past period can give way to a harmonious and happy future together.' In a much later, and almost final, letter from 1939, after Lotte's return from the USA, he expresses great happiness that Lotte and Siegi are back together again.

At the same time, Hermann had persisted with an intriguing naivety to try to persuade Siegi to return to Germany, which I can only imagine Siegi must have had to dismiss. On 26 December 1933, almost immediately after Siegi finally arrived safely in Paris, Hermann writes: 'I come to the matter of our friend Alfons [Siegi]. ..Of course the filling of the job reserved for him [in Hermann's factory] cannot be infinitely postponed...If our friend [Siegi] was to return to his homeland, it cannot be known what would befall him...For me, it is deplorable that my dream has come to nothing.' He reasserts repeatedly (January, February and March letters) in 1934 how easy it would be for 'Fritz'/'Alfons' to resume his former position in the firm. Even in a letter from 1936, he grieves that his nephew is 'not showing much desire to breathe German air again' (!) In a sad, undated letter, but probably from 1939, written on thin paper and extremely difficult to decipher, Hermann again writes that he is still hoping that this 'normally very clever man' will overcome his inhibitions, as German emigrants do not face 'a land of milk and honey.'

Yet the real situation in the Germany, even in 1933, that Hermann was hoping Siegi would return to, was revealed in this cheery, but damning, sentence : 'I am steaming all correspondence that is not of historical significance because of these considerations ['these' is left to the reader to understand]. The steam from this drove our egg mixing apparatus and made wonderful egg liqueur [advocaat – one of the liqueurs produced in their factory]. All the old bank notes, made worthless by inflation, are fuelling the boiler. I am very happy about this.' In another letter from 1933, Herman is already writing that their liqueurs and wines are having to be sold cheap: 'wines in balloons of 5–10 litres. Our rich reservoir of barrels has fallen into the well-known slumber of Sleeping Beauty.' Except of course, there was to be no Prince.

Indeed, even by 1934, Herman is lamenting to Siegi about all the relatives who are leaving Germany and how he misses them, a theme which becomes increasingly insistent (Hermann appears to try to provide many of these friends and relatives with the means to get out). In March 1934, he writes that his beloved house in Solln is difficult to sell. We can imagine what is happening. There are no letters between March 1934 and March 1936. In the first 1936 letter, Hermann writes in his coded style, though the meaning is all too clear: 'There may have been trespasses that had the injurious consequence of the revocation of the international passport.' The 'last' letters are not dated, although there a terrible one-line sentence from 1941, assuring everybody he is OK. But in letters, almost certainly from 1939, Hermann writes that he no longer has income or property.

What is also significant about these letters is what they do not mention: Hermann never refers to himself – or indeed any member of the family – as Jewish, or to the observation of any Jewish rituals or ceremonies. This was not just to avoid the censor's gaze but because these rituals and beliefs did not concern him. But he observes the growing anti-Semitism. In February 1938, he states that 'Hermann Meyer and Co has been Aryanised.' But, as always, he does not comment. (In the next sentence he complains of toothache, which may or may not be code.) In a letter dated 12 August 1938, he writes: 'The flowers, plants, trees, even the compost heap, know no difference between Aryan and non-Aryan.' Later in that letter, he says he would pay for Lotte's parents to get out using a Jewish emigration institution, but doubts, correctly, whether it would be allowed. 'Giving is always bliss,' he adds.

By the end of 1938, he is writing almost exclusively but obliquely about what is happening to his family, and in his very last brief letters, about being repeatedly forced to move, aged over 80, from one 'residence' to another. (Needless to say, his wonderful home in Munich, which survives, is still in the hands of the family who moved in after Hermann was moved out.) Hermann is emblematic of an 'integrated' group of the German high-bourgeoisie who did not perceive themselves primarily, or, possibly, even significantly, as Jewish, but as Germans. That was the influence that Siegi grew up under.

The Nazis' view was different. Hermann's life ended in Theriesenstadt, after his serious (and oh so rational) attempt at suicide failed. He was carried out of his house by the SS on a stretcher and then this wise old man 'chose' to starve himself to death in the camp. Nobody should ever have to die like that. I fear he was alone.

I do hope Hermann knew that Siegi and Lotte were expecting a baby, but I very much doubt it. The letters, from friends, not officialdom, informing Siegi of Hermann's death arrived about the same time I was born. I am the grandchild he yearned for and never had. In 1937 he wrote: 'If you have prospects of having an addition to the family [a baby]...I would be very happy if I was granted to have the child with me and if possible, care for it.'

Below are substantial extracts from Hermann's letters. I am including them because they give a sense of how important Siegi and Lotte were to him and give us a rare, if not unique, 'primary source' about what is happening in Siegi and Lotte's lives between about 1933 and 1939; also because the letters give both a sense of the iron boot descending in Germany and the poignancy of Hermann's response. Hermann referred to my father sometimes as Fritz, sometimes as Friedl, sometimes in terms of 'My Beloved Ones' (indeed, when I first read the translations, I did not appreciate he was writing to my father). I assume these names were in part an attempt to conceal Siegi's identity. Hermann regularly writes in code and it has not always been possible to establish his meaning. I have cut out his 'address' to make understanding these letters easier, except for the letter addressed specifically to Lotte.

12 December 1933
My dear Lotte, My congratulations to your moving [to Britain]. May contentment and blessing come from it for you and dear Louise. Every hour my thoughts and my heart are with you both.

20 February 1934
I congratulate you both that you can be together again and that you dear Fritz got out of the Paris pandemonium. I've been worried sick.

12 March 1934
Today you would have had occasion to compare the English and Bavarian beers. The Bavarian gets my vote. For today the Salvator festival started on the Nockherberg. You, dear Fritz, can

tell dear Lotte a long story about the Nockherberg. And may your mouth, dear Lotte, be watering now and so prevent many tears that you might otherwise cry. It is a pity that there isn't a service, similar to Interflora, to send you the special sausages and beer.

Let's hope that one day luck – long yearned for and well deserved – will come to you and will help you overcome all miseries.

30 March 1934
Between you, me and the gatepost, my evening menu includes a special kind of cheese, dark rye bread, grated reddish, vinegar, oil and ¾ litre Löwenbräu Bock. Cheers.

7 February 1936
I'm burning all correspondence that is not of historical significance, because of considerations. The steam from this drives our egg mixing apparatus and made wonderful egg liqueur. Lots of other material, including old inflationary bank notes, has turned our apparatus into a boiler! I'm very happy about this.

12 March 1936
The revocation of the international passport has taken away from me the possibility of seeing and speaking to you again. I have anxiously taken care not to violate the laws and rules, which are in force after all, by one iota. The longing for you would have helped me overcome all physical difficulties, even if I had suffered from it for weeks afterwards. After a few exchanges of letters with your dear parents I have now gained the opinion that you have thought through this plan to emigrate again.

10 April 1936
As your dear wife is not with you, I can confess that I can surely understand your feeling of being deserted. But you can thank God look forward to seeing each other again soon and sharing a

hopefully very long, happy and successful journey through life.

I eat quite well and in summer I'll offer my stomach reddish salad, cheese and dark bread again.

21April 1936

Dear Fritz, I haven't heard from Louise directly but my dear friend Sam [no doubt code] mentioned in his latest letter that she is fine and heading for her goal. Let's hope that you remain healthy and that the separation won't last long.

17 October 1936

Today, I'll work with the flower boxes in the loggia and cellar, and repair the shutters but also I'll pack and send a sausage which found the special approval of my guests in Solln... Let's hope the parcel will arrive well and you'll both like its taste.

24 April 1937

If you have prospects of having an addition to the family, I would be very happy for you, your dear parents and very much so for myself, if I could have your offspring with me and if possible to care for them. If this family addition comes often, if you are yourself in a secured position, it'll be easier for you and a child in every respect to overcome any financial difficulties.

7 February 1938

That you have got wobbly tables is not as bad as if your feet were wobbly. How easily I could share some of my plates and bowls with you without missing them, but it is not worth the freight. You my dear Lotte are a troubled child and I feel sorry for you that you have to run around such a lot and haven't got the success hoped for. But untroubled joy of life has never been granted to any earthly being, so just take courage. Arriving together with yours, is a negative letter from America – the prospect hinted at has met a setback. [This could refer to early attempts to get Lotte's parents an American visa but it could equally apply to many other family members wishing to get out.]

23 April 1938
So today you are probably moving into your new home [in Oxford]. Accept my fondest and sincerest wishes for your moving. May this new home be the starting point of a very happy, satisfying and successful life for you. Even if perhaps not all your wishes will be granted, you can still be happy with your fate, compared to all those who can't see a light. I can tell long stories of disappointment and cold attitude of people who have obviously not yet heard about our fate. In spite of that, I don't give up.

29 July 1938
I won't leave anything untried to help you as much as possible – of course only totally legally – with starting a new existence in the USA.

12 August 1938
As long as one breathes one has to remain faithful to one's patriotic attitude and one's honest feeling and thinking, even if the environment does not see or acknowledge it.

I want to let you know that descendants of my family tree live in Pittsburgh. I wish for you that you can make and shape your journey through life alone with your own strength, but it can't do any harm if you can find access to local families through family support. I have written to your dear parents in Berlin about purchasing tickets through a Jewish emigration institution. I have offered my help, but your parents doubt whether it is allowed in the time in question. Money fulfils its ideal value only if it is used for noble purposes. Giving is always bliss.

7 December 1938
As you can imagine I am trembling for my home and I hope I can keep it, if not I'll have to bear that as well. A. and B. will have got the necessary papers for emigration together, but the winding up of the businesses will still take months.

27 April 1939
You can imagine that due to all the incidents I haven't got the income any more and also not the property as before. Also the circle of needy relatives and good friends, as well as charities, has grown. I am unfortunately subjected to restriction in this respect. The Berlin family is very close to me.

17 July 1939
Yesterday afternoon I could admire an absolutely wonderful sea of flowers in the garden so that wandering from one tree and bush to the next, I forgot all that could sadden me. The very first pear tree on the espalier the 'good Louise of Arranches' has to suffer under the very massive group of birch trees that take a lot of light, air and also food away, but it survives and bears its beautiful and delicious fruits year by year delighting heart and also stomach until the beginning spring.

You'll be as pleased as I am with the prospect of our dear children being together again soon and hopefully being healthy. Let us wait calmly until it will be realized.

No date. (Last letter)
I have stayed in this pension for the last 16 days and have every reason to be content. But both of us would be very happy to have a home of our own again.

Appendix 4

Brief biographies of some of the members of the committee of the illegal cell of the Proletarian Freethinkers

Though this falls outside the period where we can trace Siegi's movements in Germany, it is nevertheless worth spending a moment in memory of these courageous fighters against Nazism. Fomferra's letter also gives us a brief glimpse of how illegal work was organized – as well as its terrible risks.

Fomferra, born 1895, in Essen, from a working-class family, joined the SPD in 1912, the USPD between 1918 and 1922, the Communist Workers' Party between 1920 and 1923. He was sentenced to 18 months' imprisonment for assault on a bank. From 1923, he was a member of KPD in Ruhr and leader of the Proletarian Hundreds, followed by another 16 months' prison stint for explosive offences. In 1929–1930, he went to the Comintern school in Moscow and worked for the secret underground intelligence department of the KPD.

In Berlin, Fomferra's responsibility was for print and distribution of all illegal papers and printed matters. Printing was done by Eugen Schonhaar, who was arrested or murdered/executed at the Kilometraberg, in connection with the Kattner affair. (The leader of this unit was Willy Reimers, arrested in 1933. Fritz Brilla took over responsibility for printing until April 1934, along with Comrade Countess von Hardenberg, Fritz Domnick and others, as well as the comrades in charge of the District.)

In March 1934, five comrades were arrested in different places, including Fomferra; Brilla at Dahlem Dorf tube station, Comrade von Hardenberg in her flat, the messenger at Templehof Station and Fritz Domnick at Dortmund. They had been observed for weeks, as they found out during interrogation.

Fomferra spent three years in Luckau Suchthaus (hard labour camp) till May1937, after which he became active in the Mett group, before being re-arrested in 1939 as part of the Munich special action following the failed attempt on Hitler's life in Munich. He was released after five weeks interrogation. He was active in Unit 6A with comrade Seigewam, Uhrig, Pfeifer and others. After the arrest of Mett and Uhrich, Fomferra apparently became active in the group Matthils Coehnen until the collapse of Germany. He died a natural death in 1979.

Walter Weidauer, a member of the Proletarian Freethinkers, was born on 28 July 1889 in Saxony, the son of a basket maker. He became a carpenter, joining the *Proletarischen Jugendbewegung* in 1916 (proletarian youth movement); in 1920, he joined the USPD, (the Independent Social Democratic party) and early in 1922, the KPD, and became a city councillor in Zwickau. In 1929, he was expelled from the CC of the carpenters' union for KPD activity, and then began his main work for the KPD. Until 1932, he was the leader of the KPD publishers in Essen, and the 'election leader' of the KPD Proletarian Freethinkers in Saxony.

He seems to have combined legal and illegal activities in the crucial 1932–1933 period. His 'career' suggests the degree to which these two worlds were not discrete during this period. In July 1932, Weidauer was elected as a KPD-nominated delegate to the Reichstag, until his arrest in February/March 1933, when he was held in 'protective custody'. He was released in December 1933.

He then continued with illegal work in the Freethinkers, though, interestingly, this is not included in his CV presented by the German Parliament (probably because the record is based on Weidauer's submission in 1932, when he would not have included any illegal activity). In April 1934, he was re-arrested and in November 1934, charged by the central court in Saxony, Dresden. On 28 February 1935, he was surprisingly set free. He then escaped to Denmark till the Nazis caught up with him – in 1940, he was arrested by Danish police, and in January 1941 handed over to Gestapo in Hamburg, where he was sentenced to 15 years in prison.

He survived to join the SED in 1946, becoming mayor of Dresden around 1948. He died a natural death in 1986 in Dresden (from German parliamentary notes on *Bundestag* membership).

Fritz Bischoff, another member of the Proletarian Freethinkers, was born in 1900, near Berlin, into a working-class family. He trained in a business school and later worked in Universal Films. He joined the Sparticist group in 1916 and the KPD in 1918. He was employed by the Soviet trade delegation in Berlin and Hamburg until December 1930. Nominally, he led the KPD agitprop department in Berlin - Brandenburg and in Wasser Kante, Hamburg. By the end of 1930, he was the head of Proletarian Freethinkers in Hessen, Frankfurt. So he and Siegi overlapped in two spheres and must have known each other well.

Unlike Siegi, Fritz stayed in Germany and in September 1934, was arrested in Heidelberg and, in December 1934, sentenced to eight years in prison. In 1942, he was moved from prison in Kastel to Sachenhausen Concentration Camp, then, in 1944, to Neuengamme Concentration Camp. At the very end of the war, he was one of 45 prisoners who were put on the ship Ancona, and died two days before the end of the Second World War. (Source: Reimann papers.)

Nothing could be found about Hans Mainz or Walter Jopp, other committee members of the Berlin Proletarian Freethinkers.

Appendix 5

The divisions among the revolutionary left in Germany, 1929

For those interested in such matters, it is worth noting in passing the fate of the KPDO and of the *Lenin Bund*. In Offenbach, Frankfurt, only the KPDO won over a majority of the membership, functionaries and the Communist electorate on the issue of the left turn in 1928–1929. They did, however, have significant influence within the KPD in the districts of Württemberg, centred on Stuttgart, in Silesia, centred on Breslau, and in Saxony, especially the southwest of the region with an epicentre in Chemnitz. Brandler was one of the leading figures. Leaflets were distributed at factory gates and meetings held, for example, by Paul Fröhlich, but the CC had control of the channels of communication. The strength of support for the right among trade-union Communists also brought invitations (for example, to Brandler) from cell groups to speak on the implications for factory work, but the CC used force to prevent this happening. Drawing from Weber's *Wandlung*, LaPorte (2002) reveals the fate of the right. On 22 December 1928, they were accused of attempting to re-found a *Spartacus Bund*, of representing a 'socialist current in the communist movement', and of having broken with Leninism. At the end of December, eight prominent leaders (J.Walcher, A. Schreiner, Max Koehler, P. Fröhlich, A. Enderle, Hans Tittel, A.Schmidt and Karl Rehbein) were expelled; Brandler and Thalheimer were also purged (LaPorte, 2002). The CC acted against supporters of the right who remained in the KPD by imposing a solidarity declaration. The formation of the KPDO as an independent party at the end of 1928 only organized between 4,000 and 6,000 former members of the KPD (LaPorte, 2002). But the right opposition had comprised full-time trade-union officials, party union functionaries, factory councillors and councillors in the local government, part of the militant workers' movement who regarded left-wing SPD members as potential Communists rather than the social basis of 'social fascism'.

The *Lenin Bund*, an unstable political construction led by the expelled Left Opposition leaders around Fischer, Maslow, Urbahns and Scholem, was an attempt to unite the left factions in the KPD with those already expelled from it in a campaign for a left-wing policy, but few in the KPD joined them and, once the KPD had again turned ultra-left in 1928, one faction, under Fischer, attempted to rejoin and the majority were allowed to return on condition that they desisted from oppositional activities for six months (LaPorte, 2002: 182). LaPorte (2002), drawing on Szejnmann, C.C.W. (1994), gives the figure of only some 50 SPD members in Leipzig joining the left-socialist SAPD (Socialist Workers Party of Germany, sometimes just called SAP) in 1931; in Zwickau the party lost 20 per cent of its membership – significant, but not a viable alternative (Szejnmann, C.C.W. 1994, *The Rise of the Nazi Party in Saxony between 1921 and 1933*, Ph.D. thesis (King's College, University of London). But even in Leipzig, there is no evidence of organized cooperation between rank-and-file members of the KPD and the KPDO, which comprised some 500 members in Leipzig's skilled textile and printing trades (LaPorte, 2002: 361).

Appendix 6

The Weber/LaPorte debate about the Stalinization of the KPD

Much of the following is drawn from the article by LaPorte, Morgan and Worley, in Matthew Worley, Kevin Morgan, Norman LaPorte, *Bolshevism, Stalinism and the Comintern.*

Weber, in his *Wandlung des deutschen Kommunismus*, sought to explain how, in the years soon after its formation, a mass working-class party with a high level of internal democracy became subordinated to the Comintern and the priorities of Soviet foreign policy, in a way which had never happened before in the history of the workers' movement. Weber particularly looked to the period from the mid- to late 1920s in which, as Stalin established his authority in Moscow, the Comintern exploited factional tensions from 1924. As argued throughout its work, the KPD which had already become Stalinized by the end of the 1920s, proved incapable of significantly modifying the Comintern's assessment that social democracy rather than Nazism was Communism's 'main enemy', resulting in Nazi victory. LaPorte suggests the distinctiveness of Weber's analysis is that he combined four separate but interrelated variables: the domination of the party by the party apparatus; the role of internal factionalism, which prevented the KPD developing its distinct ideological stance and gave the Centre a far more important directional role than it otherwise would have had; political and material dependence on the Comintern, in part because of the decline of its activist base and therefore the level of subs; and the KPD's marginality to German politics, particularly following the failures of 1918 and 1923 (discussed later in the text).

This model, while broadly accepted, has been questioned including in terms of Weber's periodizing, and that his approach is not bottom up, one of the strengths of LaPorte's approach. Another approach, also discussed within the text itself, is to analyse the relative appeals of, and disastrous divisions between, the SPD and KPD in class terms. Finally, Mallman (1996),* also referred to in the text, in a more recent critique of Weber's approach, argues that the KPD had greater relative autonomy, in which there was a divergence of local experiences in the relationship between KPD and SPD members. While LaPorte analyses the 'exceptionalism' of Saxony, Mallman studied the Saarland (contested as another atypical region of Germany) and argues for the existence of a 'left-proletarian milieu' where workers could unite in struggle, and not be dominated by the Party line.

Many other debates have taken place which this is not the space to enter into: about whether the KPD was 'Stalinized' before Stalin, about how far the differences with other Communist parties illuminate KPD specificity, etc.

* Mallman, K.M. (1996) *Kommunisten in der Weimarer Republik: Sozialgeschichte einer revolutionären Bewegung* (Wissenschaftliche Buchgesellschaft, Darmstadt).

Appendix 7

The Russian Oil Products (ROP)

This appendix refers only to matters of relevance to the biography and therefore ends in 1932, the last year that Siegi could have had dealings with the ROP – though the little evidence available actually suggests his role was restricted to 1931 and 1932. So this appendix, which is drawn from files at the Public Records Office, is in no way an overview of the information on this company. It is also worth mentioning that most of these files were supposedly to be held secret for up to another 30 years but that a Freedom of Information request resulted in their going into the public domain in 2007. However, some of the material is still redacted!

To start with a brief background of the company Russian Oil Products in the UK: it was created in 1924, and subsequently registered, set up an office in London (and Dublin) and started building a network of 35 depots (HO KV5/73, HO144/17916 and 7, Competition Commission publication on petrol distribution in the UK, 1914–1970) for cut price petrol. Serious price wars with larger distributors broke out and there was even a sustained media campaign in the 1930s to boycott Russian oil.

It is clear that, from 1926 to 1932 (c.f. Letter from 12 December 1932, signed by the Under-Secretary of State, directing attention to a report from March 1932), the Home Office, the Secret Service and parts of the police thought the ROP, unlike other Russian companies, was not just a commercial company but also an organization that hid potential spies, and was the seat of political propaganda in the UK for the Communist cause, financed, it was suggested, by the sale of oil, and could provide the basis for insurrection. In a couple of HO documents from the late 1920s and early 1930s (HO 144/17917), MI5 explicitly states that ROP's facilities and staff would or could be used to bring about acts of espionage for the USSR and sabotage in the event of hostilities with the USSR. Unlike the other oil companies, ROP cannot be discounted in terms of sabotage ('Secret' document 'Dangers to Internal Security... in an Emergency'): 'Definite orders have been found from Moscow that in the event of a declaration of war, workers must be able to frustrate the campaign by a general disorganization' (dated 8 May 1932 in HO144/17916). Note, amid the political hysteria, the assumption that the USSR would inevitably be on the opposite side.

It was also believed that ROP provided links with underground elements of the British Communist Party (HOKV 5/73) and that the CPGB had a cell in the ROP which developed networks with other Communists working in factories across the UK, and fed the USSR with relevant commercial, as well as political, information, although it was not clear how this actually took place. On page 7, the report suggests that the Soviet government 'hoped to make use of the pseudo-Communist Drug and Chemical Workers' Union, which was built up under the auspices of ROP', and whose membership largely overlapped with theirs. The Home Office had an extraordinarily detailed knowledge of the Communist activists and employees working at ROP, Russian and British (e.g. a HO document, 'ROP and their employees', dated 23 February 1932 and sent to Kell at MI5 (see below), and list of names submitted by 'Josh' of the Metropolitan Police, 14 January 1931, to five initialled recipients (KV 5/73)). (One source is clear – a disgruntled British employee, hoping for consequent rewards from HM Government.) At one point (6), the Report on 'Russian Oil' states: 'The most influential British Communist ... is Ross Shar who is known to be concerned with espionage and to make occasional visits to Moscow.' There follow copious details of his contacts in Moscow. Clearly, MI5 kept a close watch on the company.

Unfortunately, the papers do not mention Siegi but do on a

couple of occasions mention a German link. For example, towards the end of the document dated 5 May 1932, referred to above, it states: 'The Company in Germany [DEROP, ROP's sister company] is very definitely a centre for political intrigue and espionage and is so regarded by the German authorities.' In another brief reference to DEROP, the report states: 'The political and revolutionary uses of DEROP are more [than in the UK] clearly visible.' In another reference to Germany, the report marked 'secret' from 7 December 1932 on ROP in India (HO144/17917) states: 'We have definite information that Wilhelm Münzenberg the prominent German Communist and head of the League against Imperialism in Berlin received direct from the German branch of the Naptha Syndicate a large sum which was not entered in any cash books of the company.' Though Naptha was nominally in competition with ROP (but appears to have held shares in it at the same time), this style of link was unlikely to be a one-off and increases the possibility of a similar sort of arrangement with Siegi.

The report (HO144/17917) on ROP in India, dated 10 January 1933, so, soon after 'Moos's' purported involvement with Vakil on behalf of ROP, analyses which Indian companies are taking ROP oil. As already referred to in the body of the biography, the report refers to Felix Bauer's mission to India at the end of 1930 to arrange for the sale of Russian petrol, to the consequent appearance of another company, YIOD, in India in January 1932, and to the return visit of Vakil and Joshi to Moscow in Bauer's company during 1931.The report (page 2) expresses the fear that although YIOD had an ostensible economic purpose, 'yet there is cause for thc suspicion that this will not always be the case.' The report continues (page 3) that this suspicion is heightened by the fact that when there was a dispute with Burma Shell Company, YIOD dispatched Vakil – again – to help sort it out. It continues that Vakil sent cables from Moscow (incredibly, quoted verbatim in the report!) about negotiations. In other words, Vakil was both a key operator between the Indian company and Russia and apparently trusted in Moscow. London was, moreover, a place where negotiations occurred on more than one occasion.

The report continues (page 4) by expressing a fear that 'political suspects', such as Congressmen (!), Communists and agitators might become more significant. Again quoting from intercepted correspondence, the report suggests (pages 4, 5) that the ROP link may not be successful. It concludes: 'Until the results of the negotiations in Moscow [by Vakil] are known, it is difficult to see how the wind is blowing. The dangers of the position are only too apparent.' The Home Office and MI5 were clearly exceedingly concerned about the operations of ROP in India, maybe even more so because oil was involved.

A telling aside: the document to Kell from 2 March 1932 reveals that the previous Russian managers of ROP in the UK were being withdrawn by Moscow (page 2) and replaced (page 3) (though they too were apparently seen as incompetent!). In a report sent from Wilson on behalf of Kell, to MacIver, in their correspondence from 1931, it is stated that the Russian directors of ROP who had 'bona fide knowledge of the oil business and real commercial ability, have recently been dismissed for refusing to subordinate the commercial interests of the Company to Soviet political purposes,' later referred to as 'causing general disorganization at the time of a national emergency.' But it may not surprise all of us that, 'A letter of February 3 1930 from the OGPU (the secret police from 1922 to 1934) in Moscow contained instructions to the secret service in London to carry out a purge of such "outside elements" as still remained in ROP'! One of the intriguing aspects of all this documentation is the frequent appearance of Sir V. Kell, whom many of the accompanying letters are addressed to. To give a couple of examples: a letter and accompanying material from the Foreign Office, dated 2 March 1932, on ROP, and a reference in a letter, marked 'secret', of 12 May 1931 from J. MacIver at the Home Office to 'Holt' in which he asks for more information on the 'ROP Danger, beyond Sir Kell's letter of January 1930.' In Holt Wilson's reply 'for Col.Sir V.G. Kell', dated 1 April 1931, Wilson writes about the dangers of sabotage.

Kell was the first Director General of MI5 (and was known as 'K'!). According to Wikipedia (drawn from Popplewell: *Intelligence and Imperial Defence: British Intelligence and the Defence of the British Empire*, 1995), during the first world war, Kell headed the MI5 section, called MI5 (g), dealing with Indian revolutionaries in India and Europe and was connected to the establishment of counter-espionage networks. It would appear Kell maintained a close interest in Indian affairs.[203] When my mother was interned, much of the documentation then was signed by him, presumably before his forced resignation. Given the randomness of the 'arrests', maybe – though this seems far-fetched – Kell's earlier involvement with Indian affairs alerted him subsequently to the name of 'Moos'. But Kell was also notorious as an anti-Communist, opining in the 1930s that fascism insisted on the interests of all classes and was an understandable reaction to Communism which preached class war (Brinson and Dove, 2014).

Endnote

203. Kell was removed by Churchill in May 1940. MI5 had become overburdened with the introduction of internment. Within the first six months of the war, 64,000 citizens of Germany, Austria and Italy resident in the UK had to undergo security interviews to confirm that they were 'friendly aliens'.

Appendix 8

The Workers' Olympics

There were three internationally organized Workers' Olympics, the first in Frankfurt, organized by the Socialist Workers Sports International (SAS) associated with the SPD. Workers' sports organizations had been active as political and communal groups since the 1850s, partly providing a front for socialist political activity. (Liberal democratic politics in Germany from the 1840s to the 1870s were debated mainly within gymnastic associations that were less prone to being spied on by the Prussian government.) (I would like to thank Ulrich Lehmann for a copy of his paper *Action as Property: Sport in Modernism,* originally delivered at the Victoria and Albert Museum.)

Soon after the LSI began in 1922 to plan for a Workers' Olympiad in Frankfurt in 1925, the RSI, which was a separate organization, demanded that the four RSI sections (Russia, Czechoslovakia, France and Norway) participate with full privileges. Although LSI rules specified that participation in its activities be restricted to members, they were initially flexible, hoping for a unified international movement but the LSI's (sectarian) demand that the RSI clubs had to join the LSI, was rejected by the RSI and the LSI then rejected RSI involvement. In fact, the RSI then tried to get into the Olympics, causing further friction between the two organizations (Steinberg, 1978).

The occasion is described:

> 'Through opening ceremonies overflowing with red flags, mass free exercises in which hundreds of participants engaged in simultaneous choral movements, the mass pyramids with which the festival ended and the Weihespiel 'Kampf um die Erde' (Struggle for the World), a powerful

dramatic presentation using large speaking and acting choruses that portrayed sport as the source of strength for the creation of a new world, the Olympiad demonstrated proletarian solidarity and brotherhood' (Steinberg, 1978).

The success of these Olympics was phenomenal – about 100,000 attended, the largest sporting event ever: they embraced men and women and children and actively encouraged the participation of people in the audience in mass exercises (the most popular of all the events). It was also a statement about inclusion and internationalism after the failures of the SPD and the Second International to oppose the first world war. They believed in the importance of the body which daily was exploited and the seat of capitalist exploitation but which, during sport, the worker could regain control over and also use in the pursuit of solidarity in sport and elsewhere.

Lehmann comments:

'The aim [of the Workers' Olympics] was to promote political emancipation (socialism) for those with no ready access to economic, social and political decision making processes; reformation of working hours and structuring of leisure time through meaningful activities; improving living conditions for the largest parts of society; formation of a genuinely new (working class) culture with original expressions; and ensuring that a new generation would have improved access to education, safe working conditions and better health than their parents' (July 2012).[204]

The Workers' Olympics stressed the bourgeois character of the official Olympics and emphasized its own internationalism , for example, an absence of national flags, its educational purpose, such as the promotion of working-class culture, and the importance of mass participation (Lehmann, Paper delivered at V&A:

17). Apparently, the official Olympics, organized by Baron de Coubertin in 1924 had drawn about similar numbers, though it, unlike the Workers' Internationale, emphasized competition and prizes, severely limited the participation of women and, like the modern Olympics, did not entertain either group sporting activities or audience participation! Anybody interested in this aspect of workers' sports should try to see the film, directed by Prager: *The First Workers' Olympics*, and look at the work of Lehmann, from whose lecture at the Tate Modern, in July 2012, this information is largely drawn.

Participants in the Second Workers' Olympics, which took place in Vienna in 1931 in a period of more evident class conflict, presented more martial imagery, with an emphasis on the proletariat's need to ready itself for class struggle through workers' sports and the construction of workers' militias (Lehmann).[205]

The Communist sports groups organized a series of workers' sports festivals, starting in 1922, some of them with international participation, including from the USSR, and supported by up to 100,000, but never on the scale of the Frankfurt Olympiad. These events all had accompanying cultural activities, which appear to have been close to compulsory viewing.

Endnotes

204. Lehmann, *The New Great Power: The First Workers' Olympics, 1925,* July 2012, presented at Tate Modern.
205. I would like to thank Ulrich Lehmann for a copy of his paper: *Action as Property: Sport in Modernism,* originally delivered at the Victoria and Albert Museum.

Appendix 9

Lotte Moos

My mother's life between 1933 and 1940 was eventful in its own right. But this study is not focused on her, so this appendix will only sketch in her life and highlight the points which most affected Siegi.

Lotte was born in December 1909 to bourgeois culturally Jewish parents in Berlin. Her father was a merchant, her mother, most unusually for that time, especially for a woman and a woman from a not very distant 'Ost-Juden' background, an accountant. Lotte was the youngest of three sisters: Annamarie, Kate and her. She told me she was the apple of her father's eye, I suspect because, though he had wanted a boy, Lotte was the brightest of the three, the most adventurous and, like him, a bookworm. (She once told me she had read most of Dostoevsky by the age of 11. When I gasped, she replied, 'Why not?') She apparently had an article accepted by a Berlin daily at about the same age.

She left the *Gymnasium* (a version of grammar school) and home at a remarkably early age, probably around 15, and went to work in a photographer's shop in the early days of film. She lived, she told me, as far from her parents as possible in the eastern – and working class – reaches of Berlin. I never found out exactly what went wrong at home but know her mother used to hit Lotte on the face for being naughty (which I suspect she rarely was) and that there were serious problems about how her parents behaved towards the eldest daughter, Annamarie. I suspect that Lotte did not feel she could protect her less clever sister from her parents and that contributed to her early flight from home.

In around 1929, when she was 20, Lotte joined an agitprop

group, probably *Die Truppe*, where she met my father, who was directing, and generally a significant figure in the agitprop world. Soon afterwards, in 1931, she went to Humbolt university in Berlin to study economics where she got nothing but 'A' grades. Having lived together in a number of addresses across 'eastern' and 'middle' Berlin, from early on in their relationship, Siegi and she got married in October 1932, because, she told me, they were preparing for flight. It was a very small wedding, Siegi was late (one of my mother's few stories) and she led me to understand her parents did not approve of Siegi and did not attend (but I'm no longer so sure about this).

Lotte denied belonging to the Communist Party (KPD) even when she started to confess to me, under pressure, about other parts of her life. 'What fools,' is what she would say of the KPD members in Berlin, including my father in this embrace. But papers have come to light which suggest she was a member between 1934 and 1936. I guess her paranoia about Stalinism ran so deep she could not confess to this even when she was in her late 90s!

But Lotte was very much to the left of any brand of Social Democracy, and also, like Siegi, rejected religion, very much including Judaism. When Richard and I used to visit my parents in the 1960s and early 1970s, she would tell Richard she had supported Brandler (briefly leader of the KPD before expulsion for 'right deviationism' – see endnote 54). She became a keen reader of *Labour*, then *Socialist, Worker* in the 1960s and 1970s, and, even after Siegi's death, came out on a number of anti-Tory demonstrations when already in her 80s.

Lotte, though not an activist like Siegi, was certainly politically astute and told me that she was the one who insisted on their leaving Germany as the Nazi storm clouds gathered (discussed in the main body of the biography). She told me, maybe with hindsight, that she knew all was lost on 1 May 1929. My father, always the more optimistic one, would never have succumbed to such pessimism of the spirit!

Unlike my father, who went into hiding on the night of the Reichstag fire, Lotte felt safe enough to merely remove herself to a distant aunt's in the countryside outside Berlin – she had, she said, been unwell. She then applied openly to the police for exit papers and permission to leave. Police documents state that she officially left Germany on 27 July1933, almost five months after Siegi had gone into hiding.

Lotte told me that she caught a train to Paris in April, dressed in a neat suit as if she were going to a funeral, so as to look less suspicious. She had no idea she was leaving her parents and Berlin forever. Those Nazis would not last more than a few months, she told me, and then the German bourgeoisie would get rid of them. Or so she had believed, with a mixture of (inaccurate) class understanding and snobbery.

In Paris, she made use of a network, I suspect Jewish contacts, to get herself a job as a *bobineuse* which allowed her to support herself.[206] She found a flat in a working class block and waited for Siegi. She used to tell the story, which I believe but may nonetheless be apocryphal, that, one day in October, she went down to the Gare de L'Est for the first time, impelled by intuition, and there was Siegi sauntering off a train. The intervening six months must have been very difficult for her.

But then things started to go wrong. Until the last years of her life, most of the little she told me turned out to be at best being economic with the truth. So my sketch of the next part of her life is based partly on what she did finally tell me, partly on reconstruction, partly on input from David Perman who interviewed her when she was already in her 90s to write her biography.[207]

Whatever the cause, Lotte left Paris in 1933, at least three months before Siegi, and only a couple of months after they had met again. Maybe this was because she had relatives in the UK who could 'sponsor' her and therefore she could establish a relatively easy claim to right of entry; maybe it was because Siegi had a political role to fulfil in Paris; maybe this is an early sign of their impending domestic disturbances. She told me she had insisted that she would go to London and the LSE, whether he came with her or not, and that France was not safe. Again, it is impossible to know how far it was in order to follow her that Siegi left in February 1934, how far it was under Party instructions, and how far Siegi, too, spotted the increasing threat of the extreme right. (He left only weeks before Deladier became President.) If we believe Lotte, and on this matter I tend to, by 1934, she had twice saved my father's life.

Lotte arrived in London, and was admitted by an essentially kindly customs officer (from one of her stories). But, to her lifelong distress, LSE refused to accept her existing qualifications: she would have had to take the entry exams like an 18 year old and Lotte, probably partly out of pique (she was after all an outstanding student in Berlin), partly for financial reasons, refused.

She got herself a small job teaching German at the Linguists Club. There she met Brian Gould Vershoyles. Brian was a few years younger than Lotte, good looking and from a ruling-class Protestant liberal Irish family. (For more detailed information, refer to Barry McCloughlin's *Left to the Wolves*.) It is impossible to know for sure what their relationship became but a couple of years later, she followed Brian to the USSR, against Party instructions. He was, though she did not know this, a low-grade spy for the Russians, a courier of messages. It is not clear what passport she travelled on to Vienna but she appeared to have gone via Vienna where she met, for the last time, her beloved father. She sent Siegi (addressed to Lawn Road) a card from Vienna by Titian of 'Jesus and the adulteress', where the scribes are arguing with Jesus about whether the woman should be stoned!

Moscow turned out to be horrific. Brian and Lotte were spied on and bullied by the Party. They had to move from one seedy hotel to one that was even worse. Lotte became very ill.

Undoubtedly, their behaviour was careless, naïve even – they tried to speak to people about many sensitive issues such as food shortages and queuing (which Lotte hated), went on demonstrations and generally ignored that Russia was a place where the level of repression was heading towards the 1937 lethal show trials. The story ends dreadfully. Siegi campaigned tirelessly to get her out, contacting the great and the good in the UK in an effort to get pressure brought on the UK Embassy to get Lotte out of the USSR, even apparently sending her money. Lotte is finally allowed out – according to her, theoretically to go to a Youth Conference. When she finally spoke to me about this, she said she 'escaped, rather than being let out', but sadly refused to develop on this.

Brian, who had not been allowed out, first got sent to Spain (part of the deal which got Lotte released, I suspect) to act as a radio engineer, his trade. Lotte sent him articles and letters including supposed code supporting POUM. Brian was kidnapped and shipped to the Soviet Union. He was then interrogated and sent to a prison in Siberia where he died. In the interrogation, his inquisitors persisted in asking him questions about Lotte. It is clear from the notes from Brian's inquisition that she was thought to be a Trotskyist (false) and Brian is therefore seen as also sympathetic to Trotskyism.[208] It amounted to a death sentence.

Once safely back in London, Lotte started an insistent and fruitless search for information about Brian, even travelling down to the French side of the Pyrenees, in what one assumes was the hope of news from the other side of the border (Brian had been based in Barcelona, not very far from France). Siegi aided her fulsomely in the following years, writing letters and contacting useful people.

But not all was well between her and Siegi. Thanks to the MI5 interest in them, we know that they started to live separately soon after Siegi got to London. The MI5 transcript of Lotte's interrogation in Holloway includes reference to a letter from Siegi offering an explanation for Lotte's going off to the USSR and Brian by saying that he was not in a fit state to have an emotional relationship with Lotte after what he had been through in his escape from Berlin. He was providing her with a 'get-out-of-jail' card.

The murder of their comrades who had escaped from Germany to the USSR was a recurrent and bitter issue for my parents. My mother told a story about Ernst Busch, after I had mistakenly tried to give them, as a Christmas present, a record of Spanish Civil War songs, a present I had felt naively proud of. They refused it point blank. 'You keep it,' they said. Busch, whose music appears on the record, my mother explained, had refused to support German exile comrades persecuted by the GPU. Maybe she was referring to her own case; maybe the record was unbearable because of its association with Spain and Brian.

Even after her 'escape' from the USSR, Lotte was still restless and after a couple of trips to France, took off for the USA in early 1939, in the hope, apparently, of getting settled there with proper jobs. She resumed studying at Swarthmore College and again appears to have done outstandingly well. She made some effort to find a way of getting Siegi over but some of her letters to Siegi from the US are ill-tempered and impatient and do not unambiguously lend themselves to the interpretation that she wanted them to get back together. Her parents' letters to their daughter after the November 1938 pogrom had become far darker and started to implore her to get them out of Germany. This might have been an additional motive for Lotte's journey to the US. She put her parents down on the very long list for emigration from Germany to the US, though there is no evidence that she tried especially hard on their account.

In New York, she fatefully visited Krivitsy, who, unknown to her, was a former Soviet intelligence agent who had started to also work for the British/US. From articles of his that she had read, Lotte thought he knew what had happened to Brian. What she inadvertently set off was a process which would end with her in Holloway Prison as Krivitsky saw her as a probable spy who needed to be watched.

War clouds were looming and Lotte told me (improbably) that she caught the last boat out of the US. When I asked her why she didn't stay, she replied that she didn't have the stomach to make a new life all over again and, she added, wanted to get back to Siegi. But was that last statement for my benefit? Lotte and Siegi got back together at the end of the 1930s. They continued to live essentially at separate addresses till Siegi moved to Oxford in late 1938 and Lotte returned from the USA in mid-1939 and moved in with him there.

Lotte did not have an easy time of it when back in the UK. I suspect the reality of Nazism was beginning to strike her very hard. Her sister, Annamarie, 'disappeared' around 1939 from her mental hospital (and, as I only discovered months ago, unknown to my mother or their parents, was one of the first killed in the T4 euthanasia programme in July 1940). Lotte's parents started to send her, for the first time, desperate letters that they wanted to get out of Germany. (Why had they waited so long? My guess is that it was only when they received a completely false letter that Annamarie had died from natural causes that they felt they could leave Germany. It is also possible that their advanced age (in their late 60s/early 70s) had combined with a belief that 'it would all blow over' to keep them from seriously considering exile.)

In 1940, Lotte was arrested as a possible spy – though she protested, probably with feigned naivety, that she did not know whom she was being accused of spying for, the USSR or Germany. She was in Holloway prison for about six months, then was sent to the Isle of Man. Again, Siegi campaigned tirelessly for her. Soon after she was released, she fell terribly ill and almost died, saved by a German refugee doctor, working at the

Maudsley hospital, Oxford, with access to some of the very first and very scarce penicillin.

After her release, like Siegi, she wrote many stories and contributed regularly for *Die Zeitung,* a British government backed paper for distribution in Germany. Her stories received lavish praise and she was asked for more. She wrote about this: 'Instead of clearing up, I tried to give shape to the visions the night had left behind. A few stories appeared, were even broadcast. "Let's have more," I was told, "when the spirit moves you." But the spirit is a squeamish fellow – it feeds on tears.'

At the end of the war, Lotte and Siegi were to spend the next years in a desperate, and too often heart-breaking, search for their German families and comrades. Lotte's father had managed to get a letter to her about her mother's 'natural' death. But Lotte was always convinced her mother had been murdered. In a conversation in 2003, which I recorded, I asked my mother how her mother had died. She told me her mother died in a concentration camp. She held tightly onto my hand and I felt like scum. I then asked about her father but all she said was, 'I don't want to know. I don't want to know.'

I later established through the kindness of the Berlin Synagogue Research Centre that her mother had died naturally, though what that means – given that her daughter, Annamarie, Lotte's eldest sister, had already been murdered, supposedly dying naturally in Poland, in practice gassed up the road in Brandenburg – is another matter. Louise died in the Jewish Hospital in Berlin, which has a far from clean record in this period, so Lotte had good grounds to insist to me, choking on her words, that her mother had been murdered.

Lotte believed she had found her father. She had been receiving the heart-breaking short messages from her father, Samuel, through the Red Cross until 1942. This is a story that still makes me weep. As soon as the war was over, a mere three years later, Lotte started to make persistent enquiries through various organizations, such as the Red Cross, but they could not find her father. She did not even know for sure whether he was still at the old address in Charlottenburg. Then she received news that her father was alive. She wrote him a rapturous letter: 'Today we got the most wonderful news from the World Jewish Congress and got your address in Berlin. We dare hardly believe it…The best news first. We have a delightful little daughter, Merilyn… Merilyn's first word shall be 'Opi' [grandfather].' She was right not to believe it. Under a month after sending her letter, in August 1946, Lotte received a letter from the Jewish Community, Berlin: 'I am deeply sorry to give you news…that I must conclude that there is nobody with your father's name [alive]. My deepest regrets.' My mother never tried to find out where and when her father had died. It was left to me, years later, to trace him and acquire the 'death certificate': 'Died in Theriesenstadt.'

It is impossible to know what effect so many violent deaths had on Lotte: her sister, Brian, her father (and her mother, as far as she was concerned). And too many uncertainties: she would have suspected Brian was dead, but would never have known. I suspect Lotte never recovered. Certainly, she told me, she wished she too had died. She carried with her, I suggest, for the rest of her life an inability to come to terms with what had happened to those whom she had loved which made loving those left alive more difficult.

But Lotte and Siegi made good friends in Oxford, in particular the Worswicks. When I asked her, in her dying years, whether she had enjoyed Oxford, which she had previously suggested, she gave a resounding, 'No'. Maybe Oxford was forever associated for her with knowing too much about too many murders.

The battle for Stalingrad, as my parents saw it, made it safe for them to have a baby. A few years later, Lotte and Siegi moved to Durham, where my mother sank into domesticity and was no longer a driving force in terms of my father's life. While my father had a variety of academic and quasi-political activities outside the home, my mother had none. I think she found Durham hellish. My mother continued to write voluminously and indeed had a play put on in the West End (see main text). This is the period of my childhood and adolescence – my experience of my mother was of somebody whom I categorized as 'depressed' when I was still very young, but this was a child's view and has to be interpreted as such. She certainly did not want to leave the home for long periods of time and spent most days in my parents' bedroom. What effect this had on Siegi, I do not know.

The combination of her experiences under Stalinism, her escape from Germany, the murder of her family and her imprisonment/internment here had left my mother with a strong tendency towards paranoia. But she did not just suspect the world beyond her family, she also suspected me. Although I had learnt very young the importance of not crossing my mother, she was almost permanently suspicious that I was acting in a manner she disapproved of or, as I grew older, deliberately to oppose her. She used silence to show her displeasure, a silence she could maintain for days and the older I became, the longer her silences were maintained. I do not remember one 'heart-to-heart' at any point between her and me. Although she always prepared three meals a day, even if at unpredictable times, and ensured I was properly dressed, my memory of my childhood is of deep loneliness and insecurity. She was never able to show much emotion. Maybe she would have found mothering less difficult if she had not been so emotionally bruised, but mothering did not come easily to her. I never saw her cry, not even when Siegi died. It was as if she had cried herself dry. In the very last years of her life, as I grew braver and started to know enough to ask her the right questions, and as she started to guard her mental edges and her memories less effectively, I did finally persuade her to talk to me a little. Maybe I pushed her into talking. Maybe that wasn't right, but at least it meant I found out something of my mother's life.

It is impossible to be clear about the effect on my father of Lotte's experiences. But what seems likely is that her dreadful experiences in Moscow would have alerted him much earlier than most, to how far the USSR had strayed from its socialist path. Brian's disappearance in the USSR would have sealed his misgivings. More clear-headed than my mother, he would have suspected, long before she would have wanted to recognize this as a possibility, that Brian had been killed. Siegi would not have forgiven such excesses. Of course the small Trotskyist groupings in the UK, whose literature I suspect he would have followed avidly, were already debating what the character of the USSR had become but my guess is that Siegi always suspected Trotskyism for being too critical of the USSR, and probably too sectarian.

What the personal impact of Lotte's dalliance with Brian was can only be guessed at. Again, this is touched on in the main text. Siegi had followed Lotte to London, but his relationship with Lotte deteriorated to the point that they rapidly stopped living together and did not do so again for about five years. What were the implications of his 'taking her back' (for this is how I see the scenario in 1938/39)? Did this bind her forever to him or/and leave their relationship profoundly out of kilter? With hindsight, it would appear to me that not all was well between them when I was a child.

But in the last years of their lives together, before Siegi's death in 1988, they seemed to me to be getting on better than I had seen before. The fears around the Cold War were fading away. They were living in London, both highly active in the poetry scene around Centerprise, a local and radical Hackney community centre, and with a group of much younger men and women around them and admiring them. Lotte had at least three books of wonderful, if somewhat cerebral, poems published, almost all decrying injustice. It was a happy joint ending to such troubled lives.

But Lotte did not cope well with the remaining 20 years of living without Siegi and became increasingly remote from reality. In the end, I decided she had to go into a care home though this was certainly not what she wanted. After a series of misadventures, which would have killed most people her age, she lived her last years in a Jewish care home and died on 3 January 2008, a couple of days after I had sung her the Internationale and Lotte, by now, almost completely unresponsive, raised her fist in salute.

Endnotes

206. A *bobineuse* is somebody (usually a female 'somebody') who winds the wool yarn around a spool. It is apparently difficult work unless very experienced as the yarn regularly breaks.
207. David Perman: *Stranger in a Borrowed Land: Lotte Moos and her writing* (Grendel Publishing, 2012).
208. My thanks to Barry McLoughlin for giving me a copy of these notes.

Bibliography

Abbey, William (1995) *Between Two Languages, German-speaking exiles in Great Britain 1933–1945*, edited by William Abbey, Charmian Brinson, Richard Dove, Marian Malet and Jennifer Taylor (London: IGS / Stuttgart: Hans-Dieter Heinz)

Barnes, James and Barnes, Patience (2001) *Nazi Refugee Turned Gestapo Spy: The Life of Hans Wesemann, 1895–1971* (USA: Praeger publishers)

Berghahn, Volker (2005) *Europe in the Era of Two World Wars: From Militarism and Genocide to Civil Society, 1900–1950* (English translation 2005) (NY: Berghahn Books)

Birchall, Ian (1997) Introduction in Serge, *Witness to the German Revolution* (Chicago: Haymarket)

Blackledge, Paul (2011) 'Labourism and Socialism: Ralph Miliband's Marxism' (*ISJ*, 129, January 2011)

Bodek, Richard (1992) 'Communist Music in the Streets: Politics and Perceptions in Berlin at the End of the Weimar Republic', in James Retallack and Larry Eugene Jones (eds.) *Elections, Mass Politics, and Social Change in Modern Germany: New Perspectives* (UK: Cambridge University Press)

Bodek, Richard (1995) 'Red Song: Social Democratic Music and Radicalism at the End of the Weimar Republic' (*Central European History*, 28, No 2, February1995

Bodek, Richard (1996) 'The Not so Golden 20's: everyday life and Communist Agitprop in Weimar-era Berlin (*Journal of Social History*, Vol 30, No 1, 1996)

Brinson, Charmian and Malet, M. (1995) 'Die Zeitung', in *Between Two Languages: German Exiles in Great Britain 1933–1945*, Vol. 59, eds. Abbey, William, Brinson, Dove, Malet, Taylor (Akademischer Verlag, Stuttgart, 1995)

Brinson, Charmian and Malet, M. (1995) 'Rudolf Olden: Alerting the English', in *Between Two Languages: German Exiles in Great*

Britain 1933–1945, Vol 59, eds. Abbey, Brinson, Dove, Malet, Taylor (Akademischer Verlag, Stuttgart, 1995)

Brinson, Charmian (1998) 'The Gestapo and the German political exiles in Britain during the 1930s: the case of Hans Wosermann and others, German life and letters' (*IGRS,* Vol 11, No 1, January 1998)

Brinson, Charmian (2003) *In the Exile of Internment or Von Versuchen, aus einer Not eine Tugent zu machen; German -speaking women interned by the British during the Second World War, Politics and culture in twentieth-century Germany,* eds. Niven, Jordan, Rochester (N.Y., Camden House)

Brinson, Charmian and Dove, Richard (2010) *Politics by Other Means: The Free German League of Culture in London 1939–1946* (UK: Vallentine Mitchell)

Brinson, Charmian and Dove, Richard (2011) 'Politik mit anderen Mitteln: Der Freie Deutsche Kulturbund in London, 1939-1946' , *Focus Exil 2011. Aus der Arbeit der Weichmann-Stiftung*

Brinson, Charmian and Dove, Richard (2014) *A Matter of Intelligence:MI5 and the Surveillance of anti-Nazi refugees 1933–1950* (UK: MUP)

Broué, Pierre (2005) *The German Revolution 1917–23,* trans. Archer, ed. Birchall and Pearce (Brill, Boston)

Calder, Angus (1980) 'The Myth of 1940' (*LRB,* Vol 2, Nos 20, 18, 19, 16, October 1980)

Caron, V. (2005) 'The Path to Vichy: Antisemitism in France in the 1930s', Talk to US Holocaust Memorial Museum Center for Advanced Holocaust Studies, Occasional Paper (20 April 2005)

Carr, Edward (1982) *The twilight of the Comintern* (Macmillan Press, London)

Cohen, Gidon (2001) 'The Independent Labour Party, Disaffiliation, Revolution and Standing Orders' (*History,* 86, pp 180–199, April 2001). doi: 10.1111/1468-229X.00186, accessed 10.09,2011: http://onlinelibrary.wiley.com/doi/10.1

111/1468-229X.00186

Copper, Torsten (1988) *Workers and athletes against fascism. The struggle for Community sporting red units in Leipzig from 1933 to 1935* (Karl Marx University, Leipzig, Ph.D. thesis)

Crohn C.D. (1996) 'Dismissal and Emigration of German speaking economists after 1933', in *Forced Migration and Scientific Change* , ed. M. Ash and A. Sollneer (German Historical Institute, CUP, 1996)

Crome, Len (1988) *Unbroken: Resistance and survival in the concentration camps* (Laurence and Wishart, London)

Dewar, Margaret (1989) *The Quiet Revolutionary* (Bookmarks, London)

Dove, Richard and Lamb, S. (1995) 'A Rebel in England: Ernest Toller's Campaign against National Socialism', in *Between Two Languages: German speaking exiles in GB 1933–1945*, Vol. 59, eds. Abbey, Brinson, Dove, Malet, Taylor (Akademischer Verlag, Stuttgart, 1995)

Dove, Richard (2011) ' Flying and Spying, Claud W. Sykes, MI5 and the Carl Otten Group Politics in Exile ', in *Political Exile and Exile Politics in Britain after1933*, eds.Grenville, Anthony and Andrea Reiter (Yearbook of the Research Centre for German & Austrian Exile Studies, Vol 12, London, Amsterdam/New York, 187, January 2011)

Fischer, Conan (1991) *The German Communists and the Rise of Nazism* (Macmillan, Basingstoke and London)

Frohlich, Paul (1972) *Rosa Luxemburg* (Pluto Press, London)

Furness, N. A. (1995) 'The moral Imperative of exile: Otto Lehmann-Russbueldtr's mediations for Victims of Nazi Persecution', in *Between Two Languages: German speaking exiles in Great Britian 1933–1945,* Vol 59, eds. Abbey, Brinson, Dove, Malet, Taylor (Akademischer Verlag, Stuttgart, 1995)

Gounot, André (2001) *Sport or Political organization? Structures and Characteristics of the Red Sport International 1921–1937* (U.F.R.des sciences at techniques des activites physiques et sportives, uni Marc Bloch, 2001) http://library.la84.org/SportsLibrary/JSH/JSH2001/JSH2801/JSH2801d.pdf, accessed 21.07.11

Grant, Thomas (2004) *Stormtroopers and the crisis in the Nazi movement: activism, ideology and dissolution* (Routledge, London)

Grunberger, Richard (1973) *Red Rising in Bavaria* (Arthur Barker Ltd, London)

Hagerman, Harald (2006) 'German-speaking Economists in British Exile 1933–1945', in *Royal Economic Newsletter*, July 2006

Hansard (1933) *HC Deb*, 16 November 1933, vol 281 cc1094–5

Harman, Chris (1982) *The Lost Revolution: Germany 1918-1923* (Bookmarks, London)

Hobsbawm, Eric (1973) *Introduction to Leviné* (Saxon House)

Hobsbawm, Eric (2002) *Interesting Times* (Abacus)

Hobsbawm, Eric (2011) 'Everybody behaved perfectly' (*LRB*, Vol 33, August 2011)

Hoffmann, Ludwig and Hoffman-Ostwald, Daniel (1972) *Deutsches Arbeitertheater 1918–1933*, Vols 1 and 2 (Henschelverlag Kunst und Gesellschaft, Berlin)

HO144/17916, 8 May 1932,

HO144/17917, 10 January 1933: 'Activities of ROP in India'

HO: KV5/73, HO144/17916 and 7

'Negotiations between Jehangir Vakil with Russian Oil Products Co' (ROP), dated 1932,

Hoser, Paul, *National Socialist German Workers Party, 1920–23,* accessed 11.10.10 http://www.historisches-lexikon-bayerns.de/suche/abfrage?type=volltext&schnellsuche=Hoser&x=-163&y=-209

Hrebeniak, Michael (2005) Obituary on Gunther Reimann (*Guardian*, 1March 2005)

Institute of Statistics (1944): *The Economics of Full Employment* (Reprints of Economic Classics, New York, 1967, originally

Blackwell, Oxford)

Kruger, Arnd (1996) 'The German Way of Worker Sport,' in A. Kruger and J. Riordan (eds.) *The Story of Worker Sport* (Champaigne, 11, Human Kinetics, 1996)

Kushner, Tony (1989) *The persistence of prejudice: antisemitism in British society during the Second World War* (MUP)

Landauer, Carl (1959) *European socialism* (University of California Press, Berkeley)

LaPorte, Norman (2002) *The German Communist Party in Saxony, 1924–33: Factionalism, Fratricide and Political Failure* (Peter Lang, Bern)

LaPorte, Norman; Morgan, Kevin and Worley, Matthew (2008) 'Stalinisation and Communist Historiography', in Matthew Worley, Kevin Morgan, Norman LaPorte, *Bolshevism, Stalinism and the Comintern: Perspectives on Stalinisation 1917–53* (Palgrave Macmillan, 2008)

Lehmann, Ulrich (2012) 'The New Great Power: The First Workers' Olympics, 1925' (Talk at Tate Modern, London, 30 July 2012)

Leske, Birgid (1983) *Des Eingen der Organization der KPD in Grossbritannien um die Verwirklichung der Einheits-und Volksfront-politik der KPD, 1934 bis Mai 1945* (Ph.D: Institut fur Marxisme-Leninismus beim CC der SPD, 1983)

Leviné-Meyer, Rosa (1973) *Leviné: The life of a Revolutionary* (Saxon House)

London, Louise (2000a) *Whitehall and the Jewish Refugees* (Archive of the Society for Protection of Science and Learning)

London, Louise (2000b) *Whitehall and the Jews,1933–1948:British Immigration Policy, Jewish Refugees and the Holocaust* (CUP)

Marxists.org/archive: Election results in Germany: 1930–33

McCloughlin, Barry (2007) *Left to the Wolves: Irish Victims of Stalinist Terror* (Irish Academic Press, Dublin)

McMeekin, Sean (2003) *The Red Millionaire: A Political Biography of Willi Münzenberg* (Yale University Press)

Merson, Alan (1986) *Communist Resistance in Nazi Germany* (Laurence and Wishart, London)

Mitchell, Allan (1965) *Revolution in Bavaria* (Princeton University Press, US)

Moos, Margarette C. (Lotte) (1965) *Come back with Diamonds* (in personal possession)

Moos, M.C. (Lotte) (1981) *Time to be Bold* (Centerprise Trust, London)

Moos, M.C. (Lotte) (1992) *A Heart in Transit* (Approach Poets, London)

Moos, M.C. (Lotte) (1993) *Collected Poems* (Rockingham Press, Ware)

Moos, Merilyn (2010) *The Language of Silence* (Cressida Press)

Moos, Siegfried (1971) *Aspects of monopoly and restrictive practices legislation in relation to small firms* (Research reports/Great Britain. Committee of Inquiry on Small Firms, HMSO, 1971)

Moos, Siegfried (1989) *Mind the Gap* (private publication by Lotte Moos)

Morris, William (1888) *A Dream of John Ball* (serialised 1886–1887, book version 1888) from John Ball's sermon on Blackheath in 1381

Mühldorfer, Friedbert, *KPD in Bavaria 1918–1933* (www.histor ische lexicon Bayern, accessed November 2012)

Newman, Michael (2002) *Ralph Miliband* (Merlin Press, UK)

Palmier, Jean-Michel (2006) *Weimar in exile: the anti-fascist emigration in Europe and America* (UK: Verso)

Pennybacker, Susan D. (2009) *From Scottsboro to Munich. Race and Political Culture in 1930's Britain* (US: Princeton University Press)

Perman, David (2012) *Stranger in a Borrowed Land: Lotte Moos and her writing* (UK: Grendel Publishing)

Peterson, Fredrik (2008) 'In Control of solidarity: Willi Münzenberg, the Workers International relief and the league against imperialism, 1921–35', in *Comintern Working papers* 8,

2008. Accessed 6.07.12 http://www.academia.edu/437174/In_Control_of_Solidarity_Willi_Münzenberg_the_Workers_International_Relief_and_League_against_Imperialism_1921-1935

Peterson, Johannes (2009) *Our Street. A Chronicle written in the Heart of Fascist Germany* (Faber and Faber, London)

Price, Morgan Philips (1999) *Dispatches from the Weimar Republic*, ed. Tania Rose (Pluto Press, London)

Pritt, Denis Nowel (1965) *From Right to Left* (Lawrence and Wishart, London)

Purcell, Hugh (2004) *Last English Revolutionary: Tom Wintringham 1898–1949* (Sutton Publishing Ltd)

Reiter, A. (2011) 'Political Exiles and Exile Politics in Britain', in *Political Exile and Exile Politics in Britain after 1933*, eds. Grenville and Reiter (The Yearbook of the German and Austrian Exile Studies, Vol 12, 2011)

Richardson, Michael (2007) *Revolutionary Theatre and the Classical Heritage* (Suny, New Paltz)

Roos, Walter (1998) *Die Rote Armee der Bayerischen Räterepublik in München 1919 (The Red Army of the Bavarian Soviet Republic in Munich 1919)* (Heidelberg, 1998) Accessed 10.10.10 http://www.historisches-lexikon-bayerns.de/artikel/artikel_44654 (12/11/2009)

Rosenhaft, Eve (1983) *Beating the Fascists? The German Communists and Political Violence 1929–1933* (CUP)

Rosenhaft, Eve (2006) 'Brecht's Germany1898–1933', in *Brecht*, eds. Thompson, P. and Sacks G. (CUP, 2nd edition, 2006)

Serge, Victor (1972) *Year One of the Russian Revolution* (Holt, Reinhart, and Winston)

Serge, Victor (1997) *Witness to the German Revolution* (Haymarket Books, Chicago, USA)

Steinberg, D. (1978) 'The Workers' Sport Internationals 1920–28', in *Journal of Contemporary History*, Vol 13, No 2, Special Issue: Workers' Culture (April, 1978, pp 233–251, Sage)

Stibb, Matthew (2011) 'Jürgen Kuczynski and the Search for a

(Non-Existent) Western Spy Ring in the East German Communist Party in 1953', in *Contemporary European History,* 20, 1, 2011, pp 61–79 (Cambridge University Press)

Trotsky, Leon (1971) *The Struggle against Fascism in Germany* (Pathfinder, New York)

Vietor-Englānder, D. (1995) 'I cannot prophesy. I cannot assert. But I can guess. And I can warn. Alfred Kerr in London', in *Between Two Languages: German speaking exiles in GB 1933–1945,* Vol. 59, eds. Abbey, Brinson, Dove, Malet, Taylor (Akademischer Verlag, Stuttgart,1995)

Wallerstein, B. (1979) *Britain and the Jews of Europe 1939–45* (Oxford, UK)

Weber, Hermann (1969) *Die Wandlung des Deutschen Kommunismus* (Europ.Verlag-anst)

Weber, Hermann (1974) 'Arbeiter Bühne und Film, Zentralorgan des Arbeiter – Theatre – Bundes Juni 1930–Juni 1931', *Kulturpolitische Dokumente der revolutionairen Arbeiterbewegung* (Verlag Gaehme Henke, Koln, 1974)

Weber, Hermann (1982) *Hauptfiend, Social democratic Strategie und tactik der KPD 1929–33* (Dusseldorf)

Weber, Hermann (2008) *Deutsche Kommunisten Biographisches handbuch 1918 bis 1945* (Karl Dietz Verlag, Berlin, 2nd edition)

Weindling, Paul (1996) 'The Impact of German medical scientists on British medicine: A Case-study of Oxford 1933–45', in *Forced Migration and Scientific change,* ed. M. Borden, pp 86–114 (CUP, UK, 1996)

Young, W. and Lee, F.S. (1993) *Oxford Economics and Oxford Economists* (Macmillan, London)